AWS CloudTrail User Guide

A catalogue record for this book is available from the Hong Kong Public Libraries.

Published in Hong Kong by Samurai Media Limited.

Email: info@samuraimedia.org

ISBN 9789888408214

Contents

What Is AWS CloudTrail?

AWS CloudTrail is an AWS service that helps you enable governance, compliance, and operational and risk auditing of your AWS account. Actions taken by a user, role, or an AWS service are recorded as events in CloudTrail. Events include actions taken in the AWS Management Console, AWS Command Line Interface, and AWS SDKs and APIs.

CloudTrail is enabled on your AWS account when you create it. When activity occurs in your AWS account, that activity is recorded in a CloudTrail event. You can easily view recent events in the CloudTrail console by going to Event history. For an ongoing record of activity and events in your AWS account, create a trail.

Visibility into your AWS account activity is a key aspect of security and operational best practices. You can use CloudTrail to view, search, download, archive, analyze, and respond to account activity across your AWS infrastructure. You can identify who or what took which action, what resources were acted upon, when the event occurred, and other details to help you analyze and respond to activity in your AWS account.

You can integrate CloudTrail into applications using the API, automate trail creation for your organization, check the status of trails you create, and control how users view CloudTrail events.

- How CloudTrail Works
- CloudTrail Workflow
- CloudTrail Concepts
- CloudTrail Supported Regions
- CloudTrail Log File Examples
- CloudTrail Supported Services and Integrations
- Limits in AWS CloudTrail

How CloudTrail Works

CloudTrail is enabled on your AWS account when you create it. When activity occurs in your AWS account, that activity is recorded in a CloudTrail event. You can easily view events in the CloudTrail console by going to **Event history**.

Event history allows you to view, search, and download the past 90 days of activity in your AWS account. In addition, you can create a CloudTrail trail to archive, analyze, and respond to changes in your AWS resources. A trail is a configuration that enables delivery of events to an Amazon S3 bucket that you specify. You can also deliver and analyze events in a trail with Amazon CloudWatch Logs and Amazon CloudWatch Events. You can create a trail with the CloudTrail console, the AWS CLI, or the CloudTrail API.

You can create two types of trails:

** A trail that applies to all regions **
When you create a trail that applies to all regions, CloudTrail records events in each region and delivers the CloudTrail event log files to an S3 bucket that you specify. If a region is added after you create a trail that applies to all regions, that new region is automatically included, and events in that region are logged. This is the default option when you create a trail in the CloudTrail console. For more information, see Creating a Trail in the Console.

** A trail that applies to one region **
When you create a trail that applies to one region, CloudTrail records the events in that region only. It then delivers the CloudTrail event log files to an Amazon S3 bucket that you specify. If you create additional single trails, you can have those trails deliver CloudTrail event log files to the same Amazon S3 bucket or to separate buckets. This is the default option when you create a trail using the AWS CLI or the CloudTrail API. For more information, see Creating a Trail with the AWS Command Line Interface.

Note
For both types of trails, you can specify an Amazon S3 bucket from any region.

You can change the configuration of a trail after you create it, including whether it logs events in one region or all regions. You can also change whether it logs data events. Changing whether a trail logs events in one region or in all regions affects which events are logged. For more information, see Updating a Trail (console), Managing Trails (AWS CLI), and Logging Data and Management Events for Trails.

By default, CloudTrail event log files are encrypted using Amazon S3 server-side encryption (SSE). You can also choose to encrypt your log files with an AWS Key Management Service (AWS KMS) key. You can store your log files in your bucket for as long as you want. You can also define Amazon S3 lifecycle rules to archive or delete log files automatically. If you want notifications about log file delivery and validation, you can set up Amazon SNS notifications.

CloudTrail typically delivers log files within 15 minutes of account activity. In addition, CloudTrail publishes log files multiple times an hour, about every five minutes. These log files contain API calls from services in the account that support CloudTrail. For more information, see CloudTrail Supported Services and Integrations.

Note
CloudTrail captures actions made directly by the user or on behalf of the user by an AWS service. For example, an AWS CloudFormation `CreateStack` call can result in additional API calls to Amazon EC2, Amazon RDS, Amazon EBS, or other services as required by the AWS CloudFormation template. This behavior is normal and expected. You can identify if the action was taken by an AWS service with the `invokedby` field in the CloudTrail event.

To get started with CloudTrail, see Getting Started with CloudTrail.

For CloudTrail pricing, see AWS CloudTrail Pricing. For Amazon S3 and Amazon SNS pricing, see Amazon S3 Pricing and Amazon SNS Pricing.

CloudTrail Workflow

View event history for your AWS account
You can view and search the last 90 days of events recorded by CloudTrail in the CloudTrail console or by using the AWS CLI. For more information, see Viewing Events with CloudTrail Event History.

Download events
You can download a CSV or JSON file containing up to the past 90 days of CloudTrail events for your AWS account. For more information, see Downloading Events.

** Create a trail **
A trail enables CloudTrail to deliver log files to your Amazon S3 bucket. By default, when you create a trail in the console, the trail applies to all regions. The trail logs events from all regions in the AWS partition and delivers the log files to the S3 bucket that you specify. For more information, see Overview for Creating a Trail.

** Create and subscribe to an Amazon SNS topic**
Subscribe to a topic to receive notifications about log file delivery to your bucket. Amazon SNS can notify you in multiple ways, including programmatically with Amazon Simple Queue Service. For information, see Configuring Amazon SNS Notifications for CloudTrail.
If you want to receive SNS notifications about log file deliveries from all regions, specify only one SNS topic for your trail. If you want to programmatically process all events, see Using the CloudTrail Processing Library.

** View your log files **
Use Amazon S3 to retrieve log files. For information, see Getting and Viewing Your CloudTrail Log Files.

** Manage user permissions **
Use AWS Identity and Access Management (IAM) to manage which users have permissions to create, configure, or delete trails; start and stop logging; and access buckets that have log files. For more information, see Controlling User Permissions for CloudTrail.

** Monitor events with CloudWatch Logs **
You can configure your trail to send events to CloudWatch Logs. You can then use CloudWatch Logs to monitor your account for specific API calls and events. For more information, see Monitoring CloudTrail Log Files with Amazon CloudWatch Logs.
If you configure a trail that applies to all regions to send events to a CloudWatch Logs log group, CloudTrail sends events from all regions to a single log group.

** Log management and data events **
Configure your trails to log read-only, write-only, or all management and data events. By default, trails log management events. For more information, see Logging Data and Management Events for Trails.

** Enable log encryption **
Log file encryption provides an extra layer of security for your log files. For more information, see Encrypting CloudTrail Log Files with AWS KMS–Managed Keys (SSE-KMS).

** Enable log file integrity **
Log file integrity validation helps you verify that log files have remained unchanged since CloudTrail delivered them. For more information, see Validating CloudTrail Log File Integrity.

Share log files with other AWS accounts
You can share log files between accounts. For more information, see Sharing CloudTrail Log Files Between AWS Accounts.

** Aggregate logs from multiple accounts **
You can aggregate log files from multiple accounts to a single bucket. For more information, see Receiving CloudTrail Log Files from Multiple Accounts.

** Work with partner solutions **
Analyze your CloudTrail output with a partner solution that integrates with CloudTrail. Partner solutions offer

a broad set of capabilities, such as change tracking, troubleshooting, and security analysis. For more information, see the AWS CloudTrail partner page.

CloudTrail Concepts

This section summarizes basic concepts related to CloudTrail.

What Are CloudTrail Events?

An event in CloudTrail is the record of an activity in an AWS account. This activity can be an action taken by a user, role, or service that is monitorable by CloudTrail. CloudTrail events provide a history of both API and non-API account activity made through the AWS Management Console, AWS SDKs, command line tools, and other AWS services. There are two types of events that can be logged in CloudTrail: management events and data events. By default, trails log management events, but not data events.

Both management events and data events use the same CloudTrail JSON log format. You can identify them by the value in the `managementEvent` field.

Note
CloudTrail does not log all AWS services. Some AWS services do not enable logging of all APIs and events. Even if you configure logging all management and data events in a trail, you will not create a log with all possible AWS events. For more information about unsupported services, see CloudTrail Unsupported Services. For details about which APIs are logged for a specific service, see documentation for that service in CloudTrail Supported Services and Integrations.

What Are Management Events?

Management events provide insight into management operations that are performed on resources in your AWS account. These are also known as *control plane operations*. Example management events include:

- Configuring security (for example, IAM `AttachRolePolicy` API operations).
- Registering devices (for example, Amazon EC2 `CreateDefaultVpc` API operations).
- Configuring rules for routing data (for example, Amazon EC2 `CreateSubnet` API operations).
- Setting up logging (for example, AWS CloudTrail `CreateTrail` API operations).

Management events can also include non-API events that occur in your account. For example, when a user signs in to your account, CloudTrail logs the `ConsoleLogin` event. For more information, see Non-API Events Captured by CloudTrail. For a list of management events that CloudTrail logs for AWS services, see CloudTrail Supported Services and Integrations.

What Are Data Events?

Data events provide insight into the resource operations performed on or in a resource. These are also known as *data plane operations*. Data events are often high-volume activities. Example data events include:

- Amazon S3 object-level API activity (for example, `GetObject`, `DeleteObject`, and `PutObject` API operations).
- AWS Lambda function execution activity (the `Invoke` API).

Data events are disabled by default when you create a trail. To record CloudTrail data events, you must explicitly add to a trail the supported resources or resource types for which you want to collect activity. For more information, see Creating a Trail and Data Events.

Additional charges apply for logging data events. For CloudTrail pricing, see AWS CloudTrail Pricing.

What Is CloudTrail Event History?

CloudTrail event history provides a viewable, searchable, and downloadable record of the past 90 days of CloudTrail events. You can use this history to gain visibility into actions taken in your AWS account in the AWS Management Console, AWS SDKs, command line tools, and other AWS services. You can customize your view of event history in the CloudTrail console by selecting which columns are displayed.

What Are Trails?

A trail is a configuration that enables delivery of CloudTrail events to an Amazon S3 bucket, CloudWatch Logs, and CloudWatch Events. You can use a trail to filter the CloudTrail events you want delivered, encrypt your CloudTrail event log files with an AWS KMS key, and set up Amazon SNS notifications for log file delivery.

How Do You Manage CloudTrail?

CloudTrail Console

You can use and manage the CloudTrail service with the AWS CloudTrail console. The console provides a user interface for performing many CloudTrail tasks such as:

- Viewing recent events and event history for your AWS account.
- Downloading a filtered or complete file of the last 90 days of events.
- Creating and editing CloudTrail trails.
- Configuring CloudTrail trails, including:
  - Selecting an Amazon S3 bucket.
  - Setting a prefix.
  - Configuring delivery to CloudWatch Logs.
  - Using AWS KMS keys for encryption.
  - Enabling Amazon SNS notifications for log file delivery.

For more information about the AWS Management Console, see AWS Management Console.

CloudTrail CLI

The AWS Command Line Interface is a unified tool that you can use to interact with CloudTrail from the command line. For more information, see the AWS Command Line Interface User Guide. For a complete list of CloudTrail CLI commands, see Available Commands.

CloudTrail APIs

In addition to the console and the CLI, you can also use the CloudTrail RESTful APIs to program CloudTrail directly. For more information, see the AWS CloudTrail API Reference.

AWS SDKs

As an alternative to using the CloudTrail API, you can use one of the AWS SDKs. Each SDK consists of libraries and sample code for various programming languages and platforms. The SDKs provide a convenient way to create programmatic access to CloudTrail. For example, you can use the SDKs to sign requests cryptographically, manage errors, and retry requests automatically. For more information, see the Tools for Amazon Web Services page.

How Do You Control Access to CloudTrail?

AWS Identity and Access Management is a web service that enables Amazon Web Services (AWS) customers to manage users and user permissions. Use IAM to create individual users for anyone who needs access to AWS CloudTrail. Create an IAM user for yourself, give that IAM user administrative privileges, and use that IAM user for all of your work. By creating individual IAM users for people accessing your account, you can give each IAM user a unique set of security credentials. You can also grant different permissions to each IAM user. If necessary, you can change or revoke an IAM user's permissions at any time. For more information, see Controlling User Permissions for CloudTrail.

How Do You Log Management and Data Events?

By default, trails log all management events for your AWS account and don't include data events. You can choose to create or update trails to log data events. Only events that match your trail settings are delivered to your Amazon S3 bucket and Amazon CloudWatch Events, and optionally to an Amazon CloudWatch Logs log group. If the event doesn't match the settings for a trail, the trail doesn't log the event. For more information, see Logging Data and Management Events for Trails.

How Do You Perform Monitoring with CloudTrail?

CloudWatch Logs and CloudTrail

Amazon CloudWatch is a web service that collects and tracks metrics to monitor your Amazon Web Services (AWS) resources and the applications that you run on AWS. Amazon CloudWatch Logs is a feature of CloudWatch that you can use specifically to monitor log data. Integration with CloudWatch Logs enables CloudTrail to send events containing API activity in your AWS account to a CloudWatch Logs log group. CloudTrail events that are sent to CloudWatch Logs can trigger alarms according to the metric filters you define. You can optionally configure CloudWatch alarms to send notifications or make changes to the resources that you are monitoring based on log stream events that your metric filters extract. Using CloudWatch Logs, you can also track CloudTrail events alongside events from the operating system, applications, or other AWS services that are sent to CloudWatch Logs. For more information, see Monitoring CloudTrail Log Files with Amazon CloudWatch Logs.

How Does CloudTrail Behave Regionally and Globally?

A trail can be applied to all regions or a single region. As a best practice, create a trail that applies to all regions in the AWS partition in which you are working. This is the default setting when you create a trail in the CloudTrail console.

Note
Turning on a trail means that you create a trail and start delivery of CloudTrail event log files to an Amazon S3 bucket. In the CloudTrail console, logging is turned on automatically when you create a trail.

What Are the Advantages of Applying a Trail to All Regions?

A trail that applies to all regions has the following advantages:

- The configuration settings for the trail apply consistently across all regions.
- You receive CloudTrail events from all regions in a single S3 bucket and, optionally, in a CloudWatch Logs log group.
- You manage trail configuration for all regions from one location.
- You immediately receive events from a new region. When a new region is launched, CloudTrail automatically creates a trail for you in the new region with the same settings as your original trail.
- You can create trails in regions that you don't use often to monitor for unusual activity.

What Happens When You Apply a Trail to All Regions?

When you apply a trail to all regions, CloudTrail uses the trail that you create in a particular region to create trails with identical configurations in all other regions in your account.

This has the following effects:

- CloudTrail delivers log files for account activity from all regions to the single Amazon S3 bucket that you specify, and, optionally, to a CloudWatch Logs log group.
- If you configured an Amazon SNS topic for the trail, SNS notifications about log file deliveries in all regions are sent to that single SNS topic.
- If you enabled it, log file integrity validation is enabled for the trail in all regions. For information, see Validating CloudTrail Log File Integrity.

Multiple Trails per Region

If you have different but related user groups, such as developers, security personnel, and IT auditors, you can create multiple trails per region. This allows each group to receive its own copy of the log files.

CloudTrail supports five trails per region. A trail that applies to all regions counts as one trail in every region.

The following example is a region with five trails:

- You create two trails in the US West (N. California) Region that apply to this region only.
- You create two more trails in US West (N. California) Region that apply to all regions.
- You create a trail in the Asia Pacific (Sydney) Region that applies to all regions. This trail also exists as a trail in the US West (N. California) Region.

You can see a list of your trails in all regions on the **Trails** page of the CloudTrail console. For more information, see Updating a Trail. For CloudTrail pricing, see AWS CloudTrail Pricing.

AWS Security Token Service (AWS STS) and CloudTrail

AWS STS is a service that has a global endpoint and also supports region-specific endpoints. An endpoint is a URL that is the entry point for web service requests. For example, `https://cloudtrail.us-west-2.amazonaws.com` is the US West (Oregon) regional entry point for the AWS CloudTrail service. Regional endpoints help reduce latency in your applications.

When you use an AWS STS region-specific endpoint, the trail in that region delivers only the AWS STS events that occur in that region. For example, if you are using the endpoint `sts.us-west-2.amazonaws.com`, the trail in us-west-2 delivers only the AWS STS events that originate from us-west-2. For more information about AWS STS regional endpoints, see Activating and Deactivating AWS STS in an AWS Region in the *IAM User Guide*.

For a complete list of AWS regional endpoints, see AWS Regions and Endpoints in the *AWS General Reference*. For details about events from the global AWS STS endpoint, see About Global Service Events.

About Global Service Events

For most services, events are recorded in the region where the action occurred. For global services such as AWS Identity and Access Management (IAM), AWS STS, Amazon CloudFront, and Route 53, events are delivered to any trail that includes global services, and are logged as occurring in US East (N. Virginia) Region.

To avoid receiving duplicate global service events, remember the following:

- Global service events are delivered by default to trails that are created using the CloudTrail console. Events are delivered to the bucket for the trail.

- If you have multiple single region trails, consider configuring your trails so that global service events are delivered in only one of the trails. For more information, see Enabling and disabling logging global service events.

- If you change the configuration of a trail from logging all regions to logging a single region, global service event logging is turned off automatically for that trail. Similarly, if you change the configuration of a trail from logging a single region to logging all regions, global service event logging is turned on automatically for that trail.

   For more information about changing global service event logging for a trail, see Enabling and disabling logging global service events.

Example:

1. You create a trail in the CloudTrail console. By default, this trail logs global service events.

2. You have multiple single region trails.

3. You do not need to include global services for the single region trails. Global service events are delivered for the first trail. For more information, see Creating a Trail with the AWS Command Line Interface.

Note
When you create or update a trail with the AWS CLI, AWS SDKs, or CloudTrail API, you can specify whether to include or exclude global service events for trails. You cannot configure global service event logging from the CloudTrail console.

How Does CloudTrail Relate to Other AWS Monitoring Services?

CloudTrail adds another dimension to the monitoring capabilities already offered by AWS. It does not change or replace logging features you might already be using, such as those for Amazon S3 or Amazon CloudFront subscriptions. Amazon CloudWatch focuses on performance monitoring and system health. CloudTrail focuses on API activity. Although CloudTrail does not report on system performance or health, you can use CloudTrail with CloudWatch alarms to notify you about activity that you might be interested in.

Partner Solutions

AWS partners with third-party specialists in logging and analysis to provide solutions that use CloudTrail output. For more information, visit the CloudTrail detail page at AWS CloudTrail.

CloudTrail Supported Regions

Region Name	Region	Endpoint	Protocol	AWS Account ID	Support Date
US East (Ohio)	us-east-2	cloudtrail.us-east-2.amazon-aws.com	HTTPS	475085895292	10/17/2016
US East (N. Virginia)	us-east-1	cloudtrail.us-east-1.amazon-aws.com	HTTPS	086441151436	11/13/2013
US West (N. California)	us-west-1	cloudtrail.us-west-1.amazon-aws.com	HTTPS	388731089494	05/13/2014
US West (Oregon)	us-west-2	cloudtrail.us-west-2.amazon-aws.com	HTTPS	113285607260	11/13/2013
Canada (Central)	ca-central-1	cloudtrail.ca-central-1.amazonaws.com	HTTPS	819402241893	12/08/2016
Asia Pacific (Mumbai)	ap-south-1	cloudtrail.ap-south-1.amazonaws.com	HTTPS	977081816279	06/27/2016
Asia Pacific (Osaka-Local)	ap-northeast-3	cloudtrail.ap-northeast-3.amazon-aws.com	HTTPS	765225791966	02/12/2018
Asia Pacific (Seoul)	ap-northeast-2	cloudtrail.ap-northeast-2.amazon-aws.com	HTTPS	492519147666	01/06/2016
Asia Pacific (Singapore)	ap-southeast-1	cloudtrail.ap-southeast-1.amazon-aws.com	HTTPS	903692715234	06/30/2014
Asia Pacific (Sydney)	ap-southeast-2	cloudtrail.ap-southeast-2.amazon-aws.com	HTTPS	284668455005	05/13/2014
Asia Pacific (Tokyo)	ap-northeast-1	cloudtrail.ap-northeast-1.amazon-aws.com	HTTPS	216624486486	06/30/2014
China (Ningxia)	cn-northwest-1	cloudtrail.cn-northwest-1.amazon-aws.com.cn	HTTPS	681348832753	12/11/2017
EU (Frankfurt)	eu-central-1	cloudtrail.eu-central-1.amazonaws.com	HTTPS	035351147821	10/23/2014
EU (Ireland)	eu-west-1	cloudtrail.eu-west-1.amazon-aws.com	HTTPS	859597730677	05/13/2014

Region Name	Region	Endpoint	Protocol	AWS Account ID	Support Date
EU (London)	eu-west-2	cloudtrail.eu-west-2.amazon-aws.com	HTTPS	282025262664	12/13/2016
EU (Paris)	eu-west-3	cloudtrail.eu-west-3.amazon-aws.com	HTTPS	262312530599	12/18/2017
South America (São Paulo)	sa-east-1	cloudtrail.sa-east-1.amazon-aws.com	HTTPS	814480443879	06/30/2014

For information about using CloudTrail in the AWS GovCloud (US), Region, see AWS GovCloud (US) Endpoints in the *AWS GovCloud (US) User Guide*.

For information about using CloudTrail in the China (Beijing) Region, see China (Beijing) Region Endpoints in the *Amazon Web Services General Reference*.

CloudTrail Log File Examples

CloudTrail monitors events for your account. If you create a trail, it delivers those events as log files to your Amazon S3 bucket. See the following to learn more about log files.

- CloudTrail Log File Name Format
- Log File Examples

CloudTrail Log File Name Format

CloudTrail uses the following file name format for the log file objects that it delivers to your Amazon S3 bucket:

```
1 AccountID_CloudTrail_RegionName_YYYYMMDDTHHmmZ_UniqueString.FileNameFormat
```

- The YYYY, MM, DD, HH, and mm are the digits of the year, month, day, hour, and minute when the log file was delivered. Hours are in 24-hour format. The Z indicates that the time is in UTC. **Note** A log file delivered at a specific time can contain records written at any point before that time.

- The 16-character UniqueString component of the log file name is there to prevent overwriting of files. It has no meaning, and log processing software should ignore it.

- FileNameFormat is the encoding of the file. Currently, this is json.gz, which is a JSON text file in compressed gzip format.

Example CloudTrail Log File Name

```
1 111122223333_CloudTrail_us-east-2_20150801T0210Z_Mu0KsOhtH1ar15ZZ.json.gz
```

Log File Examples

A log file contains one or more records. The following examples are snippets of logs that show the records for an action that started the creation of a log file.

Amazon EC2 Log Examples

Amazon Elastic Compute Cloud (Amazon EC2) provides resizeable computing capacity in the AWS Cloud. You can launch virtual servers, configure security and networking, and manage storage. Amazon EC2 can also scale up or down quickly to handle changes in requirements or spikes in popularity, thereby reducing your need to forecast server traffic. For more information, see the Amazon EC2 User Guide for Linux Instances.

The following example shows that an IAM user named Alice used the AWS CLI to call the Amazon EC2 StartInstances action by using the ec2-start-instances command for instance i-ebeaf9e2.

```
1  {"Records": [{
2      "eventVersion": "1.0",
3      "userIdentity": {
4          "type": "IAMUser",
5          "principalId": "EX_PRINCIPAL_ID",
6          "arn": "arn:aws:iam::123456789012:user/Alice",
7          "accessKeyId": "EXAMPLE_KEY_ID",
8          "accountId": "123456789012",
9          "userName": "Alice"
10     },
11     "eventTime": "2014-03-06T21:22:54Z",
12     "eventSource": "ec2.amazonaws.com",
```

```
13      "eventName": "StartInstances",
14      "awsRegion": "us-east-2",
15      "sourceIPAddress": "205.251.233.176",
16      "userAgent": "ec2-api-tools 1.6.12.2",
17      "requestParameters": {"instancesSet": {"items": [{"instanceId": "i-ebeaf9e2"}]}},
18      "responseElements": {"instancesSet": {"items": [{
19          "instanceId": "i-ebeaf9e2",
20          "currentState": {
21              "code": 0,
22              "name": "pending"
23          },
24          "previousState": {
25              "code": 80,
26              "name": "stopped"
27          }
28      }]}}
29  }]}
```

The following example shows that an IAM user named Alice used the AWS CLI to call the Amazon EC2 StopInstancesaction by using the ec2-stop-instances.

```
1  {"Records": [{
2      "eventVersion": "1.0",
3      "userIdentity": {
4          "type": "IAMUser",
5          "principalId": "EX_PRINCIPAL_ID",
6          "arn": "arn:aws:iam::123456789012:user/Alice",
7          "accountId": "123456789012",
8          "accessKeyId": "EXAMPLE_KEY_ID",
9          "userName": "Alice"
10     },
11     "eventTime": "2014-03-06T21:01:59Z",
12     "eventSource": "ec2.amazonaws.com",
13     "eventName": "StopInstances",
14     "awsRegion": "us-east-2",
15     "sourceIPAddress": "205.251.233.176",
16     "userAgent": "ec2-api-tools 1.6.12.2",
17     "requestParameters": {
18         "instancesSet": {"items": [{"instanceId": "i-ebeaf9e2"}]},
19         "force": false
20     },
21     "responseElements": {"instancesSet": {"items": [{
22         "instanceId": "i-ebeaf9e2",
23         "currentState": {
24             "code": 64,
25             "name": "stopping"
26         },
27         "previousState": {
28             "code": 16,
29             "name": "running"
30         }
31     }]}}
32 }]}
```

The following example shows that the Amazon EC2 console backend called the CreateKeyPair action in response to requests initiated by the IAM user Alice. Note that the `responseElements` contain a hash of the key pair and that the key material has been removed by AWS.

```
1  {"Records": [{
2      "eventVersion": "1.0",
3      "userIdentity": {
4          "type": "IAMUser",
5          "principalId": "EX_PRINCIPAL_ID",
6          "arn": "arn:aws:iam::123456789012:user/Alice",
7          "accountId": "123456789012",
8          "accessKeyId": "EXAMPLE_KEY_ID",
9          "userName": "Alice",
10         "sessionContext": {"attributes": {
11             "mfaAuthenticated": "false",
12             "creationDate": "2014-03-06T15:15:06Z"
13         }}
14     },
15     "eventTime": "2014-03-06T17:10:34Z",
16     "eventSource": "ec2.amazonaws.com",
17     "eventName": "CreateKeyPair",
18     "awsRegion": "us-east-2",
19     "sourceIPAddress": "72.21.198.64",
20     "userAgent": "EC2ConsoleBackend, aws-sdk-java/Linux/x.xx.fleetxen Java_HotSpot(TM)_64-
           Bit_Server_VM/xx",
21     "requestParameters": {"keyName": "mykeypair"},
22     "responseElements": {
23         "keyName": "mykeypair",
24         "keyFingerprint": "30:1d:46:d0:5b:ad:7e:1b:b6:70:62:8b:ff:38:b5:e9:ab:5d:b8:21",
25         "keyMaterial": "\u003csensitiveDataRemoved\u003e"
26     }
27 }]}
```

IAM Log Examples

AWS Identity and Access Management (IAM) is a web service that enables AWS customers to manage users and user permissions. With IAM, you can manage users, security credentials such as access keys, and permissions that control which AWS resources users can access. For more information, see the IAM User Guide.

The following example shows that the IAM user Alice used the AWS CLI to call the `CreateUser` action to create a new user named Bob.

```
1  {"Records": [{
2      "eventVersion": "1.0",
3      "userIdentity": {
4          "type": "IAMUser",
5          "principalId": "EX_PRINCIPAL_ID",
6          "arn": "arn:aws:iam::123456789012:user/Alice",
7          "accountId": "123456789012",
8          "accessKeyId": "EXAMPLE_KEY_ID",
9          "userName": "Alice"
10     },
11     "eventTime": "2014-03-24T21:11:59Z",
12     "eventSource": "iam.amazonaws.com",
13     "eventName": "CreateUser",
14     "awsRegion": "us-east-2",
```

```
15      "sourceIPAddress": "127.0.0.1",
16      "userAgent": "aws-cli/1.3.2 Python/2.7.5 Windows/7",
17      "requestParameters": {"userName": "Bob"},
18      "responseElements": {"user": {
19          "createDate": "Mar 24, 2014 9:11:59 PM",
20          "userName": "Bob",
21          "arn": "arn:aws:iam::123456789012:user/Bob",
22          "path": "/",
23          "userId": "EXAMPLEUSERID"
24      }}
25  }]}
```

The following example shows that the IAM user Alice used the AWS Management Console to call the AddUserToGroup action to add Bob to the administrator group.

```
1  {"Records": [{
2      "eventVersion": "1.0",
3      "userIdentity": {
4          "type": "IAMUser",
5          "principalId": "EX_PRINCIPAL_ID",
6          "arn": "arn:aws:iam::123456789012:user/Alice",
7          "accountId": "123456789012",
8          "accessKeyId": "EXAMPLE_KEY_ID",
9          "userName": "Alice",
10         "sessionContext": {"attributes": {
11             "mfaAuthenticated": "false",
12             "creationDate": "2014-03-25T18:45:11Z"
13         }}
14     },
15     "eventTime": "2014-03-25T21:08:14Z",
16     "eventSource": "iam.amazonaws.com",
17     "eventName": "AddUserToGroup",
18     "awsRegion": "us-east-2",
19     "sourceIPAddress": "127.0.0.1",
20     "userAgent": "AWSConsole",
21     "requestParameters": {
22         "userName": "Bob",
23         "groupName": "admin"
24     },
25     "responseElements": null
26  }]}
```

The following example shows that the IAM user Alice used the AWS CLI to call the CreateRole action to create a new IAM role.

```
1  {
2      "Records": [{
3          "eventVersion": "1.0",
4          "userIdentity": {
5              "type": "IAMUser",
6              "principalId": "EX_PRINCIPAL_ID",
7              "arn": "arn:aws:iam::123456789012:user/Alice",
8              "accountId": "123456789012",
9              "accessKeyId": "EXAMPLE_KEY_ID",
10             "userName": "Alice"
11         },
```

```
12    "eventTime": "2014-03-25T20:17:37Z",
13    "eventSource": "iam.amazonaws.com",
14    "eventName": "CreateRole",
15    "awsRegion": "us-east-2",
16    "sourceIPAddress": "127.0.0.1",
17    "userAgent": "aws-cli/1.3.2 Python/2.7.5 Windows/7",
18    "requestParameters": {
19        "assumeRolePolicyDocument": "{\n  \"Version\": \"2012-10-17\",\n  \"Statement\": [\n
                {\n        \"Sid\": \"\",
20        \n\"Effect\": \"Allow\",\n       \"Principal\": {\n           \"AWS\": \"arn:aws:iam
                ::210987654321:root\"\n      },\n      \"Action\": \"sts:AssumeRole\"\n    }\n
                ]\n}",
21        "roleName": "TestRole"
22    },
23    "responseElements": {
24        "role": {
25            "assumeRolePolicyDocument": "%7B%0A%20%20%22Version%22%3A%20%222012-10-17%22%2C
                %0A%20%20%22Statement%22%3A%20%5B%0A%20%20%20%20%7B%0A%20%20%20%20%20%20%22
                Sid%22%3A%20%22%22%2C%0A%20%20%20%20%20%20%22Effect%22%3A%20%22Allow%22%2C%0
                A%20%20%20%20%20%20%22Principal%22%3A%20%7B%0A%20%20%20%20%20%20%20%20%22AWS
                %22%3A%20%22arn%3Aaws%3Aiam%3A%3A803981987763%3Aroot%22%0A
                %20%20%20%20%20%20%7D%2C%0A%20%20%20%20%20%20%22Action%22%3A%20%22sts%3
                AAssumeRole%22%0A%20%20%20%20%7D%0A%20%20%5D%0A%7D",
26            "roleName": "TestRole",
27            "roleId": "AROAIUU2EOWSWPGX2UJUO",
28            "arn": "arn:aws:iam::123456789012:role/TestRole",
29            "createDate": "Mar 25, 2014 8:17:37 PM",
30            "path": "/"
31        }
32    }
33  }]
34 }
```

Error Code and Message Log Example

The following example shows that the IAM user Alice used the AWS CLI to call the UpdateTrail action to update a trail named myTrail2, but the trail name was not found. The log shows this error in the errorCode and errorMessage elements.

```
1  {"Records": [{
2      "eventVersion": "1.04",
3      "userIdentity": {
4          "type": "IAMUser",
5          "principalId": "EX_PRINCIPAL_ID",
6          "arn": "arn:aws:iam::123456789012:user/Alice",
7          "accountId": "123456789012",
8          "accessKeyId": "EXAMPLE_KEY_ID",
9          "userName": "Alice"
10     },
11     "eventTime": "2016-07-14T19:15:45Z",
12     "eventSource": "cloudtrail.amazonaws.com",
13     "eventName": "UpdateTrail",
14     "awsRegion": "us-east-2",
15     "sourceIPAddress": "205.251.233.182",
```

```
16    "userAgent": "aws-cli/1.10.32 Python/2.7.9 Windows/7 botocore/1.4.22",
17    "errorCode": "TrailNotFoundException",
18    "errorMessage": "Unknown trail: myTrail2 for the user: 123456789012",
19    "requestParameters": {"name": "myTrail2"},
20    "responseElements": null,
21    "requestID": "5d40662a-49f7-11e6-97e4-d9cb6ff7d6a3",
22    "eventID": "b7d4398e-b2f0-4faa-9c76-e2d316a8d67f",
23    "eventType": "AwsApiCall",
24    "recipientAccountId": "123456789012"
25 }]}
```

CloudTrail Supported Services and Integrations

CloudTrail supports logging events for many AWS services. You can find the specifics for each supported service in that service's guide. Links to those service-specific topics are provided below. In addition, some AWS services can be used to analyze and act upon data collected in CloudTrail logs. You can browse an overview of those service integrations here.

Note
To see the list of supported regions for each service, see Regions and Endpoints in the *Amazon Web Services General Reference.*

- AWS Service Integrations With CloudTrail Logs
- AWS Service Topics for CloudTrail
- CloudTrail Unsupported Services

AWS Service Integrations With CloudTrail Logs

You can configure other AWS services to further analyze and act upon the event data collected in CloudTrail logs. For more information, see the following topics.

AWS Service	Topic	Description
Amazon Athena	Querying AWS CloudTrail Logs	Using Athena with CloudTrail logs is a powerful way to enhance your analysis of AWS service activity. For example, you can use queries to identify trends and further isolate activity by attribute, such as source IP address or user. You can automatically create tables for querying logs directly from the CloudTrail console, and use those tables to run queries in Athena. For more information, see Creating a Table for CloudTrail Logs in the CloudTrail Console in the Amazon Athena User Guide. Running queries in Amazon Athena incurs additional costs. For more information, see Amazon Athena Pricing.

AWS Service	Topic	Description
Amazon CloudWatch Logs	Monitoring CloudTrail Log Files with Amazon Cloud-Watch Logs	You can configure CloudTrail with CloudWatch Logs to monitor your trail logs and be notified when specific activity occurs. For example, you can define CloudWatch Logs metric filters that will trigger CloudWatch alarms and send notifications to you when those alarms are triggered. Standard pricing for Amazon CloudWatch and Amazon CloudWatch Logs applies. For more information, see Amazon CloudWatch Pricing.

AWS Service Topics for CloudTrail

You can learn more about how the events for individual AWS services are recorded in CloudTrail logs, including example events for that service in log files. For more information about how specific AWS services integrate with CloudTrail, see the topic about integration in the individual guide for that service.

AWS Service	CloudTrail Topics	Support began
Alexa for Business	Logging Alexa for Business Administration Calls Using AWS CloudTrail	11/29/2017
Amazon API Gateway	Log API management calls to Amazon API Gateway Using AWS CloudTrail	07/09/2015
Application Auto Scaling	Logging Application Auto Scaling API calls with AWS CloudTrail	10/31/2016
AWS Application Discovery Service	Application Discovery Service API Reference	05/12/2016
AWS AppSync	Logging AWS AppSync API Calls with AWS CloudTrail	02/13/2018
Amazon Athena	Logging Amazon Athena API Calls with AWS CloudTrail	05/19/2017
Amazon EC2 Auto Scaling	Logging Auto Scaling API Calls By Using CloudTrail	07/16/2014
AWS Batch	Logging AWS Batch API Calls with AWS CloudTrail	1/10/2018
AWS Billing and Cost Management	Logging AWS Billing and Cost Management API Calls with AWS CloudTrail	06/07/2018
AWS Certificate Manager	Using AWS CloudTrail	03/25/2016
Amazon Chime	Log Amazon Chime Administration Calls Using AWS CloudTrail	09/27/2017

AWS Service	CloudTrail Topics	Support began
Amazon Cloud Directory	Logging Cloud Directory API calls Using AWS CloudTrail	01/26/2017
AWS CloudFormation	Logging AWS CloudFormation API Calls in AWS CloudTrail	04/02/2014
Amazon CloudFront	Using AWS CloudTrail to Capture Requests Sent to the CloudFront API	05/28/2014
AWS CloudHSM	Logging AWS CloudHSM API Calls By Using AWS CloudTrail	01/08/2015
Amazon CloudSearch	Logging Amazon CloudSearch Configuration Service Calls Using AWS CloudTrail	10/16/2014
AWS CloudTrail	AWS CloudTrail API Reference	11/13/2013
Amazon CloudWatch	Logging Amazon CloudWatch API Calls in AWS CloudTrail	04/30/2014
CloudWatch Events	Logging Amazon CloudWatch Events API Calls in AWS CloudTrail	01/16/2016
CloudWatch Logs	Logging Amazon CloudWatch Logs API Calls in AWS CloudTrail	03/10/2016
AWS CodeBuild	Logging AWS CodeBuild API Calls with AWS CloudTrail	12/01/2016
AWS CodeCommit	Logging AWS CodeCommit API Calls with AWS CloudTrail	01/11/2017
AWS CodeDeploy	Monitoring Deployments with AWS CloudTrail	12/16/2014
AWS CodePipeline	Logging AWS CodePipeline API Calls By Using AWS CloudTrail	07/09/2015
AWS CodeStar	Logging AWS CodeStar API Calls with AWS CloudTrail	06/14/2017
Amazon Cognito	Logging Amazon Cognito API Calls with AWS CloudTrail	02/18/2016
AWS Config	Logging AWS Config API Calls By with AWS CloudTrail	02/10/2015
AWS Data Pipeline	Logging AWS Data Pipeline API Calls by using AWS CloudTrail	12/02/2014
AWS Database Migration Service (AWS DMS)	Logging AWS Database Migration Service API Calls Using AWS CloudTrail	02/04/2016
AWS Device Farm	Logging AWS Device Farm API Calls By Using AWS CloudTrail	07/13/2015
AWS Direct Connect	Logging AWS Direct Connect API Calls in AWS CloudTrail	03/08/2014

AWS Service	CloudTrail Topics	Support began
AWS Directory Service	Logging AWS Directory Service API Calls by Using CloudTrail	05/14/2015
Amazon DynamoDB	Logging DynamoDB Operations By Using AWS CloudTrail	05/28/2015
Amazon Elastic Container Registry (Amazon ECR)	Logging Amazon ECR API Calls By Using AWS CloudTrail	12/21/2015
Amazon Elastic Container Service (Amazon ECS)	Logging Amazon ECS API Calls By Using AWS CloudTrail	04/09/2015
Amazon EC2 Systems Manager (SSM)	Auditing SSM API Calls Using AWS CloudTrail	11/13/2013
AWS Elastic Beanstalk (Elastic Beanstalk)	Using Elastic Beanstalk API Calls with AWS CloudTrail	03/31/2014
Amazon Elastic Block Store (Amazon EBS)	Logging API Calls Using AWS CloudTrail	11/13/2013
Amazon Elastic Compute Cloud (Amazon EC2)	Logging API Calls Using AWS CloudTrail	11/13/2013
Amazon Elastic File System (Amazon EFS)	Logging Amazon EFS API Calls with AWS CloudTrail	06/28/2016
Amazon Elastic Container Service for Kubernetes (Amazon EKS)	Logging Amazon EKS API Calls with AWS CloudTrail	06/05/2018
Elastic Load Balancing	AWS CloudTrail Logging for Your Classic Load Balancer and AWS CloudTrail Logging for Your Application Load Balancer	04/04/2014
Amazon Elastic Transcoder	Logging Elastic Transcoder API Calls Using CloudTrail	10/27/2014
Amazon ElastiCache	Logging Amazon ElastiCache API Calls Using AWS CloudTrail	09/15/2014
Amazon Elasticsearch Service	Auditing Amazon Elasticsearch Service Domains with AWS CloudTrail	10/01/2015
AWS Elemental MediaConvert	Logging AWS Elemental MediaConvert API Calls with CloudTrail	11/27/2017
AWS Elemental MediaStore	Logging AWS Elemental MediaStore API Calls with CloudTrail	11/27/2017
Amazon EMR	Logging Amazon EMR API Calls in AWS CloudTrail	04/04/2014
Amazon GameLift	Logging Amazon GameLift API Calls with AWS CloudTrail	01/27/2016
Amazon Glacier	Logging Amazon Glacier API Calls By Using AWS CloudTrail	12/11/2014

AWS Service	CloudTrail Topics	Support began
AWS Glue	Logging AWS Glue Operations Using AWS CloudTrail	11/07/2017
Amazon GuardDuty	Logging Amazon GuardDuty API Calls with AWS CloudTrail	02/12/2018
AWS Health	Logging AWS Health API Calls with AWS CloudTrail	11/21/2016
AWS Identity and Access Management (IAM)	Logging IAM Events with AWS CloudTrail	11/13/2013
Amazon Inspector	Logging Amazon Inspector API calls with AWS CloudTrail	04/20/2016
AWS IoT	Logging AWS IoT API Calls with AWS CloudTrail	04/11/2016
AWS IoT Analytics	Logging AWS IoT Analytics API calls with AWS CloudTrail	04/23/2018
AWS Key Management Service (AWS KMS)	Logging AWS KMS API Calls using AWS CloudTrail	11/12/2014
Amazon Kinesis Data Firehose	Monitoring Amazon Kinesis Data Firehose API Calls with AWS CloudTrail	03/17/2016
Amazon Kinesis Data Streams	Logging Amazon Kinesis Data Streams API Calls Using AWS CloudTrail	04/25/2014
AWS Lambda	Logging AWS Lambda API Calls By Using AWS CloudTrail Using Lambda with AWS CloudTrail	Management events: 04/09/2015 Data events: 11/30/2017
Amazon Lex	Logging Amazon Lex API Calls with CloudTrail	08/15/2017
Amazon Lightsail	Logging Lightsail API Calls with AWS CloudTrail	12/23/2016
Amazon Machine Learning	Logging Amazon ML API Calls By Using AWS CloudTrail	12/10/2015
AWS Managed Services	AWS Managed Services	12/21/2016
AWS Marketplace	AWS Marketplace Metering Service API Reference	05/02/2017
AWS Migration Hub	Logging AWS Migration Hub API Calls with AWS CloudTrail	08/14/2017
AWS OpsWorks	Logging AWS OpsWorks API Calls By Using AWS CloudTrail	06/04/2014
AWS OpsWorks for Chef Automate	Logging AWS OpsWorks for Chef Automate API Calls with AWS CloudTrail	11/23/2016
AWS Organizations	Logging AWS Organizations Events with AWS CloudTrail	02/27/2017
AWS Personal Health Dashboard	Logging AWS Health API Calls with AWS CloudTrail	12/01/2016

AWS Service	CloudTrail Topics	Support began
Amazon Pinpoint	Logging Amazon Pinpoint API Calls with AWS Cloud-Trail	02/06/2018
Amazon Polly	Logging Amazon Polly API Calls with AWS CloudTrail	11/30/2016
AWS Private Certificate Authority (PCA)	Using CloudTrail	04/04/2018
Amazon QuickSight	Logging Operations with CloudTrail	04/28/2017
Amazon Redshift	Amazon Redshift API Reference	06/10/2014
Amazon Rekognition	Logging Amazon Rekognition API Calls Using AWS Cloud-Trail	04/6/2018
Amazon Relational Database Service (Amazon RDS)	Logging Amazon RDS API Calls Using AWS CloudTrail	11/13/2013
Route 53	Using AWS CloudTrail to Capture Requests Sent to the Route 53 API	02/11/2015
Amazon SageMaker	Logging Amazon SageMaker API Calls with AWS Cloud-Trail	01/11/2018
AWS Secrets Manager	Monitor the Use of Your AWS Secrets Manager Secrets	04/05/2018
AWS Security Token Service (AWS STS)	Logging IAM Events with AWS CloudTrail The IAM topic includes information for AWS STS.	11/13/2013
AWS Server Migration Service	AWS SMS API Reference	11/14/2016
AWS Service Catalog	Logging AWS Service Catalog API Calls with AWS Cloud-Trail	07/06/2016
AWS Shield	Logging Shield Advanced API Calls with AWS CloudTrail	02/08/2018
Amazon Simple Email Service (Amazon SES)	Logging Amazon SES API Calls By Using AWS Cloud-Trail	05/07/2015
Amazon Simple Notification Service (Amazon SNS)	Logging Amazon Simple Notification Service API Calls By Using AWS CloudTrail	10/09/2014
Amazon Simple Queue Service (Amazon SQS)	Logging Amazon SQS API Actions Using AWS CloudTrail	07/16/2014
Amazon Simple Storage Service	Logging Amazon S3 API Calls By Using AWS CloudTrail	Management events: 09/01/2015 Data events: 11/21/2016
Amazon Simple Workflow Service (Amazon SWF)	Logging Amazon Simple Workflow Service API Calls with AWS CloudTrail	05/13/2014
AWS Single Sign-On (AWS SSO)	Logging AWS SSO API Calls with AWS CloudTrail	12/07/2017
AWS Step Functions	Logging AWS Step Functions API Calls with AWS Cloud-Trail	12/01/2016

AWS Service	CloudTrail Topics	Support began
AWS Storage Gateway	Logging AWS Storage Gateway API Calls by Using AWS CloudTrail	12/16/2014
AWS Support	Logging AWS Support API Calls with AWS CloudTrail	04/21/2016
Amazon Virtual Private Cloud (Amazon VPC)	Logging API Calls Using AWS CloudTrail The Amazon VPC API is a subset of the Amazon EC2 API.	11/13/2013
AWS WAF	Logging AWS WAF API Calls with AWS CloudTrail	04/28/2016
Amazon WorkDocs	Logging Amazon WorkDocs API Calls By Using AWS CloudTrail	08/27/2014
Amazon WorkMail	Logging Amazon WorkMail API Calls Using AWS CloudTrail	12/12/2017
Amazon WorkSpaces	Logging Amazon WorkSpaces API Calls by Using CloudTrail	04/09/2015
AWS X-Ray	Logging AWS X-Ray API Calls With CloudTrail	04/25/2018

CloudTrail Unsupported Services

The following AWS services are not yet supported with AWS CloudTrail.

For a list of supported AWS services, see CloudTrail Supported Services and Integrations.

AWS service	Launch date
Amazon AppStream 2.0	December 1, 2016
Amazon Comprehend	November 29, 2017
Amazon FreeRTOS	November 29, 2017
Amazon Kinesis Video Streams	November 29, 2017
Amazon Mobile Analytics	December 17, 2014
Amazon MQ	November 28, 2017
Amazon Sumerian	November 27, 2017
Amazon Transcribe	November 29, 2017
Amazon Translate	November 29, 2017
AWS Cloud9	November 30, 2017
AWS DeepLens	November 29, 2017
AWS Elemental MediaLive	November 27, 2017
AWS Elemental MediaPackage	November 27, 2017
AWS Elemental MediaTailor	November 27, 2017
AWS Greengrass	June 7, 2017
AWS Snowball	October 7, 2015
AWS Trusted Advisor	April 30, 2013

The following AWS services do not have public API operations.

AWS service	Launch date
Amazon Connect	March 28, 2017
Amazon Macie	August 14, 2017
Amazon WorkSpaces Application Manager	April 9, 2015
AWS Artifact	November 30, 2016
AWS Mobile Hub	February 9, 2016
AWS Snowball Edge	November 30, 2016
AWS Snowmobile	November 30, 2016

Limits in AWS CloudTrail

The following table describes limits within CloudTrail. CloudTrail has no adjustable limits. For information about other limits in AWS, see AWS Service Limits.

Resource	Default Limit	Comments
Trails per region	5	This limit cannot be increased.
Get, describe, and list APIs	10 transactions per second (TPS)	The maximum number of operation requests you can make per second without being throttled. The LookupEvents API is not included in this category.This limit cannot be increased.
All other APIs	1 transaction per second (TPS)	The maximum number of operation requests you can make per second without being throttled. This limit cannot be increased.
Event selectors	5 per trail	This limit cannot be increased.
Data resources in event selectors	250 across all event selectors in a trail	The total number of data resources cannot exceed 250 across all event selectors in a trail. The limit of number of resources on an individual event selector is configurable up to 250. This upper limit is allowed only if the total number of data resources does not exceed 250 across all event selectors. Examples: [See the AWS documentation website for more details]This limit cannot be increased.

Getting Started with CloudTrail

CloudTrail is enabled by default for your AWS account. You can use CloudTrail to view, search, download, archive, analyze, and respond to account activity across your AWS infrastructure. This includes activity made through the AWS Management Console, AWS Command Line Interface, and AWS SDKs and APIs.

- Viewing Events with CloudTrail Event History
- Overview for Creating a Trail
- Getting and Viewing Your CloudTrail Log Files
- Configuring Amazon SNS Notifications for CloudTrail
- Controlling User Permissions for CloudTrail

Viewing Events with CloudTrail Event History

You can troubleshoot operational and security incidents over the past 90 days in the CloudTrail console by viewing **Event history**. You can look up events related to creation, modification, or deletion of resources (such as IAM users or Amazon EC2 instances) in your AWS account on a per-region basis. Events can be viewed and downloaded by using the AWS CloudTrail console. You can customize the view of event history in the console by selecting which columns are displayed and which are hidden. You can programmatically look up events by using the AWS SDKs or AWS Command Line Interface.

Note
CloudTrail began logging all CloudTrail management events in **Event history** on June 14, 2018, but these events are not logged retroactively. A full 90-day record of all management event activity in your AWS account will not be available in **Event history** until after 90 days have passed.
Over time, AWS services might add additional events. CloudTrail will record these events in **Event history**, but a full 90-day record of activity that includes added events will not be available until 90 days after the events are added.

This section describes how to look up events by using the CloudTrail console and the AWS CLI. It also describes how to download a file of events. For information on using the `LookupEvents` API to retrieve information from CloudTrail events, see the AWS CloudTrail API Reference.

For information on creating a trail so that you have a record of events that extends past 90 days, see Creating a Trail and Getting and Viewing Your CloudTrail Log Files.

- Viewing CloudTrail Events in the CloudTrail Console
- Viewing CloudTrail Events with the AWS CLI

Viewing CloudTrail Events in the CloudTrail Console

You can use the CloudTrail console to view the last 90 days of recorded API activity and events in an AWS Region. You can also download a file with that information, or a subset of information based on the filter and time range you choose. You can customize your view of event history by selecting which columns are displayed in the console. You can also look up and filter events by the resource types available for a particular service.

CloudTrail logging varies between AWS services. While most AWS services support CloudTrail logging of all events, some services only support logging a subset of APIs and events, and a few services are unsupported. You can learn more about the specifics of how CloudTrail logs events for a specific service by consulting the documentation for that service. For more information, see CloudTrail Supported Services and Integrations and CloudTrail Unsupported Services.

Note
For an ongoing record of activity and events, create a trail. Creating a trail also enables you to take advantage of the following integrations:
Analyze your AWS service activity with queries in Amazon Athena. For more information, see Creating a Table for CloudTrail Logs in the CloudTrail Console in the Amazon Athena User Guide, or simply choose the option to create a table directly from **Event history** in the CloudTrail console. Monitor your trail logs and be notified when specific activity occurs with Amazon CloudWatch Logs. For more information, see Monitoring CloudTrail Log Files with Amazon CloudWatch Logs.

To view CloudTrail events

1. Sign in to the AWS Management Console and open the CloudTrail console at https://console.aws.amazon. com/cloudtrail/home/.

2. In the navigation pane, choose **Event history**.

A list of events appears in the content pane with the latest event first. Scroll down to see more events.

Displaying CloudTrail Events

You can customize the display of event history by selecting which columns to display in the CloudTrail console. By default, the following columns are displayed:

- **Event time**
- **User name**
- **Event name**
- **Resource type**
- **Resource name**

You cannot change the order of the columns.

To customize the columns displayed in event history

1. Sign in to the AWS Management Console and open the CloudTrail console at https://console.aws.amazon. com/cloudtrail/home/.

2. In the navigation pane, choose **Event history**.

3. Choose the gear icon.

4. In **Show/Hide Columns**, select the columns you want to display. Clear the columns you do not want to display. When you have finished, choose **Save**.

Filtering CloudTrail Events

You can filter events by the following attributes. You can filter by time range and one other attribute.

** Event ID **
The CloudTrail ID of the event. Each event has a unique ID.

** Event name **
The name of the event. For example, you can filter on IAM events, such as `CreatePolicy`, or Amazon EC2 events, such as `RunInstances`.

** Event source **
The AWS service to which the request was made, such as `iam.amazonaws.com` or `s3.amazonaws.com`. You can scroll through a list of event sources after you choose the **Event source** filter.

** Resource name **
The name or ID of the resource referenced by the event. For example, the resource name might be "auto-scaling-test-group" for an Auto Scaling group or "i-1234567" for an EC2 instance.

** Resource type **
The type of resource referenced by the event. For example, a resource type can be `Instance` for EC2 or `DBInstance` for RDS. Resource types vary for each AWS service.

** Time range **
The time range in which you want to filter events. You can filter events for the last 90 days.

** User name **
The name of the user referenced by the event. For example, this can be an IAM user.

If there are no events logged for the attribute or time that you choose, the results list is empty. You can apply only one attribute filter in addition to the time range. If you choose a different attribute filter, your specified time range is preserved.

The following steps describe how to filter by attribute.

To filter by attribute

1. To filter the results by an attribute, choose **Select attribute**, and then type or choose a value in the **Enter lookup value** box.

2. To remove an attribute filter, choose the **X** on the right of the attribute filter box.

The following steps describe how to filter by a start and end date and time.

To filter by a start and end date and time

1. To narrow the time range for the events that you want to see, choose **Select time range**.

2. To remove a time range filter, choose the calendar icon on the right of the **Time range** box, and then choose **Remove**.

Viewing Details for an Event

1. Choose an event in the results list to show its details.

2. If the event referenced more than one resource, the additional resources are listed at the bottom of the details pane.

3. Some referenced resources have links. Choose the link to open the console for that resource.

4. Choose **View Event** in the details pane to view the event in JSON format.

5. Choose the event again to close the details pane.

Downloading Events

You can download recorded event history as a file in CSV or JSON format. Use filters and time ranges to reduce the size of the file you download.

Note
CloudTrail event history files are data files that contain information (such as resource names) that can be configured by individual users. Some data can potentially be interpreted as commands in programs used to read and analyze this data (CSV injection). For example, when CloudTrail events are exported to CSV and imported to a spreadsheet program, that program might warn you about security concerns. You should choose to disable this content to keep your system secure. Always disable links or macros from downloaded event history files.

1. Specify the filter and time range for events you want to download. For example, you can specify the event name, `StartInstances`, and specify a time range for the last three days of activity.

2. Choose the and then choose **Export to CSV** or **Export to JSON**. The download starts immediately. **Note**
Your download might take some time to complete. For faster results, before you start the download process, use a more specific filter or a shorter time range to narrow the results.

3. After your download is complete, open the file to view the events that you specified.

4. To cancel your download, choose **Cancel download**.

Viewing Resources Referenced with AWS Config

AWS Config records configuration details, relationships, and changes to your AWS resources.

On the **Resources Referenced** pane, choose the in the **Config timeline** column to view the resource in the AWS Config console.

If the icon is gray, AWS Config is not turned on, or it's not recording the resource type. Choose the icon to go to the AWS Config console to turn on the service or start recording that resource type. For more information, see Set Up AWS Config Using the Console in the *AWS Config Developer Guide*.

If **Link not available** appears in the column, the resource can't be viewed for one of the following reasons:

- AWS Config doesn't support the resource type. For more information, see Supported Resources, Configuration Items, and Relationships in the *AWS Config Developer Guide*.

- AWS Config recently added support for the resource type, but it's not yet available from the CloudTrail console. You can look up the resource in the AWS Config console to see the timeline for the resource.

- The resource is owned by another AWS account.

- The resource is owned by another AWS service, such as a managed IAM policy.

- The resource was created and then deleted immediately.

- The resource was recently created or updated.

Example

1. You configure AWS Config to record IAM resources.

2. You create an IAM user, Bob-user. The **Event history** page shows the `CreateUser` event and Bob-user as an IAM resource. You can choose the AWS Config icon to view this IAM resource in the AWS Config timeline.

3. You update the user name to Bob-admin.

4. The **Event history** page shows the `UpdateUser` event and Bob-admin as the updated IAM resource.

5. You can choose the icon to view the Bob-admin IAM resource in the timeline. However, you can't choose the icon for Bob-user, because the resource name changed. AWS Config is now recording the updated resource.

To grant users read-only permission to view resources in the AWS Config console, see Granting Permission to View AWS Config Information on the CloudTrail Console.

For more information about AWS Config, see the AWS Config Developer Guide.

Viewing CloudTrail Events with the AWS CLI

You can look up CloudTrail events for the last 90 days using the aws cloudtrail lookup-events command. `lookup-events` has the following options:

- `--max-results`
- `--start-time`
- `--lookup-attributes`
- `--next-token`
- `--generate-cli-skeleton`
- `--cli-input-json`

These options are explained in this topic. For general information on using the AWS Command Line Interface, see the AWS Command Line Interface User Guide.

Prerequisites

- To run AWS CLI commands, you must install the AWS CLI. For information, see Installing the AWS Command Line Interface.
- Make sure your AWS CLI version is greater than 1.6.6. To verify the CLI version, run aws --version on the command line.
- To set the account, region, and default output format for an AWS CLI session, use the aws configure command. For more information, see Configuring the AWS Command Line Interface.

Note
The CloudTrail AWS CLI commands are case-sensitive.

Getting command line help

To see the command line help for `lookup-events`, type the following command:

```
1 aws cloudtrail lookup-events help
```

Looking up events

To see the ten latest events, type the following command:

```
1 aws cloudtrail lookup-events
```

A returned event looks similar to the following fictitious example, which has been formatted for readability:

```
1 {
2     "NextToken": "kbOt5LlZe++
        mErCebpy2TgaMgmDvF1kYGFcH64JSjIbZFjsuvrSqg66b5YGssKutDYIyII4lrP4IDbeQdiObkp9YAlju3oXd12juy3CI
        =",
3     "Events": [
4         {
5             "EventId": "0ebbaee4-6e67-431d-8225-ba0d81df5972",
6             "Username": "root",
7             "EventTime": 1424476529.0,
```

```
 8          "CloudTrailEvent": "{
 9              \"eventVersion\":\"1.02\",
10              \"userIdentity\":{
11                  \"type\":\"Root\",
12                  \"principalId\":\"111122223333\",
13                  \"arn\":\"arn:aws:iam::111122223333:root\",
14                  \"accountId\":\"111122223333\"},
15              \"eventTime\":\"2015-02-20T23:55:29Z\",
16              \"eventSource\":\"signin.amazonaws.com\",
17              \"eventName\":\"ConsoleLogin\",
18              \"awsRegion\":\"us-east-2\",
19              \"sourceIPAddress\":\"203.0.113.4\",
20              \"userAgent\":\"Mozilla/5.0\",
21              \"requestParameters\":null,
22              \"responseElements\":{\"ConsoleLogin\":\"Success\"},
23              \"additionalEventData\":{
24                  \"MobileVersion\":\"No\",
25                  \"LoginTo\":\"https://console.aws.amazon.com/console/home",
26                  \"MFAUsed\":\"No\"},
27              \"eventID\":\"0ebbaee4-6e67-431d-8225-ba0d81df5972\",
28              \"eventType\":\"AwsApiCall\",
29              \"recipientAccountId\":\"111122223333\"}",
30          "EventName": "ConsoleLogin",
31          "Resources": []
32      }
33    ]
34 }
```

For an explanation of the lookup-related fields in the output, see the section Lookup Output Fields later in this document. For an explanation of the fields in the CloudTrail event, see CloudTrail Record Contents.

Specifying the number of events to return

To specify the number of events to return, type the following command:

```
1 aws cloudtrail lookup-events --max-results <integer>
```

The default value for is 10. Possible values are 1 through 50. The following example returns one result.

```
1 aws cloudtrail lookup-events --max-results 1
```


Looking up events by time range

Events from the past 90 days are available for lookup. To specify a time range, type the following command:

```
1 aws cloudtrail lookup-events --start-time <timestamp> --end-time <timestamp>
```

--start-time <timestamp> specifies that only events that occur after or at the specified time are returned. If the specified start time is after the specified end time, an error is returned.

--end-time <timestamp> specifies that only events that occur before or at the specified time are returned. If the specified end time is before the specified start time, an error is returned.

The default start time is the earliest date that data is available within the last 90 days.The default end time is the time of the event that occurred closest to the current time.

Valid formats

The `--start-time` and `--end-time` attributes take UNIX time values or valid equivalents.

The following are examples of valid formats. Date, month, and year values can be separated by hyphens or forward slashes. Double quotes must be used if spaces are present.

```
1  1422317782
2  1422317782.0
3  01-27-2015
4  01-27-2015,01:16PM
5  "01-27-2015, 01:16 PM"
6  "01/27/2015, 13:16"
7  2015-01-27
8  "2015-01-27, 01:16 PM"
```

Looking up events by attribute

To filter by an attribute, type the following command:

```
1  aws cloudtrail lookup-events --lookup-attributes AttributeKey=<attribute>,AttributeValue=<string
   >
```

You can specify only one attribute key/value pair for each lookup-events command. The following are values for `AttributeKey`. Value names are case sensitive.

- EventId
- EventName
- EventSource
- ResourceName
- ResourceType
- Username

Attribute lookup examples

The following example command returns the event for the specified CloudTrail `EventId`.

```
1  aws cloudtrail lookup-events --lookup-attributes AttributeKey=EventId,AttributeValue=b5cc8c40-12
   ba-4d08-a8d9-2bceb9a3e002
```

The following example command returns events in which the value of `EventName` is `RunInstances`.

```
1  aws cloudtrail lookup-events --lookup-attributes AttributeKey=EventName,AttributeValue=
   RunInstances
```

The following example command returns events in which the value of `EventSource` is `iam.amazonaws.com`.

```
1  aws cloudtrail lookup-events --lookup-attributes AttributeKey=EventSource,AttributeValue=iam.
   amazonaws.com
```

The following example command returns events in which the value of `ResourceName` is `CloudTrail_CloudWatchLogs_Role`.

```
1  aws cloudtrail lookup-events --lookup-attributes AttributeKey=ResourceName,AttributeValue=
   CloudTrail_CloudWatchLogs_Role
```

The following example command returns events in which the value of `ResourceType` is `AWS::S3::Bucket`.

```
1 aws cloudtrail lookup-events --lookup-attributes AttributeKey=ResourceType,AttributeValue=AWS::
    S3::Bucket
```

The following example command returns events in which the value of `Username` is `root`.

```
1 aws cloudtrail lookup-events --lookup-attributes AttributeKey=Username,AttributeValue=root
```

Specifying the next page of results

To get the next page of results from a `lookup-events` command, type the following command:

```
1 aws cloudtrail lookup-events <same parameters as previous command> --next-token=<token>
```

where the value for is taken from the first field of the output of the previous command.

When you use `--next-token` in a command, you must use the same parameters as in the previous command. For example, suppose you run the following command:

```
1 aws cloudtrail lookup-events --lookup-attributes AttributeKey=Username,AttributeValue=root
```

To get the next page of results, your next command would look like this:

```
1 aws cloudtrail lookup-events --lookup-attributes AttributeKey=Username,AttributeValue=root --
    next-token=kbOt5LlZe++
    mErCebpy2TgaMgmDvF1kYGFcH64JSjIbZFjsuvrSqg66b5YGssKutDYIyII4lrP4IDbeQdiObkp9YAlju3oXd12juy3CIZW8
    =
```

Getting JSON input from a file

The AWS CLI for some AWS services has two parameters, `--generate-cli-skeleton` and `--cli-input-json`, that you can use to generate a JSON template which you can modify and use as input to the `--cli-input-json` parameter. This section describes how to use these parameters with `aws cloudtrail lookup-events`. For more general information, see Generate CLI Skeleton and CLI Input JSON Parameters.

To look up CloudTrail events by getting JSON input from a file

1. Create an input template for use with `lookup-events` by redirecting the `--generate-cli-skeleton` output to a file, as in the following example.

   ```
   1 aws cloudtrail lookup-events --generate-cli-skeleton > LookupEvents.txt
   ```

   The template file generated (in this case, LookupEvents.txt) looks like this:

   ```
    1 {
    2     "LookupAttributes": [
    3         {
    4             "AttributeKey": "",
    5             "AttributeValue": ""
    6         }
    7     ],
    8     "StartTime": null,
    9     "EndTime": null,
   10     "MaxResults": 0,
   11     "NextToken": ""
   12 }
   ```

2. Use a text editor to modify the JSON as needed. The JSON input must contain only values that are specified. **Important**

   All empty or null values must be removed from the template before you can use it.

   The following example specifies a time range and maximum number of results to return.

```
1 {
2     "StartTime": "2015-01-01",
3     "EndTime": "2015-01-27",
4     "MaxResults": 2
5 }
```

3. To use the edited file as input, use the syntax `--cli-input-json file://`, as in the following example:

```
1 aws cloudtrail lookup-events --cli-input-json file://LookupEvents.txt
```

Note
You can use other arguments on the same command line as `--cli-input-json` .

Lookup Output Fields

Events
A list of lookup events based on the lookup attribute and time range that were specified. The events list is sorted by time, with the latest event listed first. Each entry contains information about the lookup request and includes a string representation of the CloudTrail event that was retrieved.
The following entries describe the fields in each lookup event.

CloudTrailEvent
A JSON string that contains an object representation of the event returned. For information about each of the elements returned, see Record Body Contents.

EventId
A string that contains the GUID of the event returned.

EventName
A string that contains the name of the event returned.

EventSource
The AWS service that the request was made to.

EventTime
The date and time, in UNIX time format, of the event.

Resources
A list of resources referenced by the event that was returned. Each resource entry specifies a resource type and a resource name.

ResourceName
A string that contains the name of the resource referenced by the event.

ResourceType
A string that contains the type of a resource referenced by the event. When the resource type cannot be determined, null is returned.

Username
A string that contains the user name of the account for the event returned.

NextToken
A string to get the next page of results from a previous `lookup-events` command. To use the token, the parameters must be the same as those in the original command. If no `NextToken` entry appears in the output, there are no more results to return.

Overview for Creating a Trail

You can configure the following settings when you create or update a trail with the CloudTrail console or the AWS Command Line Interface (AWS CLI). Both methods follow the same steps:

1. Turn on CloudTrail by creating a trail. By default, when you create a trail in a region in the CloudTrail console, the trail applies to all regions.

2. Create an Amazon S3 bucket or specify an existing bucket where you want the log files delivered. By default, log files from all regions in your account are delivered to the bucket that you specify.

3. Configure your trail to log read-only, write-only, or all management and data events. By default, trails log all management events.

4. Create an Amazon SNS topic to receive notifications when log files are delivered. Delivery notifications from all regions are sent to the topic that you specify.

5. Configure CloudWatch Logs to receive your logs from CloudTrail so that you can monitor for specific log events.

6. Turn on log file encryption. This encrypts your files for added security.

7. Turn on integrity validation for log files. This enables the delivery of digest files that you can use to validate the integrity of log files after CloudTrail has delivered them.

8. Add tags (custom key-value pairs) to your trail.

- Creating a Trail with the Console
- Creating a Trail with the AWS Command Line Interface
- CloudTrail Trail Naming Requirements
- Amazon S3 Bucket Naming Requirements
- Amazon S3 Bucket Policy for CloudTrail
- AWS KMS Alias Naming Requirements
- Tips for Managing Trails

Creating a Trail with the Console

You can create, update, or delete your trails with the CloudTrail console. You can create up to five trails for each region. After you create a trail, CloudTrail automatically starts logging API calls and related events in your account to the Amazon S3 bucket that you specify. To stop logging, you can turn off logging for the trail or delete it.

- Creating a Trail
- Updating a Trail
- Deleting a Trail
- Turning off Logging for a Trail

Creating a Trail

Follow the procedure to create a trail that applies to all regions. A trail that applies to all regions delivers log files from all regions to an S3 bucket. After you create the trail, CloudTrail automatically starts logging the events that you specified.

Note
After you create a trail, you can configure other AWS services to further analyze and act upon the event data collected in CloudTrail logs. For more information, see CloudTrail Supported Services and Integrations.

Creating a Trail in the Console

You can configure your trail for the following:

- Specify if you want the trail to apply to all regions or a single region.
- Specify an Amazon S3 bucket to receive log files.
- For management and data events, specify if you want to log read-only, write-only, or all events.

To create a CloudTrail trail with the AWS Management Console

1. Sign in to the AWS Management Console and open the CloudTrail console at https://console.aws.amazon.com/cloudtrail/.

2. Choose the region where you want the trail to be created.

3. Choose **Get Started Now. Tip**
   If you do not see **Get Started Now**, choose **Trails**, and then choose **Create trail**.

4. On the **Create Trail** page, for **Trail name**, type a name for your trail. For more information, see CloudTrail Trail Naming Requirements.

5. For **Apply trail to all regions**, choose **Yes** to receive log files from all regions. This is the default and recommended setting. If you choose **No**, the trail logs files only from the region in which you create the trail.

6. For **Management events**, for **Read/Write events**, choose if you want your trail to log **All**, **Read-only**, **Write-only**, or **None**, and then choose **Save**. By default, trails log all management events. For more information, see Management Events.

7. For **Data events**, you can specify logging data events for Amazon S3 buckets, for AWS Lambda functions, or both. By default, trails don't log data events. Additional charges apply for logging data events. For CloudTrail pricing, see AWS CloudTrail Pricing.

   You can select the option to log all S3 buckets and Lambda functions, or you can specify individual buckets or functions.

   For Amazon S3 buckets:

   - Choose the **S3** tab.

   - To specify a bucket, choose **Add S3 bucket**. Type the S3 bucket name and prefix (optional) for which you want to log data events. For each bucket, specify whether you want to log **Read** events, such as `GetObject`, **Write** events, such as `PutObject`, or both. For more information, see Data Events.

   - To log data events for all S3 buckets in your AWS account, select **Select all S3 buckets in your account**. Then choose whether you want to log **Read** events, such as `GetObject`, **Write** events, such as `PutObject`, or both. This setting takes precedence over individual settings you configure for individual buckets. For example, if you specify logging **Read** events for all S3 buckets, and then

choose to add a specific bucket for data event logging, **Read** is already selected for the bucket you added. You cannot clear the selection. You can only configure the option for **Write. Note**
Selecting the **Select all S3 buckets in your account** option enables data event logging for all buckets currently in your AWS account and any buckets you create after you finish creating the trail. It also enables logging of data event activity performed by any user or role in your AWS account, even if that activity is performed on a bucket that belongs to another AWS account.

If the trail applies only to one region, selecting the **Select all S3 buckets in your account** option enables data event logging for all buckets in the same region as your trail and any buckets you create later in that region. It will not log data events for Amazon S3 buckets in other regions in your AWS account.

For Lambda functions:

- Choose the **Lambda** tab.

- To specify logging individual functions, select them from the list. **Note**
If you have more than 15,000 Lambda functions in your account, you cannot view or select all functions in the CloudTrail console when creating a trail. You can still select the option to log all functions, even if they are not displayed. If you want to log data events for specific functions, you can manually add a function if you know its ARN. You can also finish creating the trail in the console, and then use the AWS CLI and the put-event-selectors command to configure data event logging for specific Lambda functions. For more information, see Managing Trails.

- To log data events for all Lambda functions in your AWS account, select **Log all current and future functions**. This setting takes precedence over individual settings you configure for individual functions. All functions are logged, even if all functions are not displayed. **Note**
If you are creating a trail for all regions, this selection enables data event logging for all functions currently in your AWS account, and any Lambda functions you might create in any region after you finish creating the trail. If you are creating a trail for a single region, this selection enables data event logging for all functions currently in that region in your AWS account, and any Lambda functions you might create in that region after you finish creating the trail. It does not enable data event logging for Lambda functions created in other regions.
Logging data events for all functions also enables logging of data event activity performed by any user or role in your AWS account, even if that activity is performed on a function that belongs to another AWS account.

8. For **Storage location**, for **Create a new S3 bucket**, choose **Yes** to create a bucket. When you create a bucket, CloudTrail creates and applies the required bucket policies. **Note**
If you chose **No**, choose an existing S3 bucket. The bucket policy must grant CloudTrail permission to write to it. For information about manually editing the bucket policy, see Amazon S3 Bucket Policy for CloudTrail.

9. For **S3 bucket**, type a name for the bucket you want to designate for log file storage. The name must be globally unique. For more information, see Amazon S3 Bucket Naming Requirements.

10. To configure advanced settings, see Configuring Advanced Settings for Your Trail. Otherwise, choose **Create**.

11. The new trail appears on the **Trails** page. The **Trails** page shows the trails in your account from all regions. In about 15 minutes, CloudTrail publishes log files that show the AWS API calls made in your account. You can see the log files in the S3 bucket that you specified.

Note
You can't rename a trail after it has been created. Instead, you can delete the trail and create a new one.

Configuring Advanced Settings for Your Trail

You can configure the following settings for your trail:

- Specify a log file prefix for the S3 bucket receiving log files.

- Encrypt log files with AWS Key Management Service.

- Enable log file validation for logs.

- Configure Amazon SNS to notify you when log files are delivered.

To configure advanced settings for your trail

1. For **Storage location**, choose **Advanced**.

2. In the **Log file prefix** field, type a prefix for your Amazon S3 bucket. The prefix is an addition to the URL for an Amazon S3 object that creates a folder-like organization in your bucket. The location where your log files will be stored appears under the text field.

3. For **Encrypt log files**, choose **Yes** if you want AWS KMS to encrypt your log files.

4. For **Create a new KMS key**, choose **Yes** to create a key or **No** to use an existing one.

5. If you chose **Yes**, in the **KMS key** field, type an alias. CloudTrail encrypts your log files with the key and adds the policy for you. **Note**
If you chose **No**, choose an existing KMS key. You can also type the ARN of a key from another account. For more information, see Updating a Trail to Use Your CMK. The key policy must allow CloudTrail to use the key to encrypt your log files, and allow the users you specify to read log files in unencrypted form. For information about manually editing the key policy, see AWS KMS Key Policy for CloudTrail.

6. For **Enable log file validation**, choose **Yes** to have log digests delivered to your S3 bucket. You can use the digest files to verify that your log files did not change after CloudTrail delivered them. For more information, see Validating CloudTrail Log File Integrity.

7. For **Send SNS notification for every log file delivery**, choose **Yes** if you want to be notified each time a log is delivered to your bucket. CloudTrail stores multiple events in a log file. SNS notifications are sent for every log file, not for every event.

8. For **Create a new SNS topic**, choose **Yes** to create a topic, or choose **No** to use an existing topic. If you are creating a trail that applies to all regions, SNS notifications for log file deliveries from all regions are sent to the single SNS topic that you create. **Note**
If you chose **No**, choose an existing topic. You can also enter the ARN of a topic from another region or from an account with appropriate permissions. For more information, see Amazon SNS Topic Policy for CloudTrail.

9. If you chose **Yes**, in the **SNS topic** field, type a name.

   If you create a topic, you must subscribe to the topic to be notified of log file delivery. You can subscribe from the Amazon SNS console. Due to the frequency of notifications, we recommend that you configure the subscription to use an Amazon SQS queue to handle notifications programmatically. For more information, see the Amazon Simple Notification Service Getting Started Guide.

10. Choose **Create**.

Next Steps

After you create your trail, you can return to the trail to make changes:

- Configure CloudTrail to send log files to CloudWatch Logs. For more information, see Sending Events to CloudWatch Logs.

- Create a table and use it to run a query in Amazon Athena to analyze your AWS service activity. For more information, see Creating a Table for CloudTrail Logs in the CloudTrail Console in the Amazon Athena User Guide.

- Add custom tags (key-value pairs) to the trail.

- To create another trail, return to the **Trails** page and choose **Add new trail**.

Note

When configuring a trail, you can choose an S3 bucket and SNS topic that belong to another account. However, if you want CloudTrail to deliver events to a CloudWatch Logs log group, you must choose a log group that exists in your current account.

Updating a Trail

To change trail settings, use the following procedure.

To update a trail with the AWS Management Console

1. Sign in to the AWS Management Console and open the CloudTrail console at https://console.aws.amazon.com/cloudtrail/.

2. Choose **Trails** and then choose a trail.

3. To make updates for **Trail settings**, choose the pencil icon, specify if you want your trail to apply to a single region or all regions, and then choose **Save**.

4. For **Management events**, choose the pencil icon, make your changes, and then choose **Save**. Your trail can log **All**, **Read-only**, **Write-only**, or **None**. By default, trails log **All** management events. For more information, see Management Events.

5. For **Data events**, choose the pencil icon or **Configure**, make your changes, and then choose **Save**. By default, trails don't log data events. For more information, see Data Events.

6. For **Storage location**, choose the pencil icon to update the settings for the following:

   - The S3 bucket (with optional prefix) that is receiving your log files.

   - Log file encryption with AWS KMS.

   - Log file validation for logs.

   - The Amazon SNS topic to notify you when log files are delivered.

   For more information, see Configuring Advanced Settings for Your Trail.

7. Choose **Save**.

To configure CloudWatch Logs and tags for your trail

1. To configure CloudTrail to deliver events to CloudWatch Logs for monitoring, for **CloudWatch Logs **, choose **Configure**. For more information about these settings, see Sending Events to CloudWatch Logs.

2. To configure tags (custom key-value pairs) for your trail, for **Tags**, click the pencil icon. You can add up to 50 key-value pairs per trail. Trail tags must be configured from the region in which the trail was created.

3. When finished, choose **Apply**.

Deleting a Trail

You can delete trails with the CloudTrail console. If you want to delete a trail that receives log files from all regions, you must choose the region where you originally created the trail.

To delete a trail with the CloudTrail console

1. Sign in to the AWS Management Console and open the CloudTrail console at https://console.aws.amazon.com/cloudtrail/.

2. Navigate to the **Trails** page of the CloudTrail console for the region in which the trail was created.

3. Choose the trail name.

4. At the top of the configuration page, click the trash icon.

5. Choose **Delete** to delete the trail permanently. The trail will be removed from the list of trails for the region. Log files that were already delivered to the Amazon S3 bucket will not be deleted. **Note** Content delivered to Amazon S3 buckets might contain customer content. For more information about removing personally identifiable information, see How Do I Empty an S3 Bucket? or How Do I Delete an S3 Bucket?.

Turning off Logging for a Trail

When you create a trail, logging is turned on automatically. You can turn off logging for a trail. Previous logs will still be accessible.

To turn off logging for a trail with the CloudTrail console

1. Sign in to the AWS Management Console and open the CloudTrail console at https://console.aws.amazon.com/cloudtrail/.

2. In the navigation pane, choose **Trails**, and then choose the trail that you want to configure.

3. At the top of the configuration page, choose **Logging** to turn off logging for the trail.

4. When the **stop logging** message appears, choose **Continue**. CloudTrail stops logging activity for that trail.

5. To resume logging for that trail, choose **Logging** again.

Creating a Trail with the AWS Command Line Interface

Note
You need the AWS command line tools to run the AWS Command Line Interface (AWS CLI) commands in this topic. For more information, see the AWS Command Line Interface User Guide. For help with CloudTrail commands at the AWS CLI command line, type `aws cloudtrail help`.

Two options for creating and updating trails

When creating or updating a trail with the AWS CLI, you have two sets of options:

- `create-trail` and `update-trail`
- `create-subscription` and `update-subscription`

create-trail and update-trail

The `create-trail` and `update-trail` commands offer the following functionality that the `create-subscription` and `update-subscription` commands do not:

- Create a trail that receives logs across regions, or update a trail with the `--is-multi-region-trail` option.
- Convert a multi-region trail to single-region trail with the `--no-is-multi-region-trail` option.
- Enable or disable log file encryption with the `--kms-key-id` option. The option specifies an AWS KMS key that you have already created and to which you have attached a policy that allows CloudTrail to encrypt your logs. For more information, see Enabling and disabling CloudTrail log file encryption with the AWS CLI.
- Enable or disable log file validation with the `--enable-log-file-validation` and `--no-enable-log-file-validation` options. For more information, see Validating CloudTrail Log File Integrity.
- Specify a CloudWatch Logs log group and role so that CloudTrail can deliver events to a CloudWatch Logs log group. For more information, see Monitoring CloudTrail Log Files with Amazon CloudWatch Logs.

create-subscription and update-subscription

The `create-subscription` and `update-subscription` commands offer the following advantages:

- You can have CloudTrail create an S3 bucket for you. With the `create-trail` command, you must specify an existing bucket in which you have already applied the bucket policy for CloudTrail.
- The `create-subscription` command starts logging for the trail. With the `create-trail` command, you must run the `start-logging` command.

Using create-trail

Creating a single-region trail

The following command creates a single-region trail. The specified Amazon S3 bucket must already exist and have the appropriate CloudTrail permissions applied. For more information, see Amazon S3 Bucket Policy for CloudTrail.

```
1 aws cloudtrail create-trail --name my-trail --s3-bucket-name my-bucket
```

For more information, see CloudTrail Trail Naming Requirements.

Sample output:

```
1 {
2     "IncludeGlobalServiceEvents": true,
3     "Name": "my-trail",
4     "TrailARN": "arn:aws:cloudtrail:us-east-2:123456789012:trail/my-trail",
5     "LogFileValidationEnabled": false,
6     "IsMultiRegionTrail": false,
7     "S3BucketName": "my-bucket"
8 }
```

By default, the `create-trail` command creates a single-region trail and that trail does not enable log file validation.

Start logging for the trail

After the `create-trail` command completes, run the `start-logging` command to start logging for that trail.

Note

When you create a trail with the CloudTrail console or the `create-subscription` command, logging is turned on automatically.

The following example starts logging for a trail:

```
1 aws cloudtrail start-logging --name my-trail
```

This command doesn't return an output, but you can use the `get-trail-status` command to verify that logging has started:

```
1 aws cloudtrail get-trail-status --name my-trail
```

To confirm that the trail is logging, the `IsLogging` element in the output shows `true`:

```
1  {
2      "LatestDeliveryTime": 1441139757.497,
3      "LatestDeliveryAttemptTime": "2015-09-01T20:35:57Z",
4      "LatestNotificationAttemptSucceeded": "2015-09-01T20:35:57Z",
5      "LatestDeliveryAttemptSucceeded": "2015-09-01T20:35:57Z",
6      "IsLogging": true,
7      "TimeLoggingStarted": "2015-09-01T00:54:02Z",
8      "StartLoggingTime": 1441068842.76,
9      "LatestDigestDeliveryTime": 1441140723.629,
10     "LatestNotificationAttemptTime": "2015-09-01T20:35:57Z",
11     "TimeLoggingStopped": ""
12 }
```

Creating a trail that applies to all regions

To create a trail that applies to all regions, use the `--is-multi-region-trail` option.

The following example creates a trail that delivers logs from all regions to an existing bucket named **my-bucket**:

```
1 aws cloudtrail create-trail --name my-trail --s3-bucket-name my-bucket --is-multi-region-trail
```

To confirm that your trail exists in all regions, the `IsMultiRegionTrail` element in the output shows `true`:

```
1 {
2     "IncludeGlobalServiceEvents": true,
3     "Name": "my-trail",
4     "TrailARN": "arn:aws:cloudtrail:us-east-2:123456789012:trail/my-trail",
5     "LogFileValidationEnabled": false,
6     "IsMultiRegionTrail": true,
7     "S3BucketName": "my-bucket"
8 }
```

Note

Use the `start-logging` command to start logging for your trail.

Creating a trail that applies to all regions and that has log file validation enabled

To enable log file validation when using `create-trail`, use the `--enable-log-file-validation` option.

For information about log file validation, see Validating CloudTrail Log File Integrity.

The following example creates a trail that delivers logs from all regions to the specified bucket. The command uses the `--enable-log-file-validation` option.

```
1 aws cloudtrail create-trail --name my-trail --s3-bucket-name my-bucket --is-multi-region-trail
      --enable-log-file-validation
```

To confirm that log file validation is enabled, the `LogFileValidationEnabled` element in the output shows `true`:

```
1 {
2     "IncludeGlobalServiceEvents": true,
3     "Name": "my-trail",
4     "TrailARN": "arn:aws:cloudtrail:us-east-2:123456789012:trail/my-trail",
5     "LogFileValidationEnabled": true,
6     "IsMultiRegionTrail": true,
7     "S3BucketName": "my-bucket"
8 }
```

Using update-trail

You can use the `update-trail` command to change the configuration settings for a trail.

Note

If you use the AWS CLI or one of the AWS SDKs to modify a trail, be sure that the trail's bucket policy is up-to-date. In order for your bucket to automatically receive events from a new AWS Region, the policy must contain the full service name, `cloudtrail.amazonaws.com`. For more information, see Amazon S3 Bucket Policy for CloudTrail.

Note

You can run the `update-trail` command only from the region in which the trail was created.

Converting a trail that applies to one region to apply to all regions

To change an existing trail so that it applies to all regions use the `--is-multi-region-trail` option:

```
1 aws cloudtrail update-trail --name my-trail --is-multi-region-trail
```

To confirm that the trail now applies to all regions, the `IsMultiRegionTrail` element in the output shows `true`:

```
1 {
2     "IncludeGlobalServiceEvents": true,
3     "Name": "my-trail",
4     "TrailARN": "arn:aws:cloudtrail:us-east-2:123456789012:trail/my-trail",
5     "LogFileValidationEnabled": false,
6     "IsMultiRegionTrail": true,
7     "S3BucketName": "my-bucket"
8 }
```

Converting a multi-region trail to a single-region trail

To change an existing multi-region trail so that it appliesonly to the region in which it was created, use the `--no-is-multi-region-trail` option.

```
1 aws cloudtrail update-trail --name my-trail --no-is-multi-region-trail
```

To confirm that the trail now applies to a single region, the `IsMultiRegionTrail` element in the output shows `false`:

```
1 {
2     "IncludeGlobalServiceEvents": true,
3     "Name": "my-trail",
4     "TrailARN": "arn:aws:cloudtrail:us-east-2:123456789012:trail/my-trail",
5     "LogFileValidationEnabled": false,
6     "IsMultiRegionTrail": false,
7     "S3BucketName": "my-bucket"
8 }
```

Enabling and disabling logging global service events

To change a trail so that it does not log global service events, use the `--no-include-global-service-events` option.

```
1 aws cloudtrail update-trail --name my-trail --no-include-global-service-events
```

To confirm that the trail no longer logs global service events, the `IncludeGlobalServiceEvents` element in the output shows `false`:

```
1 {
2     "IncludeGlobalServiceEvents": false,
3     "Name": "my-trail",
4     "TrailARN": "arn:aws:cloudtrail:us-east-2:123456789012:trail/my-trail",
5     "LogFileValidationEnabled": false,
6     "IsMultiRegionTrail": false,
7     "S3BucketName": "my-bucket"
8 }
```

To change a trail so that it logs global service events, use the `--include-global-service-events` option.

Enabling log file validation

To enable log file validation for a trail, use the `--enable-log-file-validation` option. Digest files are delivered to the Amazon S3 bucket for that trail.

```
1 aws cloudtrail update-trail --name my-trail --enable-log-file-validation
```

To confirm that log file validation is enabled, the `LogFileValidationEnabled` element in the output shows true:

```
1 {
2     "IncludeGlobalServiceEvents": true,
3     "Name": "my-trail",
4     "TrailARN": "arn:aws:cloudtrail:us-east-2:123456789012:trail/my-trail",
5     "LogFileValidationEnabled": true,
6     "IsMultiRegionTrail": false,
7     "S3BucketName": "my-bucket"
8 }
```

Disabling log file validation

To disable log file validation for a trail, use the `--no-enable-log-file-validation` option.

```
1 aws cloudtrail update-trail --name my-trail-name --no-enable-log-file-validation
```

To confirm that log file validation is disabled, the `LogFileValidationEnabled` element in the output shows false:

```
1 {
2     "IncludeGlobalServiceEvents": true,
3     "Name": "my-trail",
4     "TrailARN": "arn:aws:cloudtrail:us-east-2:123456789012:trail/my-trail",
5     "LogFileValidationEnabled": false,
6     "IsMultiRegionTrail": false,
7     "S3BucketName": "my-bucket"
8 }
```

To validate log files with the AWS CLI, see Validating CloudTrail Log File Integrity with the AWS CLI.

Using create-subscription

The `create-subscription` command creates a trail. You can also use this command to create an Amazon S3 bucket for log file delivery and an Amazon SNS topic for notifications. The `create-subscription` command also starts logging for the trail that it creates.

The `create-subscription` command includes the following options:

- `--name` specifies the name of the trail. This option is required. For more information, see CloudTrail Trail Naming Requirements.

- `--s3-use-bucket` specifies an existing Amazon S3 bucket for log file storage.

- `--s3-new-bucket` specifies the name of the new bucket created when the command executes. The name of the bucket must be globally unique. For more information, see Amazon S3 Bucket Naming Requirements.

- `--s3-prefix` specifies a prefix for the log file delivery path (optional). The maximum length is 200 characters. **Note**
  If you want to use a new log file prefix for an existing bucket, add the prefix to the bucket policy first. For more information, see Changing a Prefix for an Existing Bucket.

- `--sns-new-topic` specifies the name of the Amazon SNS topic to which you can subscribe for notification of log file delivery to your bucket (optional).

Note

Type `aws cloudtrail create-subscription help` to see the list of options.

The following example creates a trail, an Amazon S3 bucket for log file delivery, an S3 bucket prefix, and an SNS topic.

```
1 aws cloudtrail create-subscription --name=awscloudtrail-example --s3-new-bucket=awscloudtrail-
    new-bucket-example --s3-prefix=prefix-example --sns-new-topic=awscloudtrail-example-log-
    deliverytopic
```

If the command executes successfully, you see output similar to the following:

```
1 Setting up new S3 bucket awscloudtrail-new-bucket-example...
2 Setting up new SNS topic awscloudtrail-example-log-deliverytopic...
3 Creating/updating CloudTrail configuration...
4 CloudTrail configuration:
5 {
6    "trailList": [
7       {
8          "IncludeGlobalServiceEvents": true,
9          "Name": "awscloudtrail-example",
10         "S3KeyPrefix": "prefix-example",
11         "TrailARN": "arn:aws:cloudtrail:us-east-2:123456789012:trail/awscloudtrail-example",
12         "LogFileValidationEnabled": false,
13         "IsMultiRegionTrail": false,
14         "HasCustomEventSelectors": false,
15         "S3BucketName": "awscloudtrail-new-bucket-example",
16         "SnsTopicName": "awscloudtrail-example-log-deliverytopic",
17         "HomeRegion": "us-east-2"
18      }
19   ],
20   "ResponseMetadata": {
21      "HTTPStatusCode": 200,
22      "RequestId": "4c55c744-a0ea-4aea-b3b9-eb63dfe68383"
23   }
24 }
25 Starting CloudTrail service...
26 Logs will be delivered to awscloudtrail-new-bucket-example:prefix-example
```

Using update-subscription

You can update your trail by using the **update-subscription** command and setting the options to new values. The following example uses the **--s3-use-bucket** option to designate a different, existing Amazon S3 bucket. If you want a trail with a different name, delete the trail with the **delete-trail** command and then run the **create-subscription** command.

```
1 aws cloudtrail update-subscription --name=awscloudtrail-example --s3-use-bucket=awscloudtrail-
    new-bucket-example2 --s3-prefix=prefix-example
```

If the command executes successfully, the **S3BucketName** value is updated to *awscloudtrail-new-bucket-example2*:

```
1 CloudTrail configuration:
2 {
3    "trailList": [
4       {
5          "IncludeGlobalServiceEvents": true,
```

```
 6        "Name": "awscloudtrail-example",
 7        "S3KeyPrefix": "prefix-example",
 8        "TrailARN": "arn:aws:cloudtrail:us-east-2:123456789012:trail/awscloudtrail-example",
 9        "LogFileValidationEnabled": false,
10        "IsMultiRegionTrail": false,
11        "HasCustomEventSelectors": false,
12        "S3BucketName": "awscloudtrail-new-bucket-example2"
13        "SnsTopicName": "awscloudtrail-example-log-deliverytopic",
14        "HomeRegion": "us-east-2"
15      }
16    ]
17 }
```

Note

If you specify an existing Amazon S3 bucket and that bucket was not created with CloudTrail, you need to attach the appropriate policy. See Amazon S3 Bucket Policy for CloudTrail.

Managing Trails

The CloudTrail CLI includes several other commands that help you manage your trails.

Retrieving trail settings and the status of a trail

Use the `describe-trails` command to retrieve trail settings:

```
1 aws cloudtrail describe-trails
```

If the command succeeds, you see output similar to the following:

```
 1 {
 2   "trailList": [
 3     {
 4       "IncludeGlobalServiceEvents": true,
 5       "Name": "my-trail",
 6       "S3KeyPrefix": "my-prefix",
 7       "TrailARN": "arn:aws:cloudtrail:us-east-2:123456789012:trail/my-trail",
 8       "LogFileValidationEnabled": false,
 9       "IsMultiRegionTrail": false,
10       "HasCustomEventSelectors": false,
11       "S3BucketName": "my-bucket"
12       "SnsTopicName": "my-topic",
13       "HomeRegion": "us-east-2"
14     }
15   ]
16 }
```

Run the `get-trail-status` command to retrieve the status of a trail.

```
1 aws cloudtrail get-trail-status --name awscloudtrail-example
```

If the command succeeds, you see output similar to the following:

```
1 {
2     "LatestDeliveryTime": 1441139757.497,
3     "LatestDeliveryAttemptTime": "2015-09-01T20:35:57Z",
```

```
4    "LatestNotificationAttemptSucceeded": "2015-09-01T20:35:57Z",
5    "LatestDeliveryAttemptSucceeded": "2015-09-01T20:35:57Z",
6    "IsLogging": true,
7    "TimeLoggingStarted": "2015-09-01T00:54:02Z",
8    "StartLoggingTime": 1441068842.76,
9    "LatestDigestDeliveryTime": 1441140723.629,
10   "LatestNotificationAttemptTime": "2015-09-01T20:35:57Z",
11   "TimeLoggingStopped": ""
12 }
```

In addition to the fields shown in the preceding JSON code, the status contains the following fields if there are Amazon SNS or Amazon S3 errors:

- LatestNotificationError. Contains the error emitted by Amazon SNS if a subscription to a topic fails.

- LatestDeliveryError. Contains the error emitted by Amazon S3 if CloudTrail cannot deliver a log file to a bucket.

Configuring event selectors

To view the event selector settings for a trail, run the get-event-selectors command:

```
1 aws cloudtrail get-event-selectors --trail-name TrailName
```

The following example returns the default settings for an event selector for a trail.

```
1 {
2    "EventSelectors": [
3        {
4            "IncludeManagementEvents": true,
5            "DataResources": [],
6            "ReadWriteType": "All"
7        }
8    ],
9    "TrailARN": "arn:aws:cloudtrail:us-east-2:123456789012:trail/TrailName"
10 }
```

To create an event selector, run the put-event-selectors command. When an event occurs in your account, CloudTrail evaluates the configuration for your trails. If the event matches any event selector for a trail, the trail processes and logs the event. You can configure up to 5 event selectors for a trail and up to 250 data resources for a trail. For more information, see Logging Data and Management Events for Trails.

- Example: A trail with specific event selectors
- Example: A trail that logs all events

Example: A trail with specific event selectors

The following example creates an event selector for a trail named *TrailName* to include read-only and write-only management events, data events for two Amazon S3 bucket/prefix combinations, and data events for a single AWS Lambda function named *hello-world-python-function*.

```
1 aws cloudtrail put-event-selectors --trail-name TrailName --event-selectors '[{"ReadWriteType":
     "All","IncludeManagementEvents": true,"DataResources": [{"Type":"AWS::S3::Object", "Values":
     ["arn:aws:s3:::mybucket/prefix","arn:aws:s3:::mybucket2/prefix2"]},{"Type": "AWS::Lambda::
     Function","Values": ["arn:aws:lambda:us-west-2:999999999999:function:hello-world-python-
     function"]}]}]'
```

The example returns the event selector configured for the trail:

```
1  {
2      "EventSelectors": [
3          {
4              "IncludeManagementEvents": true,
5              "DataResources": [
6                  {
7                      "Values": [
8                          "arn:aws:s3:::mybucket/prefix",
9                          "arn:aws:s3:::mybucket2/prefix2"
10                     ],
11                     "Type": "AWS::S3::Object"
12                 },
13                 {
14                     "Values": [
15                         "arn:aws:lambda:us-west-2:123456789012:function:hello-world-python-
                                function"
16                     ],
17                     "Type": "AWS::Lambda::Function"
18                 },
19             ],
20             "ReadWriteType": "All"
21         }
22     ],
23     "TrailARN": "arn:aws:cloudtrail:us-east-2:123456789012:trail/TrailName"
24 }
```

Example: A trail that logs all events

The following example creates an event selector for a trail named *TrailName2* that includes all events, including read-only and write-only management events, and all data events for all Amazon S3 buckets and AWS Lambda functions in the AWS account.

Note

If the trail applies only to one region, only events in that region are logged, even though the event selector parameters specify all Amazon S3 buckets and Lambda functions. Event selectors apply only to the regions where the trail is created.

```
1  aws cloudtrail put-event-selectors --trail-name TrailName2 --event-selectors '[{"ReadWriteType":
       "All","IncludeManagementEvents": true,"DataResources": [{"Type":"AWS::S3::Object", "Values
       ": ["arn:aws:s3:::"]},{"Type": "AWS::Lambda::Function","Values": ["arn:aws:lambda"]}]}]'
```

The example returns the event selectors configured for the trail:

```
1  {
2      "EventSelectors": [
3          {
4              "IncludeManagementEvents": true,
5              "DataResources": [
6                  {
7                      "Values": [
8                          "arn:aws:s3:::"
9                      ],
10                     "Type": "AWS::S3::Object"
11                 },
```

```
12          {
13              "Values": [
14                  "arn:aws:lambda"
15              ],
16              "Type": "AWS::Lambda::Function"
17          },
18      ],
19      "ReadWriteType": "All"
20  }
21  ],
22  "TrailARN": "arn:aws:cloudtrail:us-east-2:123456789012:trail/TrailName2"
23 }
```

Stopping and starting logging for a trail

The following commands start and stop CloudTrail logging:

```
1 aws cloudtrail start-logging --name awscloudtrail-example
```

```
1 aws cloudtrail stop-logging --name awscloudtrail-example
```

Note
Before deleting a bucket, run the `stop-logging` command to stop delivering events to the bucket. If you don't stop logging, CloudTrail attempts to deliver log files to a bucket with the same name for a limited period of time.

Deleting a trail

You can delete a trail with the following command. You can delete a trail only in the region it was created.

```
1 aws cloudtrail delete-trail --name awscloudtrail-example
```

When you delete a trail, you do not delete the Amazon S3 bucket or the Amazon SNS topic associated with it. Use the AWS Management Console, AWS CLI, or service API to delete these resources separately.

CloudTrail Trail Naming Requirements

CloudTrail trail names must meet the following requirements:

- Contain only ASCII letters (a-z, A-Z), numbers (0-9), periods (.), underscores (_), or dashes (-).

- Start with a letter or number, and end with a letter or number.

- Be between 3 and 128 characters.

- Have no adjacent periods, underscores or dashes. Names like my-_namespace and my-\-namespace are invalid.

- Not be in IP address format (for example, 192.168.5.4).

Amazon S3 Bucket Naming Requirements

The Amazon S3 bucket that you use to store CloudTrail log files must have a name that conforms with naming requirements for non-US Standard regions. Amazon S3 defines a bucket name as a series of one or more labels, separated by periods, that adhere to the following rules:

- The bucket name can be between 3 and 63 characters long, and can contain only lower-case characters, numbers, periods, and dashes.

- Each label in the bucket name must start with a lowercase letter or number.

- The bucket name cannot contain underscores, end with a dash, have consecutive periods, or use dashes adjacent to periods.

- The bucket name cannot be formatted as an IP address (198.51.100.24).

Warning

Because S3 allows your bucket to be used as a URL that can be accessed publicly, the bucket name that you choose must be globally unique. If some other account has already created a bucket with the name that you chose, you must use another name. For more information, see Bucket Restrictions and Limitations in the *Amazon Simple Storage Service Developer Guide.*

Amazon S3 Bucket Policy for CloudTrail

By default, Amazon S3 buckets and objects are private. Only the resource owner (the AWS account that created the bucket) can access the bucket and objects it contains. The resource owner can grant access permissions to other resources and users by writing an access policy.

To deliver log files to an S3 bucket, CloudTrail must have the required permissions, and it cannot be configured as a Requester Pays bucket. CloudTrail automatically attaches the required permissions to a bucket when you do the following:

- Create an S3 bucket as part of creating or updating a trail in the CloudTrail console.

- Create an S3 bucket with the AWS CLI `create-subscription` and `update-subscription` commands.

CloudTrail adds the following fields in the policy for you:

- The allowed SIDs.

- The bucket name.

- The service principal name for CloudTrail.

- The name of the folder where the log files are stored, including the bucket name, a prefix (if you specified one), and your AWS account ID.

The following policy allows CloudTrail to write log files to the bucket from supported regions. For more information, see CloudTrail Supported Regions.

S3 bucket policy

```
1  {
2      "Version": "2012-10-17",
3      "Statement": [
4          {
5              "Sid": "AWSCloudTrailAclCheck20150319",
6              "Effect": "Allow",
7              "Principal": {"Service": "cloudtrail.amazonaws.com"},
8              "Action": "s3:GetBucketAcl",
9              "Resource": "arn:aws:s3:::myBucketName"
10         },
11         {
12             "Sid": "AWSCloudTrailWrite20150319",
13             "Effect": "Allow",
14             "Principal": {"Service": "cloudtrail.amazonaws.com"},
15             "Action": "s3:PutObject",
16             "Resource": "arn:aws:s3:::myBucketName/[optional prefix]/AWSLogs/myAccountID/*",
17             "Condition": {"StringEquals": {"s3:x-amz-acl": "bucket-owner-full-control"}}
18         }
19     ]
20 }
```

Specifying an Existing Bucket for CloudTrail Log Delivery

If you specified an existing S3 bucket as the storage location for log file delivery, you must attach a policy to the bucket that allows CloudTrail to write to the bucket.

Note
As a best practice, use a dedicated S3 bucket for CloudTrail logs.

To add the required CloudTrail policy to an Amazon S3 bucket

1. Open the Amazon S3 console at https://console.aws.amazon.com/s3/.

2. Choose the bucket where you want CloudTrail to deliver your log files, and then choose **Properties**.

3. Choose **Permissions**.

4. Choose **Edit Bucket Policy**.

5. Copy the S3 bucket policy to the **Bucket Policy Editor** window. Replace the placeholders in italics with the names of your bucket, prefix, and account number. If you specified a prefix when you created your trail, include it here. The prefix is an optional addition to the S3 object key that creates a folder-like organization in your bucket. **Note**
If the existing bucket already has one or more policies attached, add the statements for CloudTrail access to that policy or policies. Evaluate the resulting set of permissions to be sure that they are appropriate for the users who will access the bucket.

Receiving Log Files from Other Accounts

You can configure CloudTrail to deliver log files from multiple AWS accounts to a single S3 bucket. For more information, see Receiving CloudTrail Log Files from Multiple Accounts.

Troubleshooting the S3 Bucket Policy

The following sections describe how to troubleshoot the S3 bucket policy.

Common S3 Policy Configuration Errors

When you create a new bucket as part of creating or updating a trail, CloudTrail attaches the required permissions to your bucket. The bucket policy uses the service principal name, `"cloudtrail.amazonaws.com"`, which allows CloudTrail to deliver logs for all regions.

If CloudTrail is not delivering logs for a region, it's possible that your bucket has an older policy that specifies CloudTrail account IDs for each region. This policy gives CloudTrail permission to deliver logs only for the regions specified.

The following bucket policy allows CloudTrail to deliver logs for the specified nine regions only:

Example bucket policy with account IDs

```
1  {
2      "Version": "2012-10-17",
3      "Statement": [
4          {
5              "Sid": "AWSCloudTrailAclCheck20131101",
6              "Effect": "Allow",
7              "Principal": {"AWS": [
8                  "arn:aws:iam::903692715234:root",
9                  "arn:aws:iam::035351147821:root",
10                 "arn:aws:iam::859597730677:root",
11                 "arn:aws:iam::814480443879:root",
12                 "arn:aws:iam::216624486486:root",
13                 "arn:aws:iam::086441151436:root",
14                 "arn:aws:iam::388731089494:root",
15                 "arn:aws:iam::284668455005:root",
16                 "arn:aws:iam::113285607260:root"
```

```
17          ]},
18          "Action": "s3:GetBucketAcl",
19          "Resource": "arn:aws:s3:::bucket-1"
20       },
21       {
22          "Sid": "AWSCloudTrailWrite20131101",
23          "Effect": "Allow",
24          "Principal": {"AWS": [
25             "arn:aws:iam::903692715234:root",
26             "arn:aws:iam::035351147821:root",
27             "arn:aws:iam::859597730677:root",
28             "arn:aws:iam::814480443879:root",
29             "arn:aws:iam::216624486486:root",
30             "arn:aws:iam::086441151436:root",
31             "arn:aws:iam::388731089494:root",
32             "arn:aws:iam::284668455005:root",
33             "arn:aws:iam::113285607260:root"
34          ]},
35          "Action": "s3:PutObject",
36          "Resource": "arn:aws:s3:::bucket-1/my-prefix/AWSLogs/123456789012/*",
37          "Condition": {"StringEquals": {"s3:x-amz-acl": "bucket-owner-full-control"}}
38       }
39    ]
40 }
```

This policy uses a permission based on individual CloudTrail account IDs. To send notifications for a new region, you must manually update the policy to include the CloudTrail account ID for that region. For example, because CloudTrail added support for the US East (Ohio) Region, you must update the policy to include the account ID ARN for that region: `"arn:aws:iam::475085895292:root"`.

As a best practice, update the policy to use a permission with the CloudTrail service principal. To do this, replace the account ID ARNs with the service principal name: `"cloudtrail.amazonaws.com"`. This gives CloudTrail permission to deliver logs for current and new regions. The following is an updated version of the previous policy:

Example bucket policy with service principal name

```
1 {
2     "Version": "2012-10-17",
3     "Statement": [
4        {
5           "Sid": "AWSCloudTrailAclCheck20150319",
6           "Effect": "Allow",
7           "Principal": {"Service": "cloudtrail.amazonaws.com"},
8           "Action": "s3:GetBucketAcl",
9           "Resource": "arn:aws:s3:::bucket-1"
10       },
11       {
12          "Sid": "AWSCloudTrailWrite20150319",
13          "Effect": "Allow",
14          "Principal": {"Service": "cloudtrail.amazonaws.com"},
15          "Action": "s3:PutObject",
16          "Resource": "arn:aws:s3:::bucket-1/my-prefix/AWSLogs/123456789012/*",
17          "Condition": {"StringEquals": {"s3:x-amz-acl": "bucket-owner-full-control"}}
18       }
19    ]
20 }
```

Changing a Prefix for an Existing Bucket

If you try to add, modify, or remove a log file prefix for an S3 bucket that receives logs from a trail, you may see the error: **There is a problem with the bucket policy**. A bucket policy with an incorrect prefix can prevent your trail from delivering logs to the bucket. To resolve this issue, use the Amazon S3 console to update the prefix in the bucket policy, and then use the CloudTrail console to specify the same prefix for the bucket in the trail.

To update the log file prefix for an S3 bucket

1. Open the Amazon S3 console at https://console.aws.amazon.com/s3/.

2. Choose the bucket for which you want to modify the prefix, and then choose **Properties**.

3. Choose **Permissions**.

4. Choose **Edit Bucket Policy**.

5. In the bucket policy, under the `s3:PutObject` action, edit the `Resource` entry to add, modify, or remove the log file *prefix* as needed.

```
1 "Action": "s3:PutObject",
2       "Resource": "arn:aws:s3:::myBucketName/prefix/AWSLogs/myAccountID/*",
```

6. Choose **Save**.

7. Open the CloudTrail console at https://console.aws.amazon.com/cloudtrail/.

8. Choose your trail and for **Storage location**, click the pencil icon to edit the settings for your bucket.

9. For **S3 bucket**, choose the bucket with the prefix you are changing.

10. For **Log file prefix**, update the prefix to match the prefix that you entered in the bucket policy.

11. Choose **Save**.

Additional Resources

For more information about S3 buckets and policies, see the Amazon Simple Storage Service Developer Guide.

AWS KMS Alias Naming Requirements

When you create a customer master key (CMK), you can choose an alias to identify it. For example, you might choose the alias "KMS-CloudTrail-us-west-2" to encrypt the logs for a specific trail.

The alias must meet the following requirements:

- Between 1 and 32 characters, inclusive
- Contain alphanumeric characters (A-Z, a-z, 0-9), hyphens (-), forward slashes (/), and underscores (_)
- Cannot begin with **aws**

For more information, see Creating Keys in the *AWS Key Management Service Developer Guide*.

Tips for Managing Trails

- You can view all trails from any region in the CloudTrail console.

- To edit a trail in the list, choose the trail name. The console takes you to the region where the trail was created.

- Configure at least one trail that applies to all regions, so that you receive log files from all regions in your account.

- To log events from a specific region and deliver log files to an S3 bucket in the same region, you can update the trail to apply to a single region. This is useful if you want to keep your log files separate. For example, you may want users to manage their own logs in specific regions, or you may want to separate CloudWatch Logs alarms by region.

- Creating multiple trails will incur additional costs. For more information, see AWS CloudTrail Pricing.

Getting and Viewing Your CloudTrail Log Files

After you create a trail and configure it to capture the log files you want, you need to be able to find the log files and interpret the information they contain.

CloudTrail delivers your log files to an Amazon S3 bucket that you specify when you create the trail. Typically, log files appear in your bucket within 15 minutes of the recorded AWS API call or other AWS event. Log files are generally published every 5 minutes.

- Finding Your CloudTrail Log Files
- Downloading Your CloudTrail Log Files

Finding Your CloudTrail Log Files

CloudTrail publishes log files to your S3 bucket in a gzip archive. In the S3 bucket, the log file has a formatted name that includes the following elements:

- The bucket name that you specified when you created trail (found on the Trails page of the CloudTrail console)
- The (optional) prefix you specified when you created your trail
- The string "AWSLogs"
- The account number
- The string "CloudTrail"
- A region identifier such as us-west-1
- The year the log file was published in YYYY format
- The month the log file was published in MM format
- The day the log file was published in DD format
- An alphanumeric string that disambiguates the file from others that cover the same time period

The following example shows a complete log file object name:

```
1  bucket_name/prefix_name/AWSLogs/Account ID/CloudTrail/region/YYYY/MM/DD/file_name.json.gz
```

To retrieve a log file, you can use the Amazon S3 console, the Amazon S3 command line interface (CLI), or the API.

To find your log files with the Amazon S3 console

1. Open the Amazon S3 console.
2. Choose the bucket you specified.
3. Navigate through the object hierarchy until you find the log file you want.

   All log files have a .gz extension.

You will navigate through an object hierarchy that is similar to the following example, but with a different bucket name, account ID, region, and date.

```
1  All Buckets
2      Bucket_Name
3          AWSLogs
4              123456789012
5                  CloudTrail
6                      us-west-1
7                          2014
8                              06
9                                  20
```

A log file for the preceding object hierarchy will look like the following:

```
1  123456789012_CloudTrail_us-west-1_20140620T1255ZHdkvFTXOA3Vnhbc.json.gz
```

Note
Although uncommon, you may receive log files that contain one or more duplicate events. Duplicate events will have the same **eventID**. For more information about the **eventID** field, see CloudTrail Record Contents.

Downloading Your CloudTrail Log Files

Log files are in JSON format. If you have a JSON viewer add-on installed, you can view the files directly in your browser. Double-click the log file name in the bucket to open a new browser window or tab. The JSON displays in a readable format.

For example, if you use Mozilla Firefox, you can also download the JSONView add-on. With JSONView, you can double-click the compressed .gz file in your bucket to open the log file in JSON format.

CloudTrail log files are Amazon S3 objects. You can use the Amazon S3 console, the AWS Command Line Interface (CLI), or the Amazon S3 API to retrieve log files.

For more information, see Working with Amazon S3 Objects in the* Amazon Simple Storage Service Developer Guide.*

The following procedure describes how to download a log file with the AWS Management Console.

To download and read a log file

1. Open the Amazon S3 console at https://console.aws.amazon.com/s3/.

2. Choose the bucket and choose the log file that you want to download.

3. Choose **Download** or **Download as** and follow the prompts to save the file. This saves the file in compressed format. **Note**
   Some browsers, such as Chrome, automatically extract the log file for you. If your browser does this for you, skip to step 5.

4. Use a product such as 7-Zip to extract the log file.

5. Open the log file in a text editor such as Notepad++.

For more information about the event fields that can appear in a log file entry, see CloudTrail Log Event Reference.

AWS partners with third-party specialists in logging and analysis to provide solutions that use CloudTrail output. For more information, see AWS Partner Network - AWS CloudTrail Partners.

Note
You can also use the **Event history** feature to look up events for create, update, and delete API activity during the last 90 days.
For more information, see Viewing Events with CloudTrail Event History.

Configuring Amazon SNS Notifications for CloudTrail

You can be notified when CloudTrail publishes new log files to your Amazon S3 bucket. You manage notifications using Amazon Simple Notification Service (Amazon SNS).

Notifications are optional. If you want notifications, you configure CloudTrail to send update information to an Amazon SNS topic whenever a new log file has been sent. To receive these notifications, you can use Amazon SNS to subscribe to the topic. As a subscriber you can get updates sent to a Amazon Simple Queue Service (Amazon SQS) queue, which enables you to handle these notifications programmatically.

- Configuring CloudTrail to Send Notifications
- Amazon SNS Topic Policy for CloudTrail

Configuring CloudTrail to Send Notifications

You can configure a trail to use an Amazon SNS topic. You can use the CloudTrail console or the http://docs.aws.amazon.com/cli/latest/reference/cloudtrail/create-subscription.html CLI command to create the topic. CloudTrail creates the Amazon SNS topic for you and attaches an appropriate policy, so that CloudTrail has permission to publish to that topic.

When you create an SNS topic name, the name must meet the following requirements:

- Between 1 and 256 characters long

- Contain uppercase and lowercase ASCII letters, numbers, underscores, or hyphens

When you configure notifications for a trail that applies to all regions, notifications from all regions are sent to the Amazon SNS topic that you specify. If you have one or more region-specific trails, you must create a separate topic for each region and subscribe to each individually.

To receive notifications, subscribe to the Amazon SNS topic or topics that CloudTrail uses. You do this with the Amazon SNS console or Amazon SNS CLI commands. For more information, see Subscribe to a Topic in the *Amazon Simple Notification Service Developer Guide*.

Note

CloudTrail sends a notification when log files are written to the Amazon S3 bucket. An active account can generate a large number of notifications. If you subscribe with email or SMS, you can receive a large volume of messages. We recommend that you subscribe using Amazon Simple Queue Service (Amazon SQS), which lets you handle notifications programmatically. For more information, see Subscribing a Queue to an Amazon SNS Topic in the *Amazon Simple Queue Service Developer Guide*.

The Amazon SNS notification consists of a JSON object that includes a `Message` field. The `Message` field lists the full path to the log file, as shown in the following example:

```
1 {
2     "s3Bucket": "your-bucket-name","s3ObjectKey": ["AWSLogs/123456789012/CloudTrail/us-east
        -2/2013/12/13/123456789012_CloudTrail_us-west-2_20131213T1920Z_LnPgDQnpkSKEsppV.json.gz
        "]
3 }
```

If multiple log files are delivered to your Amazon S3 bucket, a notification may contain multiple logs, as shown in the following example:

```
1 {
2     "s3Bucket": "your-bucket-name",
3     "s3ObjectKey": [
4         "AWSLogs/123456789012/CloudTrail/us-east-2/2016/08/11/123456789012_CloudTrail_us-east-2
            _20160811T2215Z_kpaMYavMQA9Ahp7L.json.gz",
5         "AWSLogs/123456789012/CloudTrail/us-east-2/2016/08/11/123456789012_CloudTrail_us-east-2
            _20160811T2210Z_zqDkyQv3TK8ZdLr0.json.gz",
6         "AWSLogs/123456789012/CloudTrail/us-east-2/2016/08/11/123456789012_CloudTrail_us-east-2
            _20160811T2205Z_jaMVRa6JfdLCJYHP.json.gz"
7     ]
8 }
```

If you choose to receive notifications by email, the body of the email consists of the content of the `Message` field. For a complete description of the JSON structure, see Sending Amazon SNS Messages to Amazon SQS Queues in the *Amazon Simple Notification Service Developer Guide*. Only the `Message` field shows CloudTrail information. The other fields contain information from the Amazon SNS service.

If you create a trail with the CloudTrail API, you can specify an existing Amazon SNS topic that you want CloudTrail to send notifications to with the http://docs.aws.amazon.com/awscloudtrail/latest/APIReference/

API_CreateTrail.html or http://docs.aws.amazon.com/awscloudtrail/latest/APIReference/API_UpdateTrail.html operations. You must make sure that the topic exists and that it has permissions that allow CloudTrail to send notifications to it. See Amazon SNS Topic Policy for CloudTrail.

Additional Resources

For more information about Amazon SNS topics and about subscribing to them, see the Amazon Simple Notification Service Developer Guide.

Amazon SNS Topic Policy for CloudTrail

To send notifications to an SNS topic, CloudTrail must have the required permissions. CloudTrail automatically attaches the required permissions to the topic when you do the following:

- Create an SNS topic as part of creating or updating a trail in the CloudTrail console.
- Create an SNS topic with the AWS CLI `create-subscription` and `update-subscription` commands.

CloudTrail adds the following fields in the policy for you:

- The allowed SIDs.
- The service principal name for CloudTrail.
- The SNS topic, including region, account ID, and topic name.

The following policy allows CloudTrail to send notifications about log file delivery from supported regions. For more information, see CloudTrail Supported Regions.

SNS topic policy

```
1  {
2      "Version": "2012-10-17",
3      "Statement": [{
4          "Sid": "AWSCloudTrailSNSPolicy20131101",
5          "Effect": "Allow",
6          "Principal": {"Service": "cloudtrail.amazonaws.com"},
7          "Action": "SNS:Publish",
8          "Resource": "arn:aws:sns:Region:SNSTopicOwnerAccountId:SNSTopicName"
9      }]
10 }
```

Specifying an Existing Topic for Sending Notifications

You can manually add the permissions to your topic policy in the Amazon SNS console and then specify the topic in the CloudTrail console.

To manually update an SNS topic policy

1. Open the Amazon SNS console at https://console.aws.amazon.com/sns/v2/home.
2. Choose **Topics** and then choose the topic.
3. Choose **Other topic actions** and then choose **Edit topic policy**.
4. Choose **Advanced view**, and add the statement from SNS topic policy with the appropriate values for the region, account ID, and topic name.
5. Choose **Update policy**.
6. Return to the CloudTrail console and specify the topic for the trail.

Troubleshooting the SNS Topic Policy

The following sections describe how to troubleshoot the SNS topic policy.

Common SNS Policy Configuration Errors

When you create a new topic as part of creating or updating a trail, CloudTrail attaches the required permissions to your topic. The topic policy uses the service principal name, `"cloudtrail.amazonaws.com"`, which allows CloudTrail to send notifications for all regions.

If CloudTrail is not sending notifications for a region, it's possible that your topic has an older policy that specifies CloudTrail account IDs for each region. This policy gives CloudTrail permission to send notifications only for the regions specified.

The following topic policy allows CloudTrail to send notifications for the specified nine regions only:

Example topic policy with account IDs

```
1  {
2      "Version": "2012-10-17",
3      "Statement": [{
4          "Sid": "AWSCloudTrailSNSPolicy20131101",
5          "Effect": "Allow",
6          "Principal": {"AWS": [
7              "arn:aws:iam::903692715234:root",
8              "arn:aws:iam::035351147821:root",
9              "arn:aws:iam::859597730677:root",
10             "arn:aws:iam::814480443879:root",
11             "arn:aws:iam::216624486486:root",
12             "arn:aws:iam::086441151436:root",
13             "arn:aws:iam::388731089494:root",
14             "arn:aws:iam::284668455005:root",
15             "arn:aws:iam::113285607260:root"
16         ]},
17         "Action": "SNS:Publish",
18         "Resource": "aws:arn:sns:us-east-1:123456789012:myTopic"
19     }]
20 }
```

This policy uses a permission based on individual CloudTrail account IDs. To deliver logs for a new region, you must manually update the policy to include the CloudTrail account ID for that region. For example, because CloudTrail added support for the US East (Ohio) Region, you must update the policy to add the account ID ARN for that region: `"arn:aws:iam::475085895292:root"`.

As a best practice, update the policy to use a permission with the CloudTrail service principal. To do this, replace the account ID ARNs with the service principal name: `"cloudtrail.amazonaws.com"`.

This gives CloudTrail permission to send notifications for current and new regions. The following is an updated version of the previous policy:

Example topic policy with service principal name

```
1  {
2      "Version": "2012-10-17",
3      "Statement": [{
4          "Sid": "AWSCloudTrailSNSPolicy20131101",
5          "Effect": "Allow",
6          "Principal": {Service": "cloudtrail.amazonaws.com"},
7          "Action": "SNS:Publish",
8          "Resource": arn:aws:sns:us-east-1:123456789012:myTopic"
9      }]
10 }
```

Verify that the policy has the correct values:

- In the `Resource` field, specify the account number of the topic owner. For topics that you create, specify your account number.

- Specify the appropriate values for the region and SNS topic name.

Additional Resources

For more information about SNS topics and subscribing to them, see the Amazon Simple Notification Service Developer Guide.

Controlling User Permissions for CloudTrail

AWS CloudTrail integrates with AWS Identity and Access Management (IAM), which allows you to control access to CloudTrail and to other AWS resources that CloudTrail requires, including Amazon S3 buckets and Amazon Simple Notification Service (Amazon SNS) topics. You can use AWS Identity and Access Management to control which AWS users can create, configure, or delete AWS CloudTrail trails, start and stop logging, and access the buckets that contain log information.

If you work with CloudTrail as the root user in your account, you can perform all the tasks associated with trails, including creating trails, reading logs, and so on. If other people in your organization need to work with CloudTrail, you can create IAM users for those people and give them individual names and passwords. When you do that, you must also give users permissions to work with CloudTrail and with any other AWS services they need to access, such as Amazon S3. (By default, IAM users have no permissions and cannot perform any actions in AWS.)

Important

We consider it a best practice not to use root account credentials to perform everyday work in AWS. Instead, we recommend that you create an IAM administrators group with appropriate permissions, create IAM users for the people in your organization who need to perform administrative tasks (including for yourself), and add those users to the administrative group. For more information, see IAM Best Practices in the *IAM User Guide* guide.

- Granting Permissions for CloudTrail Administration
- Granting Custom Permissions for CloudTrail Users

Granting Permissions for CloudTrail Administration

To allow users to administer a CloudTrail trail, you must grant explicit permissions to IAM users to perform the actions associated with CloudTrail tasks. For most scenarios, you can do this using an AWS managed policy that contains predefined permissions.

Note
The permissions you grant to users to perform CloudTrail administration tasks are not the same as the permissions that CloudTrail itself requires in order to deliver log files to Amazon S3 buckets or send notifications to Amazon SNS topics. For more information about those permissions, see Getting and Viewing Your CloudTrail Log Files. CloudTrail also requires a role that it can assume to deliver events to an Amazon CloudWatch Logs log group. For more information, see Granting Custom Permissions for CloudTrail Users.

A typical approach is to create an IAM group that has the appropriate permissions and then add individual IAM users to that group. For example, you might create an IAM group for users who should have full access to CloudTrail actions, and a separate group for users who should be able to view trail information but not create or change trails.

To create an IAM group and users for CloudTrail access

1. Open the IAM console at https://console.aws.amazon.com/iam.

2. From the dashboard, choose **Groups** in the navigation pane, and then choose **Create New Group**.

3. Type a name, and then choose **Next Step**.

4. On the **Attach Policy** page, find and choose one of the following policies for CloudTrail:

   - **AWSCloudTrailFullAccess**. This policy gives users in the group full access to CloudTrail actions. These users have permissions to manage the Amazon S3 bucket, the log group for CloudWatch Logs, and an Amazon SNS topic for a trail.

   - **AWSCloudTrailReadOnlyAccess**. This policy lets users in the group view the CloudTrail console, including recent events and event history. These users can also view existing trails and their buckets. Users can download a file of event history, but they cannot create or update trails. **Note**
   You can also create a custom policy that grants permissions to individual actions. For more information, see Granting Custom Permissions for CloudTrail Users.

5. Choose **Next Step**.

6. Review the information for the group you are about to create. **Note**
   You can edit the group name, but you will need to choose the policy again.

7. Choose **Create Group**. The group that you created appears in the list of groups.

8. Choose the group name that you created, choose **Group Actions**, and then choose **Add Users to Group**.

9. On the **Add Users to Group** page, choose the existing IAM users, and then choose **Add Users**. If you don't already have IAM users, choose **Create New Users**, enter user names, and then choose **Create**.

10. If you created new users, choose **Users** in the navigation pane and complete the following for each user:

    1. Choose the user.

    2. If the user will use the console to manage CloudTrail, in the **Security Credentials** tab, choose **Manage Password**, and then create a password for the user.

    3. If the user will use the CLI or API to manage CloudTrail, and if you didn't already create access keys, in the **Security Credentials** tab, choose **Manage Access Keys** and then create access keys. Store the keys in a secure location.

    4. Give each user his or her credentials (access keys or password).

Additional Resources

To learn more about creating IAM users, groups, policies, and permissions, see Creating an Admins Group Using the Console and Permissions and Policies in the *IAM User Guide*.

Granting Custom Permissions for CloudTrail Users

CloudTrail policies grant permissions to users who work with CloudTrail. If you need to grant different permissions to users, you can attach a CloudTrail policy to an IAM group or to a user. You can edit the policy to include or exclude specific permissions. You can also create your own custom policy. Policies are JSON documents that define the actions a user is allowed to perform and the resources that the user is allowed to perform those actions on.

Read-only access

The following example shows a policy that grants read-only access to CloudTrail trails. It grants users permission to see trail information, but not to create or update trails. The policy also grants permission to read objects in Amazon S3 buckets, but not create or delete them.

```
1  {
2    "Version": "2012-10-17",
3    "Statement": [
4      {
5        "Effect": "Allow",
6        "Action": [
7          "s3:GetObject",
8          "s3:GetBucketLocation"
9        ],
10       "Resource": "*"
11     },
12     {
13       "Effect": "Allow",
14       "Action": [
15         "cloudtrail:DescribeTrails",
16         "cloudtrail:GetTrailStatus",
17         "cloudtrail:LookupEvents",
18         "s3:ListAllMyBuckets",
19         "kms:ListAliases"
20       ],
21       "Resource": "*"
22     }
23   ]
24 }
```

In the policy statements, the `Effect` element specifies whether the actions are allowed or denied. The `Action` element lists the specific actions that the user is allowed to perform. The `Resource` element lists the AWS resources the user is allowed to perform those actions on. For policies that control access to CloudTrail actions, the `Resource` element is always set to *, a wildcard that means "all resources."

The values in the `Action` element correspond to the APIs that the services support. The actions are preceded by `cloudtrail:` to indicate that they refer to CloudTrail actions. You can use the * wildcard character in the `Action` element , such as in the following examples:

- `"Action": ["cloudtrail:*Logging"]`

  This allows all CloudTrail actions that end with "Logging" (`StartLogging`, `StopLogging`).

- `"Action": ["cloudtrail:*"]`

  This allows all CloudTrail actions, but not actions for other AWS services.

- "Action": ["*"]

  This allows all AWS actions. This permission is suitable for a user who acts as an AWS administrator for your account.

The read-only policy doesn't grant user permission for the `CreateTrail`, `UpdateTrail`, `StartLogging`, and `StopLogging` actions. Users with this policy are not allowed to create trails, update trails, or turn logging on and off. For the list of CloudTrail actions, see the AWS CloudTrail API Reference.

Full access

The following example shows a policy that grants full access to CloudTrail. It grants users the permission to perform all CloudTrail actions. It also lets users manage files in Amazon S3 buckets, manage how CloudWatch Logs monitors CloudTrail log events, and manage Amazon SNS topics in the account that the user is associated with.

```
1  {
2    "Version": "2012-10-17",
3    "Statement": [
4      {
5        "Effect": "Allow",
6        "Action": [
7          "sns:AddPermission",
8          "sns:CreateTopic",
9          "sns:DeleteTopic",
10         "sns:ListTopics",
11         "sns:SetTopicAttributes",
12         "sns:GetTopicAttributes"
13       ],
14       "Resource": "*"
15     },
16     {
17       "Effect": "Allow",
18       "Action": [
19         "s3:CreateBucket",
20         "s3:DeleteBucket",
21         "s3:GetObject",
22         "s3:ListAllMyBuckets",
23         "s3:PutBucketPolicy",
24         "s3:GetBucketLocation",
25         "s3:GetBucketPolicy"
26       ],
27       "Resource": "*"
28     },
29     {
30       "Effect": "Allow",
31       "Action": "cloudtrail:*",
32       "Resource": "*"
33     },
34     {
35       "Effect": "Allow",
36       "Action": [
37         "logs:CreateLogGroup"
38       ],
39       "Resource": "*"
```

```
40        },
41        {
42          "Effect": "Allow",
43          "Action": [
44            "iam:PassRole",
45            "iam:ListRoles",
46            "iam:GetRolePolicy",
47            "iam:GetUser"
48          ],
49          "Resource": "*"
50        },
51        {
52          "Effect": "Allow",
53          "Action": [
54            "kms:ListKeys",
55            "kms:ListAliases"
56          ],
57          "Resource": "*"
58        }
59      ]
60    }
```

Controlling User Permissions for Actions on Specific Trails

You can use resource-level permissions to control a user's ability to perform specific actions on CloudTrail trails.

For example, you don't want users of your company's developer group to start or stop logging on a specific trail, but you want to grant them permission to perform the DescribeTrails and GetTrailStatus actions on the trail. You want the users of the developer group to perform the StartLogging or StopLogging actions on trails that they create and manage.

You can create two policy statements and then attach them to the developer user group.

In the first policy, you deny the StartLogging and StopLogging actions for the trail ARN that you specify. In the following example, the trail ARN is arn:aws:cloudtrail:us-east-2:111122223333:trail/Default.

```
1  {
2      "Version": "2012-10-17",
3      "Statement": [
4          {
5              "Sid": "Stmt1446057698000",
6              "Effect": "Deny",
7              "Action": [
8                  "cloudtrail:StartLogging",
9                  "cloudtrail:StopLogging"
10             ],
11             "Resource": [
12                 "arn:aws:cloudtrail:us-east-2:111122223333:trail/Default"
13             ]
14         }
15     ]
16 }
```

In the second policy, the DescribeTrails and GetTrailStatus actions are allowed on all CloudTrail resources:

```
1  {
```

```
2         "Version": "2012-10-17",
3         "Statement": [
4             {
5                 "Sid": "Stmt1446072643000",
6                 "Effect": "Allow",
7                 "Action": [
8                     "cloudtrail:DescribeTrails",
9                     "cloudtrail:GetTrailStatus"
10                ],
11                "Resource": [
12                    "*"
13                ]
14            }
15        ]
16 }
```

If a user of the developer group tries to start or stop logging on the trail that you specified in the first policy, that user gets an access denied exception. Users of the developer group can start and stop logging on trails that they create and manage.

The following CLI examples show that the developer group has been configured in an AWS CLI profile named `devgroup`. First, a user of `devgroup` runs the `describe-trails` command.

```
1 $ aws --profile devgroup cloudtrail describe-trails
```

The command complete successfully:

```
1 {
2     "trailList": [
3         {
4             "IncludeGlobalServiceEvents": true,
5             "Name": "Default",
6             "TrailARN": "arn:aws:cloudtrail:us-east-2:111122223333:trail/Default",
7             "IsMultiRegionTrail": false,
8             "S3BucketName": "myS3bucket ",
9             "HomeRegion": "us-east-2"
10        }
11    ]
12 }
```

The user then runs the `get-trail-status` command on the trail that you specified in the first policy.

```
1 $ aws --profile devgroup cloudtrail get-trail-status --name Default
```

The command complete successfully:

```
1 {
2     "LatestDeliveryTime": 1449517556.256,
3     "LatestDeliveryAttemptTime": "2015-12-07T19:45:56Z",
4     "LatestNotificationAttemptSucceeded": "",
5     "LatestDeliveryAttemptSucceeded": "2015-12-07T19:45:56Z",
6     "IsLogging": true,
7     "TimeLoggingStarted": "2015-12-07T19:36:27Z",
8     "StartLoggingTime": 1449516987.685,
9     "StopLoggingTime": 1449516977.332,
10    "LatestNotificationAttemptTime": "",
11    "TimeLoggingStopped": "2015-12-07T19:36:17Z"
12 }
```

Next, a user of `devgroup` runs the `stop-logging` command on the same trail.

```
1 $ aws --profile devgroup cloudtrail stop-logging --name Default
```

The command returns an access denied exception:

```
1 A client error (AccessDeniedException) occurred when calling the StopLogging operation: Unknown
```

The user runs the `start-logging` command on the same trail.

```
1 $ aws --profile devgroup cloudtrail start-logging --name Default
```

The command returns an access denied exception:

```
1 A client error (AccessDeniedException) occurred when calling the StartLogging operation: Unknown
```

With resource level permissions, you can grant or deny access to specific trails in your account.

Granting Permission to View AWS Config Information on the CloudTrail Console

You can view event information on the CloudTrail console, including resources that are related to that event. For these resources, you can choose the AWS Config icon to view the timeline for that resource in the AWS Config console. Attach this policy to your users to grant them read-only AWS Config access. The policy doesn't grant them permission to change settings in AWS Config.

```
1  {
2      "Version": "2012-10-17",
3      "Statement": [{
4          "Effect": "Allow",
5          "Action": [
6              "config:Get*",
7              "config:Describe*",
8              "config:List*"
9          ],
10         "Resource": "*"
11     }]
12 }
```

For more information, see Viewing Resources Referenced with AWS Config.

Additional Information

To learn more about creating IAM users, groups, policies, and permissions, see Creating Your First IAM User and Administrators Group and Access Management in the *IAM User Guide*.

Working with CloudTrail Log Files

You can perform more advanced tasks with your CloudTrail files.

- Create multiple trails per region.
- Monitor CloudTrail log files by sending them to CloudWatch Logs.
- Share log files between accounts.
- Use the AWS CloudTrail Processing Library to write log processing applications in Java.
- Validate your log files to verify that they have not changed after delivery by CloudTrail.
- Create Multiple Trails
- Logging Data and Management Events for Trails
- Receiving CloudTrail Log Files from Multiple Regions
- Monitoring CloudTrail Log Files with Amazon CloudWatch Logs
- Receiving CloudTrail Log Files from Multiple Accounts
- Sharing CloudTrail Log Files Between AWS Accounts
- Encrypting CloudTrail Log Files with AWS KMS–Managed Keys (SSE-KMS)
- Validating CloudTrail Log File Integrity
- Using the CloudTrail Processing Library

Create Multiple Trails

You can use CloudTrail log files to troubleshoot operational or security issues in your AWS account. You can create trails for different users, who can create and manage their own trails. You can configure trails to deliver log files to separate S3 buckets or shared S3 buckets.

Note
Creating multiple trails will incur additional costs. For more information, see AWS CloudTrail Pricing.

For example, you might have the following users:

- A security administrator creates a trail in the EU (Ireland) Region and configures KMS log file encryption. The trail delivers the log files to an S3 bucket in the EU (Ireland) Region.

- An IT auditor creates a trail in the EU (Ireland) Region and configures log file integrity validation to ensure the log files have not changed since CloudTrail delivered them. The trail is configured to deliver log files to an S3 bucket in the EU (Frankfurt) Region

- A developer creates a trail in the EU (Frankfurt) Region and configures CloudWatch alarms to receive notifications for specific API activity. The trail shares the same S3 bucket as the trail configured for log file integrity.

- Another developer creates a trail in the EU (Frankfurt) Region and configures SNS. The log files are delivered to a separate S3 bucket in the EU (Frankfurt) Region.

The following image illustrates this example.

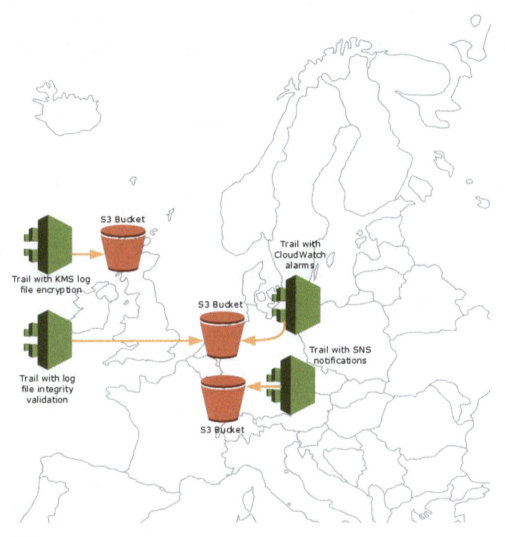

Note

You can create up to five trails per region. A trail that logs activity from all regions counts as one trail per region.

You can use resource-level permissions to manage a user's ability to perform specific operations on CloudTrail.

For example, you might grant one user permission to view trail activity, but restrict the user from starting or stopping logging for a trail. You might grant another user full permission to create and delete trails. This gives you granular control over your trails and user access.

For more information about resource-level permissions, see Controlling User Permissions for Actions on Specific Trails.

For more information about multiple trails, see the following resources:

- How Does CloudTrail Behave Regionally and Globally?
- CloudTrail FAQs

Logging Data and Management Events for Trails

When an event occurs in your account, CloudTrail evaluates whether the event matches the settings for your trails. Only events that match your trail settings are delivered to your Amazon S3 bucket and Amazon CloudWatch Logs log group.

You can configure your trails to log the following:

- **Data events**: These events provide insight into the resource operations performed on or within a resource. These are also known as data plane operations.

- **Management events**: Management events provide insight into management operations that are performed on resources in your AWS account. These are also known as control plane operations. Management events can also include non-API events that occur in your account. For example, when a user logs in to your account, CloudTrail logs the `ConsoleLogin` event. For more information, see Non-API Events Captured by CloudTrail. **Note**
  Not all AWS services support CloudTrail management events or data events. For more information about unsupported services, see CloudTrail Unsupported Services. For specific details about what APIs are logged for a specific service, see that service's documentation in CloudTrail Supported Services and Integrations.

You can configure multiple trails differently so that the trails process and log only the events that you specify. For example, one trail can log read-only data and management events, so that all read-only events are delivered to one S3 bucket. Another trail can log only write-only data and management events, so that all write-only events are delivered to a separate S3 bucket.

You can also configure your trails to have one trail log and deliver all management events to one S3 bucket, and configure another trail to log and deliver all data events to another S3 bucket.

By default, trails log all management events and don't include data events. Additional charges apply for data events. For more information, see AWS CloudTrail Pricing.

Note
The events that are logged by your trails are available in Amazon CloudWatch Events. For example, if you configure a trail to log data events for S3 objects but not management events, your trail processes and logs only data events for the specified S3 objects. The data events for these S3 objects are available in Amazon CloudWatch Events. For more information, see AWS API Call Events in the *Amazon CloudWatch Events User Guide*.

Data Events

Data events provide insight into the resource operations performed on or within a resource. These are also known as data plane operations. Data events are often high-volume activities.

Example data events include:

- Amazon S3 object-level API activity (for example, `GetObject`, `DeleteObject`, and `PutObject` API operations)

- AWS Lambda function execution activity (the `Invoke` API)

Data events are disabled by default when you create a trail. To record CloudTrail data events, you must explicitly add the supported resources or resource types for which you want to collect activity to a trail. For more information, see Creating a Trail and Data Events.

Additional charges apply for logging data events. For CloudTrail pricing, see AWS CloudTrail Pricing.

Logging Data Events with the AWS Management Console

1. Navigate to the **Trails** page of the CloudTrail console and choose the trail.

2. For **Data events**, choose the pencil icon to enable editing.

3. For Amazon S3 data events, on the **S3** tab:

    1. To configure data event logging for all Amazon S3 buckets in your AWS account, select **Select all S3 buckets in your account**. Then choose whether you want to log **Read** events, such as GetObject; **Write** events, such as PutObject; or both types of events. This setting takes precedence over any settings you configure for individual buckets. For example, if you specify logging **Read** events for all S3 buckets, and then choose to add a specific bucket for data event logging, **Read** will already be selected for that bucket. You cannot clear the selection. You can only configure the option for **Write**.
    Note
    If you select or clear an option for all buckets, that change is applied to all buckets you might have individually configured for data event logging. Consider reviewing the data event settings for individual buckets after you change the data event settings for all buckets.
    If you configure data event logging for all buckets in your AWS account, and you do not want an audit trail of data event logging, consider delivering your log files to an Amazon S3 bucket that belongs to another AWS account. For more information, see Receiving CloudTrail Log Files from Multiple Accounts and [ERROR] BAD/MISSING LINK TEXT.

    2. To configure data event logging for individual Amazon S3 buckets, choose **Add S3 bucket**. Type the bucket name and prefix (optional). For each trail, you can add up to 250 data resources, such as Amazon S3 bucket and object prefixes. The overall total of individual data event resources cannot exceed 250 in a single trail. That total includes other data resources, such as Lambda functions. This restriction does not apply if you configure data event logging for all Amazon S3 buckets.

        - To log data events for all S3 objects in a bucket, specify an S3 bucket and an empty prefix. When an event occurs on an object in that S3 bucket, the trail processes and logs the event. For more information, see Example: Logging data events for all S3 objects.

        - To log data events for S3 prefixes, specify an S3 bucket and the object prefix. When an event occurs on an object in that S3 bucket and the object starts with the specified prefix, the trail processes and logs the event. For more information, see Example: Logging data events for specific S3 objects.

        - You can also specify S3 objects that belong to other AWS accounts. For more information, see Logging Data Events for S3 Objects in Other AWS Accounts.

    3. For each resource, specify whether you want to log **Read**, **Write**, or both types of events.

    4. You can edit the bucket name, prefix, **Read/Write** option, or remove the resource by choosing the **x** icon. **Note**
    If you configured data event logging for all S3 buckets in your AWS account, the settings you configured take precedence over individual bucket settings. In this case, you cannot edit an option that is set for all buckets.

4. For Lambda data events, on the **Lambda** tab:

    1. To configure data event logging for individual Lambda functions, select them from the list. If the trail applies to all regions, you can select from functions in all regions in your AWS account. If the trail applies to only one region, you can only select from functions in that region. For each trail, you can add up to 250 data resources, such as individual Lambda functions. The overall total of individual data event resources cannot exceed 250 in a single trail. That total includes other data resources, such as Amazon S3 bucket and object prefixes. This restriction does not apply if you configure data event logging for all Lambda functions. **Note**
    If you have more than 15,000 Lambda functions in your account, you cannot view or select all functions in the CloudTrail console. You can still select the option to log all Lambda functions. You can also

manually add a function if you know its ARN, or you can use the AWS CLI and the put-event-selectors command to configure specific data event logging for resources. For more information, see Managing Trails.

2. To configure data event logging for all Lambda functions in your AWS account, and any Lambda function you might create in the future, select **Log all current and future functions**. If the trail applies to all regions, this will log all functions in all regions in your AWS account, including any you might create in any region. If the trail applies to a single region, this will log all functions in the current region and any you might create in that region, but will not enable logging of functions in other regions. Logging data events for all functions will also enable logging of data event activity performed by any user or role in your AWS account, even if that activity is performed on a function that belongs to another AWS account.

5. Choose **Save**.

Examples: Logging Data Events for Amazon S3 Objects

Logging data events for all S3 objects in an S3 bucket

The following example demonstrates how logging works when you configure logging of all data events for an S3 bucket named *bucket-1*. In this example, the CloudTrail user specified an empty prefix, and the option to log both **Read** and **Write** data events.

1. A user uploads an object to `bucket-1`.

2. The `PutObject` API operation is an Amazon S3 object-level API. It is recorded as a data event in CloudTrail. Because the CloudTrail user specified an S3 bucket with an empty prefix, events that occur on any object in that bucket are logged. The trail processes and logs the event.

3. Another user uploads an object to `bucket-2`.

4. The `PutObject` API operation occurred on an object in an S3 bucket that wasn't specified for the trail. The trail doesn't log the event.

Logging data events for specific S3 objects

The following example demonstrates how logging works when you configure a trail to log events for specific S3 objects. In this example, the CloudTrail user specified an S3 bucket named *bucket-3*, with the prefix *my-images*, and the option to log only **Write** data events.

1. A user deletes an object that begins with the `my-images` prefix in the bucket, such as `arn:aws:s3:::bucket-3/my-images/example.jpg`.

2. The `DeleteObject` API operation is an Amazon S3 object-level API. It is recorded as a **Write** data event in CloudTrail. The event occurred on an object that matches the S3 bucket and prefix specified in the trail. The trail processes and logs the event.

3. Another user deletes an object with a different prefix in the S3 bucket, such as `arn:aws:s3:::bucket-3/my-videos/example.avi`.

4. The event occurred on an object that doesn't match the prefix specified in your trail. The trail doesn't log the event.

5. A user calls the `GetObject` API operation for the object, `arn:aws:s3:::bucket-3/my-images/example.jpg`.

6. The event occurred on a bucket and prefix that are specified in the trail, but `GetObject` is a read-type Amazon S3 object-level API. It is recorded as a **Read** data event in CloudTrail, and the trail is not configured to log **Read** events. The trail doesn't log the event.

Note

If you are logging data events for specific Amazon S3 buckets, we recommend you do not use an Amazon S3 bucket for which you are logging data events to receive log files that you have specified in the data events section. Using the same Amazon S3 bucket causes your trail to log a data event each time log files are delivered to your Amazon S3 bucket. Log files are aggregated events delivered at intervals, so this is not a 1:1 ratio of event to log file; the event is logged in the next log file. For example, when the trail delivers logs, the `PutObject` event occurs on the S3 bucket. If the S3 bucket is also specified in the data events section, the trail processes and logs the `PutObject` event as a data event. That action is another `PutObject` event, and the trail processes and logs the event again. For more information, see How CloudTrail Works.

To avoid logging data events for the Amazon S3 bucket where you receive log files if you configure a trail to log all Amazon S3 data events in your AWS account, consider configuring delivery of log files to an Amazon S3 bucket that belongs to another AWS account. For more information, see Receiving CloudTrail Log Files from Multiple Accounts.

Logging Data Events for S3 Objects in Other AWS Accounts

When you configure your trail to log data events, you can also specify S3 objects that belong to other AWS accounts. When an event occurs on a specified object, CloudTrail evaluates whether the event matches any trails in each account. If the event matches the settings for a trail, the trail processes and logs the event for that account.

If you own an S3 object and you specify it in your trail, your trail logs events that occur on the object in your account. Because you own the object, your trail also logs events when other accounts call the object.

If you specify an S3 object in your trail, and another account owns the object, your trail only logs events that occur on that object in your account. Your trail doesn't log events that occur in other accounts.

Example: Logging data events for an S3 object for two AWS accounts

The following example shows how two AWS accounts configure CloudTrail to log events for the same S3 object.

1. In your account, you want your trail to log data events for all objects in your S3 bucket named `owner-bucket`. You configure the trail by specifying the S3 bucket with an empty object prefix.

2. Bob has a separate account that has been granted access to the S3 bucket. Bob also wants to log data events for all objects in the same S3 bucket. For his trail, he configures his trail and specifies the same S3 bucket with an empty object prefix.

3. Bob uploads an object to the S3 bucket with the `PutObject` API operation.

4. This event occurred in his account and it matches the settings for his trail. Bob's trail processes and logs the event.

5. Because you own the S3 bucket and the event matches the settings for your trail, your trail also processes and logs the same event.

6. You upload an object to the S3 bucket.

7. This event occurs in your account and it matches the settings for your trail. Your trail processes and logs the event.

8. Because the event didn't occur in Bob's account, and he doesn't own the S3 bucket, Bob's trail doesn't log the event.

Management Events

Management events provide insight into management operations that are performed on resources in your AWS account. These are also known as control plane operations. Example management events include:

- Configuring security (for example, IAM `AttachRolePolicy` API operations)
- Registering devices (for example, Amazon EC2 `CreateDefaultVpc` API operations)

- Configuring rules for routing data (for example, Amazon EC2 `CreateSubnet` API operations)

- Setting up logging (for example, AWS CloudTrail `CreateTrail` API operations)

Management events can also include non-API events that occur in your account. For example, when a user logs in to your account, CloudTrail logs the `ConsoleLogin` event. For more information, see Non-API Events Captured by CloudTrail. For a list of supported management events that CloudTrail logs for AWS services, see CloudTrail Supported Services and Integrations.

By default, trails are configured to log management events. For a list of supported management events that CloudTrail logs for AWS services, see CloudTrail Supported Services and Integrations.

Note
The CloudTrail **Event history **feature supports only management events. Not all management events are supported in event history. For more information, see Viewing Events with CloudTrail Event History.

Logging Management Events with the AWS Management Console

1. Navigate to the **Trails** page of the CloudTrail console and choose the trail.

2. For **Management events**, click the pencil icon.

3. For **Read/Write events**, choose if you want your trail to log **All**, **Read-only**, **Write-only**, or **None**, and then choose **Save**.

Read-only and Write-only Events

When you configure your trail to log data and management events, you can specify whether you want read-only events, write-only events, both, or none.

- **Read-only**

  Read-only events include API operations that read your resources, but don't make changes. For example, read-only events include the Amazon EC2 `DescribeSecurityGroups` and `DescribeSubnets` API operations. These operations return only information about your Amazon EC2 resources and don't change your configurations.

- **Write-only**

  Write-only events include API operations that modify (or might modify) your resources. For example, the Amazon EC2 `RunInstances` and `TerminateInstances` API operations modify your instances.

- **All**

  Your trail logs both.

- **None**

  Your trail logs neither read-only nor write-only management events.

Example: Logging read-only and write-only events for separate trails

The following example shows how you can configure trails to split log activity for an account into separate S3 buckets: one bucket receives read-only events and a second bucket receives write-only events.

1. You create a trail and choose an S3 bucket named `read-only-bucket` to receive log files. You then update the trail to specify that you want read-only management events and data events.

2. You create a second trail and choose an S3 bucket named `write-only-bucket` to receive log files. You then update the trail to specify that you want write-only management events and data events.

3. The Amazon EC2 `DescribeInstances` and `TerminateInstances` API operations occur in your account.

4. The `DescribeInstances` API operation is a read-only event and it matches the settings for the first trail. The trail logs and delivers the event to the `read-only-bucket`.

5. The `TerminateInstances` API operation is a write-only event and it matches the settings for the second trail. The trail logs and delivers the event to the `write-only-bucket`.

Logging Events with the AWS Command Line Interface

You can configure your trails to log management and data events using the AWS CLI.

To view whether your trail is logging management and data events, run the `get-event-selectors` command.

```
1 aws cloudtrail get-event-selectors --trail-name TrailName
```

The following example returns the default settings for a trail. By default, trails log all management events and don't log data events.

```
1  {
2      "EventSelectors": [
3          {
4              "IncludeManagementEvents": true,
5              "DataResources": [],
6              "ReadWriteType": "All"
7          }
8      ],
9      "TrailARN": "arn:aws:cloudtrail:us-east-2:123456789012:trail/TrailName"
10 }
```

To configure your trail to log management and data events, run the `put-event-selectors` command. The following example shows how to configure your trail to include all management and data events for two S3 objects. You can specify from 1 to 5 event selectors for a trail. You can specify from 1 to 250 data resources for a trail.

Note
The maximum number of S3 data resources is 250, regardless of the number of event selectors.

```
1 aws cloudtrail put-event-selectors --trail-name TrailName --event-selectors '[{ "ReadWriteType":
       "All", "IncludeManagementEvents":true, "DataResources": [{ "Type": "AWS::S3::Object", "
       Values": ["arn:aws:s3:::mybucket/prefix", "arn:aws:s3:::mybucket2/prefix2"] }] }]'
```

The following example returns the event selector configured for the trail.

```
1  {
2      "EventSelectors": [
3          {
4              "IncludeManagementEvents": true,
5              "DataResources": [
6                  {
7                      "Values": [
8                          "arn:aws:s3:::mybucket/prefix",
9                          "arn:aws:s3:::mybucket2/prefix2",
10                     ],
11                     "Type": "AWS::S3::Object"
12                 }
13             ],
14             "ReadWriteType": "All"
15         }
```

```
16      ],
17      "TrailARN": "arn:aws:cloudtrail:us-east-2:123456789012:trail/TrailName"
18  }
```

Logging Events with the AWS SDKs

Use the GetEventSelectors operation to see whether your trail is logging management and data events for a trail. You can configure your trails to log management and data events with the PutEventSelectors operation. For more information, see the AWS CloudTrail API Reference.

Sending Events to Amazon CloudWatch Logs

CloudTrail supports sending data and management events to CloudWatch Logs. When you configure your trail to send events to your CloudWatch Logs log group, CloudTrail sends only the events that you specify in your trail. For example, if you configure your trail to log data events only, your trail delivers data events only to your CloudWatch Logs log group. For more information, see Monitoring CloudTrail Log Files with Amazon CloudWatch Logs.

Receiving CloudTrail Log Files from Multiple Regions

You can configure CloudTrail to deliver log files from multiple regions to a single S3 bucket for a single account. For example, you have a trail in the US West (Oregon) Region that is configured to deliver log files to a S3 bucket, and a CloudWatch Logs log group. When you apply the trail to all regions, CloudTrail creates a new trail in all other regions. This trail has the original trail configuration. CloudTrail delivers log files to the same S3 bucket and CloudWatch Logs log group.

To receive CloudTrail log files from multiple regions

1. Sign in to the AWS Management Console and open the CloudTrail console at https://console.aws.amazon.com/cloudtrail/.

2. Choose **Trails**, and then choose a trail name.

3. Click the pencil icon next to **Apply trail to all regions**, and then choose **Yes**.

4. Choose **Save**. The original trail is now replicated across all regions. CloudTrail delivers log files from all regions to the specified S3 bucket.

Note
When a new region launches in the aws partition, CloudTrail automatically creates a trail for you in the new region with the same settings as your original trail.

For more information, see the following resources:

- How Does CloudTrail Behave Regionally and Globally?
- CloudTrail FAQs

Monitoring CloudTrail Log Files with Amazon CloudWatch Logs

You can configure CloudTrail with CloudWatch Logs to monitor your trail logs and be notified when specific activity occurs.

1. Configure your trail to send log events to CloudWatch Logs.

2. Define CloudWatch Logs metric filters to evaluate log events for matches in terms, phrases, or values. For example, you can monitor for `ConsoleLogin` events.

3. Assign CloudWatch metrics to the metric filters.

4. Create CloudWatch alarms that are triggered according to thresholds and time periods that you specify. You can configure alarms to send notifications when alarms are triggered, so that you can take action.

5. You can also configure CloudWatch to automatically perform an action in response to an alarm.

Standard pricing for Amazon CloudWatch and Amazon CloudWatch Logs applies. For more information, see Amazon CloudWatch Pricing.

You can configure your trails to send logs to CloudWatch Logs in the following regions:

Region Name	Region
US East (Ohio)	us-east-2
US East (N. Virginia)	us-east-1
US West (N. California)	us-west-1
US West (Oregon)	us-west-2
Canada (Central)	ca-central-1
Asia Pacific (Mumbai)	ap-south-1
Asia Pacific (Seoul)	ap-northeast-2
Asia Pacific (Singapore)	ap-southeast-1
Asia Pacific (Sydney)	ap-southeast-2
Asia Pacific (Tokyo)	ap-northeast-1
EU (Frankfurt)	eu-central-1
EU (Ireland)	eu-west-1
EU (London)	eu-west-2
South America (São Paulo)	sa-east-1
AWS GovCloud (US)*	us-gov-west-1

* This region requires a separate account. For more information, see AWS GovCloud (US).

- Sending Events to CloudWatch Logs
- Creating CloudWatch Alarms with an AWS CloudFormation Template
- Creating CloudWatch Alarms for CloudTrail Events: Examples
- Creating CloudWatch Alarms for CloudTrail Events: Additional Examples
- Configuring Notifications for CloudWatch Logs Alarms
- Stopping CloudTrail from Sending Events to CloudWatch Logs
- CloudWatch Log Group and Log Stream Naming for CloudTrail
- Role Policy Document for CloudTrail to Use CloudWatch Logs for Monitoring

Sending Events to CloudWatch Logs

When you configure your trail to send events to CloudWatch Logs, CloudTrail sends only the events that match your trail settings. For example, if you configure your trail to log data events only, your trail sends data events only to your CloudWatch Logs log group. CloudTrail supports sending data and management events to CloudWatch Logs. For more information, see Logging Data and Management Events for Trails.

To send events to a CloudWatch Logs log group:

- Create a new trail or specify an existing one. For more information, see Creating a Trail with the Console.
- Create a log group or specify an existing one.
- Specify an IAM role.
- Attach a role policy or use the default.

Configuring CloudWatch Logs Monitoring with the Console

You can use the AWS Management Console to configure your trail to send events to CloudWatch Logs for monitoring.

Creating a Log Group or Specifying an Existing Log Group

CloudTrail uses a CloudWatch Logs log group as a delivery endpoint for log events. You can create a log group or specify an existing one.

To create or specify a log group

1. Open the CloudTrail console at https://console.aws.amazon.com/cloudtrail/.

2. Choose the trail name. If you choose a trail that applies to all regions, you will be redirected to the region in which the trail was created. You can create a log group or choose an existing log group in the same region as the trail. **Note**
   A trail that applies to all regions sends log files from all regions to the CloudWatch Logs log group that you specify.

3. For **CloudWatch Logs**, choose **Configure**.

4. For **New or existing log group**, type the log group name , and then choose **Continue**. For more information, see CloudWatch Log Group and Log Stream Naming for CloudTrail.

5. For the IAM role, choose an existing role or create one. If you create an IAM role, type a role name.

6. Choose **Allow** to grant CloudTrail permissions to create a CloudWatch Logs log stream and deliver events.

Specifying an IAM Role

You can specify a role for CloudTrail to assume to deliver events to the log stream.

To specify a role

1. By default, the `CloudTrail_CloudWatchLogs_Role` is specified for you. The default role policy has the required permissions to create a CloudWatch Logs log stream in a log group that you specify, and to deliver CloudTrail events to that log stream.

   1. To verify the role, go to the AWS Identity and Access Management console at https://console.aws.amazon.com/iam/.

   2. Choose **Roles** and then choose the **CloudTrail_CloudWatchLogs_Role**.

3. To see the contents of the role policy, choose **View Policy Document**.

2. You can specify another role, but you must attach the required role policy to the existing role if you want to use it to send events to CloudWatch Logs. For more information, see Role Policy Document for CloudTrail to Use CloudWatch Logs for Monitoring.

Viewing Events in the CloudWatch Console

After you configure your trail to send events to your CloudWatch Logs log group, you can view the events in the CloudWatch console. CloudTrail typically delivers events to your log group within a few minutes of an API call.

To view events in the CloudWatch console

1. Open the CloudWatch console at https://console.aws.amazon.com/cloudwatch/.

2. Choose **Logs**.

3. Choose the log group that you specified for your trail.

4. Choose the log stream name.

5. To see the details of the event that your trail logged, choose an event.

Note
The **Time (UTC) **column in the CloudWatch console shows when the event was delivered to your log group. To see the actual time that the event was logged by CloudTrail, see the `eventTime` field.

Configuring CloudWatch Logs Monitoring with the AWS CLI

You can use the AWS CLI to configure CloudTrail to send events to CloudWatch Logs for monitoring.

Creating a Log Group

1. If you don't have an existing log group, create a CloudWatch Logs log group as a delivery endpoint for log events using the CloudWatch Logs `create-log-group` command.

```
1  aws logs create-log-group --log-group-name name
```

The following example creates a log group named `CloudTrail/logs`:

```
1  aws logs create-log-group --log-group-name CloudTrail/logs
```

2. Retrieve the log group Amazon Resource Name (ARN).

```
1  aws logs describe-log-groups
```

Creating a Role

Create a role for CloudTrail that enables it to send events to the CloudWatch Logs log group. The IAM `create-role` command takes two parameters: a role name and a file path to an assume role policy document in JSON format. The policy document that you use gives `AssumeRole` permissions to CloudTrail. The `create-role` command creates the role with the required permissions.

To create the JSON file that will contain the policy document, open a text editor and save the following policy contents in a file called `assume_role_policy_document.json`.

```
1  {
2    "Version": "2012-10-17",
3    "Statement": [
4      {
5        "Sid": "",
6        "Effect": "Allow",
7        "Principal": {
8          "Service": "cloudtrail.amazonaws.com"
9        },
10        "Action": "sts:AssumeRole"
11      }
12    ]
13  }
```

Run the following command to create the role with `AssumeRole` permissions for CloudTrail.

```
1  aws iam create-role --role-name role_name --assume-role-policy-document file://<path to
     assume_role_policy_document>.json
```

When the command completes, take a note of the role ARN in the output.

Creating a Policy Document

Create the following role policy document for CloudTrail. This document grants CloudTrail the permissions required to create a CloudWatch Logs log stream in the log group you specify and to deliver CloudTrail events to that log stream.

```
1  {
2    "Version": "2012-10-17",
3    "Statement": [
4      {
5
6        "Sid": "AWSCloudTrailCreateLogStream2014110",
7        "Effect": "Allow",
8        "Action": [
9          "logs:CreateLogStream"
10        ],
11        "Resource": [
12          "arn:aws:logs:region:accountID:log-group:log_group_name:log-stream:
               accountID_CloudTrail_region*"
13        ]
14
15      },
16      {
17        "Sid": "AWSCloudTrailPutLogEvents20141101",
18        "Effect": "Allow",
19        "Action": [
20          "logs:PutLogEvents"
21        ],
22        "Resource": [
23          "arn:aws:logs:region:accountID:log-group:log_group_name:log-stream:
               accountID_CloudTrail_region*"
24        ]
25      }
26    ]
```

```
27 }
```

Save the policy document in a file called `role-policy-document.json`.

Run the following command to apply the policy to the role.

```
1 aws iam put-role-policy --role-name role_name --policy-name cloudtrail-policy --policy-document
     file://<path to role-policy-document>.json
```

Updating the Trail

Update the trail with the log group and role information using the CloudTrail `update-trail` command.

```
1 aws cloudtrail update-trail --name trail_name --cloud-watch-logs-log-group-arn log_group_arn --
     cloud-watch-logs-role-arn role_arn
```

For more information about the AWS CLI commands, see the AWS CloudTrail Command Line Reference.

Limitation

Because CloudWatch Logs has an event size limitation of 256 KB, CloudTrail does not send events larger than 256 KB to CloudWatch Logs. For example, a call to the EC2 `RunInstances` API to launch 500 instances will exceed the 256 KB limit. CloudTrail does not send the event to CloudWatch Logs. To ensure that CloudTrail sends events to CloudWatch Logs, break large requests into smaller batches.

Creating CloudWatch Alarms with an AWS CloudFormation Template

After you configure your trail to deliver log files to your CloudWatch log group, you can create CloudWatch metric filters and alarms to monitor the events in the log files. For example, you can specify an event such as the Amazon EC2 `RunInstances` operation, so that CloudWatch sends you notifications when that event occurs in your account. You can create your filters and alarms separately or use the AWS CloudFormation template to define them all at once.

You can use the example CloudFormation template as is, or as a reference to create your own template.

- Example CloudFormation Template
- Creating a CloudFormation Stack with the Template
- CloudFormation Template Contents

Example CloudFormation Template

The CloudFormation template has predefined CloudWatch metric filters and alarms, so that you receive email notifications when specific security-related API calls are made in your AWS account.

You can download the template with the following link:

https://s3-us-west-2.amazonaws.com/awscloudtrail/cloudwatch-alarms-for-cloudtrail-api-activity/CloudWatch_Alarms_for_CloudTrail_API_Activity.json.

The template defines metric filters that monitor create, delete, and update operations for the following resource types:

- Amazon EC2 instances

- IAM policies

- Internet gateways

- Network ACLs

- Security groups

When an API call occurs in your account, a metric filter monitors that API call. If the API call exceeds the thresholds that you specify, this triggers the alarm and CloudWatch sends you an email notification.

By default, most of the filters in the template trigger an alarm when a monitored event occurs within a five-minute period. You can modify these alarm thresholds for your own requirements. For example, you can monitor for three events in a ten-minute period. To make the changes, edit the template or, after uploading the template, specify the thresholds in the CloudWatch console.

Note
Because CloudTrail typically delivers log files every five minutes, specify alarm periods of five minutes or more.

To see the metric filters and alarms in the template, and the API calls that trigger email notifications, see CloudFormation Template Contents.

Creating a CloudFormation Stack with the Template

A CloudFormation stack is a collection of related resources that you provision and update as a single unit. The following procedure describes how to create the stack and validate the email address that receives notifications.

To create a CloudFormation stack with the template

1. Configure your trail to deliver log files to your CloudWatch Logs log group. See Sending Events to CloudWatch Logs.

2. Download the CloudFormation template: https://s3-us-west-2.amazonaws.com/awscloudtrail/cloudwatch-alarms-for-cloudtrail-api-activity/CloudWatch_Alarms_for_CloudTrail_API_Activity.json.

3. Open the AWS CloudFormation console at https://console.aws.amazon.com/cloudformation.

4. Choose **Create Stack**.

5. On the **Select Template** page, for **Name**, type a stack name. The following example uses `CloudWatchAlarmsForCloudTrail`.

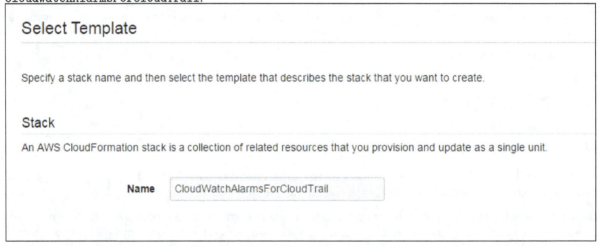

6. For **Source**, choose **Upload a template to Amazon S3**.

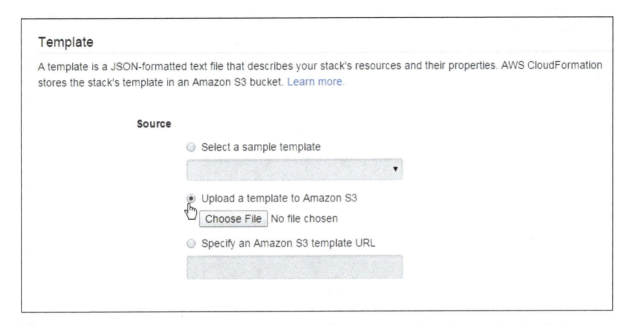

Template

A template is a JSON-formatted text file that describes your stack's resources and their properties. AWS CloudFormation stores the stack's template in an Amazon S3 bucket. Learn more.

Source

○ Select a sample template

[▼]

◉ Upload a template to Amazon S3

[Choose File] No file chosen

○ Specify an Amazon S3 template URL

[   ]

7. Choose **Choose File**, and then select the AWS CloudFormation template that you downloaded.

8. Choose **Next**.

9. On the **Specify Parameters** page, for **Email**, type the email address to receive notifications.

10. For **LogGroupName**, type the name of the log group that you specified when you configured your trail to deliver log files to CloudWatch Logs.

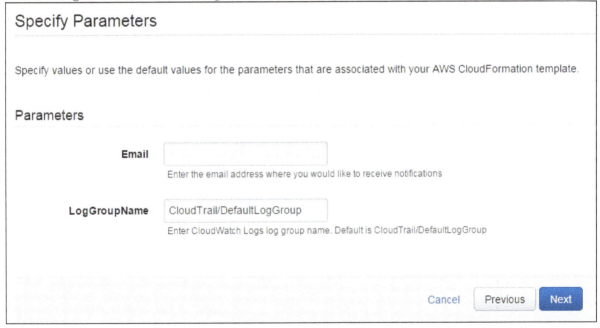

Specify Parameters

Specify values or use the default values for the parameters that are associated with your AWS CloudFormation template.

Parameters

Email	[ ]
	Enter the email address where you would like to receive notifications

LogGroupName	CloudTrail/DefaultLogGroup
	Enter CloudWatch Logs log group name. Default is CloudTrail/DefaultLogGroup

Cancel   Previous   Next

11. Choose **Next**.

12. For **Options**, you can create tags or configure other advanced options. These are not required.

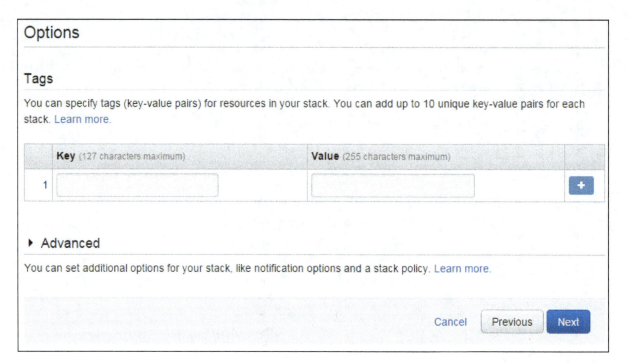

13. Choose **Next**.

14. On the **Review** page, verify that your settings are correct.

15. Choose **Create**. The stack is created in a few minutes.

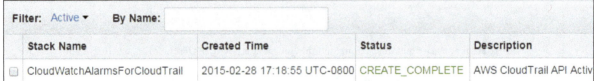

16. After the stack is created, you will receive an email at the address that you specified.

17. In the email, choose **Confirm subscription**. You receive email notifications when the alarms specified by the template are triggered.

You have chosen to subscribe to the topic:
arn:aws:sns:us-west-2:111222333444:CloudWatchAlarmsForCloudTrail-AlarmNotificationTopic-22ABC2DEFGHI2

To confirm this subscription, click or visit the link below (If this was in error no action is necessary):
Confirm subscription

Please do not reply directly to this e-mail. If you wish to remove yourself from receiving all future SNS subscription confirmation requests please send email to sns-opt-out

The following example notification was sent when an API call changed an IAM policy, which triggered the metric alarm.

Sat 2/28/2015 7:11 PM

AWS Notifications <no-reply@sns.amazonaws.com>

ALARM: "CloudTrailIAMPolicyChanges" in US-West-2

To

You are receiving this email because your Amazon CloudWatch Alarm "CloudTrailIAMPolicyChanges" in the US-West-2 region has entered the ALARM state, because "Threshold Crossed: 1 datapoint (7.0) was greater than or equal to the threshold (1.0)." at "Sunday 01 March, 2015 03:10:34 UTC".

View this alarm in the AWS Management Console:
https://console.aws.amazon.com/cloudwatch/home?region=us-west-2#s=Alarms&alarm=CloudTrailIAMPolicyChanges

Alarm Details:
- Name: CloudTrailIAMPolicyChanges
- Description: Alarms when an API call is made to change an IAM policy.
- State Change: INSUFFICIENT_DATA -> ALARM
- Reason for State Change: Threshold Crossed: 1 datapoint (7.0) was greater than or equal to the threshold (1.0).
- Timestamp: Sunday 01 March, 2015 03:10:34 UTC
- AWS Account: 111122223333

Threshold:
- The alarm is in the ALARM state when the metric is GreaterThanOrEqualToThreshold 1.0 for 300 seconds.

Monitored Metric:
- MetricNamespace: CloudTrailMetrics
- MetricName: IAMPolicyEventCount
- Dimensions:
- Period: 300 seconds
- Statistic: Sum
- Unit: not specified

State Change Actions:
- OK:
- ALARM: [arn:aws:sns:us-west-2: 111122223333:CWLAlarms1234-AlarmNotificationTopic- ABC1DEFG234H]
- INSUFFICIENT_DATA:

--
If you wish to stop receiving notifications from this topic, please click or visit the link below to unsubscribe:
https://sns.us-west-2.amazonaws.com/unsubscribe.html?SubscriptionArn=arn:aws:sns:us-west-2:111122223333:CWLAlarms1234-AlarmNotificationTopic-ABC1DEFG234H:78080d51-8221-4ff5-b4b5-0366898a7d0a&Endpoint=janedoe@amazon.com

Please do not reply directly to this e-mail. If you have any questions or comments regarding this email, please contact us at https://aws.amazon.com/support

CloudFormation Template Contents

The following tables show the metric filters and alarms in the template, their purpose, and the API calls that trigger email notifications. Notifications are triggered when one or more of the API calls for a listed filter occur in your account.

You can review the metric filter or alarm definitions in the CloudWatch console.

Amazon S3 Bucket Events

Metric Filter and Alarm	Monitor and Send Notifications for:	Notifications triggered by one or more of the following API operations:

S3BucketChangesMetricFilter S3BucketChangesAlarm	API calls that change bucket policy, lifecycle, replication, or ACLs.	`PutBucketAcl`
		`DeleteBucketPolicy`
		`PutBucketPolicy`
		`DeleteBucketLifecycle`
		`PutBucketLifecycle`
		`DeleteBucketReplication`
		`PutBucketReplication`
		`DeleteBucketCors`
		`PutBucketCors`

Network Events

Metric Filter and Alarm	Monitor and Send Notifications for:	Notifications triggered by one or more of the following API operations:

SecurityGroupChangesMetricFilter SecurityGroupChangesAlarm	API calls that create, update, and delete security groups.	`CreateSecurityGroup`
		`DeleteSecurityGroup`
		`AuthorizeSecurityGroupEgress`
		
		`RevokeSecurityGroupEgress`
		
		`AuthorizeSecurityGroupIngress`
		
		`RevokeSecurityGroupIngress`

NetworkAclChangesMetricFilter NetworkAclChangesAlarm	API calls that create, update, and delete network ACLs.	`CreateNetworkAcl`
		`DeleteNetworkAcl`
		`CreateNetworkAclEntry`
		`DeleteNetworkAclEntry`
		`ReplaceNetworkAclAssociation`
		`ReplaceNetworkAclEntry`

GatewayChangesMetricFilter GatewayChangesAlarm	API calls that create, update, and delete customer and internet gateways.	`CreateCustomerGateway`
		`DeleteCustomerGateway`
		`AttachInternetGateway`
		`CreateInternetGateway`
		`DeleteInternetGateway`
		`DetachInternetGateway`

VpcChangesMetricFilter VpcChangesAlarm	API calls that create, update, and delete virtual private clouds (VPCs), VPC peering connections, and VPC connections to classic EC2 instances using `ClassicLink`.	`CreateVpc` `DeleteVpc`
		`ModifyVpcAttribute`
		`AcceptVpcPeeringConnection`
		
		`CreateVpcPeeringConnection`
		
		`DeleteVpcPeeringConnection`
		
		`RejectVpcPeeringConnection`
		`AttachClassicLinkVpc`
		`DetachClassicLinkVpc`
		`DisableVpcClassicLink`
		`EnableVpcClassicLink`

Amazon EC2 Events

Metric Filter and Alarm	Monitor and Send Notifications for:	Notifications triggered by one or more of the following API operations:

EC2InstanceChanges-MetricFilter EC2InstanceChangesAlarm	The creation, termination, start, stop, and reboot of EC2 instances.	`RebootInstances`
		`RunInstances`
		`StartInstances`
		`StopInstances`
		`TerminateInstances`

EC2LargeInstanceChangesMetricFilter EC2LargeInstanceChangesAlarm	The creation, termination, start, stop, and reboot of 4x and 8x large EC2 instances.	**At least one of the following API operations:** `RebootInstances` `RunInstances` `StartInstances` `StopInstances` `TerminateInstances` **and at least one of the following instance types:** instancetype=*.4xlarge instancetype=*.8xlarge

CloudTrail and IAM Events

Metric Filter and Alarm	Monitor and Send Notifications for:	Notifications triggered by one or more of the following API operations:
CloudTrailChanges-MetricFilter CloudTrailChangesAlarm	Creating, deleting, and updating trails. The occurrence of starting and stopping logging for a trail.	`CreateTrail` `DeleteTrail` `StartLogging` `StopLogging` `UpdateTrail`
ConsoleSignInFailures-MetricFilter ConsoleSignInFailuresAlarm	Console login failures	`eventName` is `ConsoleLogin` and `errorMessage` is "Failed authentication"
AuthorizationFailures-MetricFilter AuthorizationFailuresAlarm	Authorization failures	Any API call that results in an error code: `AccessDenied` or `*UnauthorizedOperation`.

IAMPolicyChangesMetricFilter IAMPolicyChangesAlarm	Changes to IAM policies	`AttachGroupPolicy`
		`DeleteGroupPolicy`
		`DetachGroupPolicy`
		`PutGroupPolicy`
		`CreatePolicy DeletePolicy`
		`CreatePolicyVersion`
		`DeletePolicyVersion`
		`AttachRolePolicy`
		`DeleteRolePolicy`
		`DetachRolePolicy`
		`PutRolePolicy`
		`AttachUserPolicy`
		`DeleteUserPolicy`
		`DetachUserPolicy`
		`PutUserPolicy`

Creating CloudWatch Alarms for CloudTrail Events: Examples

This topic describes how to configure alarms for CloudTrail events using example scenarios.

Prerequisites
Before you can use the examples in this topic, you must:

- Create a trail with the console or CLI.

- Create a log group.

- Specify or create an IAM role that grants CloudTrail the permissions to create a CloudWatch Logs log stream in the log group that you specify and to deliver CloudTrail events to that log stream. The default `CloudTrail_CloudWatchLogs_Role` does this for you.

For more information, see Sending Events to CloudWatch Logs.

Create a metric filter and create an alarm
To create an alarm, you must first create a metric filter and then configure an alarm based on the filter. The procedures are shown for all examples. For more information about syntax for metric filters and patterns for CloudTrail log events, see the JSON-related sections of Filter and Pattern Syntax in the *Amazon CloudWatch Logs User Guide*.

Note
Instead of manually creating the following metric filters and alarms examples, you can use an AWS CloudFormation template to create them all at once. For more information, see Creating CloudWatch Alarms with an AWS CloudFormation Template.

- Example: Amazon S3 Bucket Activity
- Example: Security Group Configuration Changes
- Example: Network Access Control List (ACL) Changes
- Example: Network Gateway Changes
- Example: Amazon Virtual Private Cloud (VPC) Changes
- Example: Amazon EC2 Instance Changes
- Example: EC2 Large Instance Changes
- Example: CloudTrail Changes
- Example: Console Sign-In Failures
- Example: Authorization Failures
- Example: IAM Policy Changes

Example: Amazon S3 Bucket Activity

Follow this procedure to create an Amazon CloudWatch alarm that is triggered when an Amazon S3 API call is made to `PUT` or `DELETE` bucket policy, bucket lifecycle, bucket replication, or to `PUT` a bucket ACL.

The alarm also is triggered for the CORS (cross-origin resource sharing) `PUT` bucket and `DELETE` bucket events. For more information, see Cross-Origin Resource Sharing in the *Amazon Simple Storage Service Developer Guide*.

Create a Metric Filter

1. Open the CloudWatch console at https://console.aws.amazon.com/cloudwatch/.

2. In the navigation pane, choose **Logs**.

3. In the list of log groups, select the check box next to the log group that you created for CloudTrail log events.

4. Choose **Create Metric Filter**.

5. On the **Define Logs Metric Filter** screen, choose **Filter Pattern** and then type the following:

```
1 { ($.eventSource = s3.amazonaws.com) && (($.eventName = PutBucketAcl) || ($.eventName =
      PutBucketPolicy) || ($.eventName = PutBucketCors) || ($.eventName = PutBucketLifecycle)
      || ($.eventName = PutBucketReplication) || ($.eventName = DeleteBucketPolicy) || ($.
      eventName = DeleteBucketCors) || ($.eventName = DeleteBucketLifecycle) || ($.eventName
      = DeleteBucketReplication)) }
```

6. Choose **Assign Metric**.

7. For **Filter Name**, type **S3BucketActivity**.

8. For **Metric Namespace**, type **CloudTrailMetrics**.

9. For **Metric Name**, type **S3BucketActivityEventCount**.

10. Choose **Show advanced metric settings**.

11. For **Metric Value**, type **1**.

12. Choose **Create Filter**.

Create an Alarm

After you create the metric filter, follow this procedure to create an alarm.

1. On the **Filters for** *Log_Group_Name* page, next to the **S3BucketActivity** filter name, choose **Create Alarm**.

2. On the **Create Alarm** page, provide the following values.

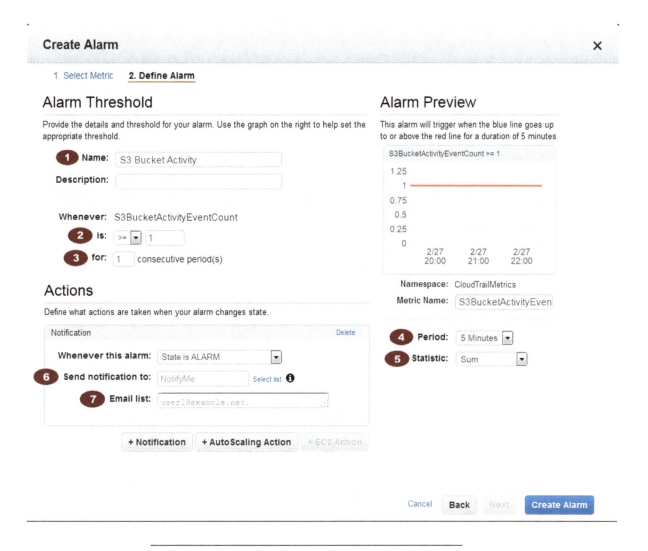

[See the AWS documentation website for more details]

1. Choose **Create Alarm**.

Testing the Alarm for S3 Bucket Activity

You can test the alarm by changing the S3 bucket policy.

To test the alarm

1. Open the Amazon S3 console at https://console.aws.amazon.com/s3/.

2. Choose an S3 bucket in a region that your trail is logging. For example, if your trail is logging in the US East (Ohio) Region only, choose a bucket in the same region. If your trail applies to all regions, choose an S3 bucket in any region.

3. Choose **Permissions** and then choose **Bucket Policy**.

4. Use the **Bucket policy editor** to change the policy and then choose **Save**.

5. Your trail logs the `PutBucketPolicy` operation, and delivers the event to your CloudWatch Logs logs group. The event triggers your metric alarm and CloudWatch Logs sends you a notification about the change.

Example: Security Group Configuration Changes

Follow this procedure to create an Amazon CloudWatch alarm that is triggered when configuration changes happen that involve security groups.

Create a Metric Filter

1. Open the CloudWatch console at https://console.aws.amazon.com/cloudwatch/.

2. In the navigation pane, choose **Logs**.

3. In the list of log groups, select the check box next to the log group that you created for CloudTrail log events.

4. Choose **Create Metric Filter**.

5. On the **Define Logs Metric Filter** screen, choose **Filter Pattern** and then type the following:

```
1 { ($.eventName = AuthorizeSecurityGroupIngress) || ($.eventName =
    AuthorizeSecurityGroupEgress) || ($.eventName = RevokeSecurityGroupIngress) || ($.
    eventName = RevokeSecurityGroupEgress) || ($.eventName = CreateSecurityGroup) || ($.
    eventName = DeleteSecurityGroup) }
```

6. Choose **Assign Metric**.

7. For **Filter Name**, type **SecurityGroupEvents**.

8. For **Metric Namespace**, type **CloudTrailMetrics**.

9. For **Metric Name**, type **SecurityGroupEventCount**.

10. Choose **Show advanced metric settings**.

11. For **Metric Value**, type **1**.

12. Choose **Create Filter**.

Create an Alarm

After you create the metric filter, follow this procedure to create an alarm.

1. On the **Filters for *Log_Group_Name*** page, next to the filter name, choose **Create Alarm**.

2. On the **Create Alarm** page, provide the following values.

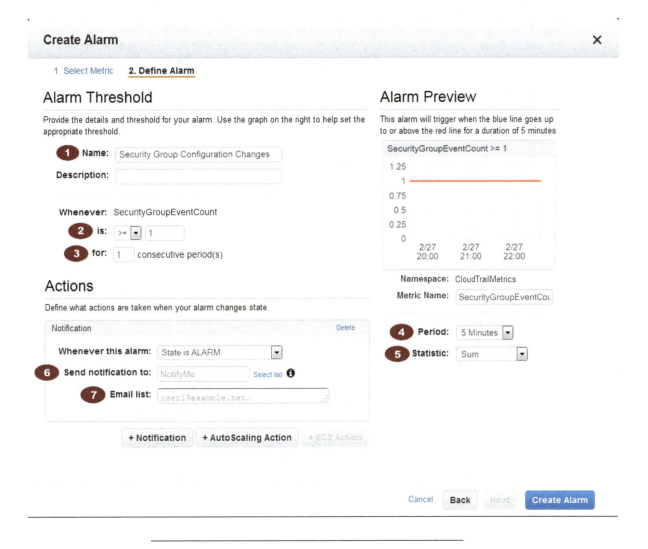

[See the AWS documentation website for more details]

1. Choose **Create Alarm**.

Example: Network Access Control List (ACL) Changes

Follow this procedure to create an Amazon CloudWatch alarm that is triggered when any configuration changes happen involving network ACLs.

Create a Metric Filter

1. Open the CloudWatch console at https://console.aws.amazon.com/cloudwatch/.

2. In the navigation pane, choose **Logs**.

3. In the list of log groups, select the check box next to the log group that you created for CloudTrail log events.

4. Choose **Create Metric Filter**.

5. On the **Define Logs Metric Filter** screen, choose **Filter Pattern** and then type the following:

```
1 { ($.eventName = CreateNetworkAcl) || ($.eventName = CreateNetworkAclEntry) || ($.eventName
    = DeleteNetworkAcl) || ($.eventName = DeleteNetworkAclEntry) || ($.eventName =
  ReplaceNetworkAclEntry) || ($.eventName = ReplaceNetworkAclAssociation) }
```

6. Choose **Assign Metric**.

7. For **Filter Name**, type **NetworkACLEvents**.

8. For **Metric Namespace**, type **CloudTrailMetrics**.

9. For **Metric Name**, type **NetworkACLEventCount**.

10. Choose **Show advanced metric settings**.

11. For **Metric Value**, type **1**.

12. Choose **Create Filter**.

Create an Alarm

After you create the metric filter, follow this procedure to create an alarm.

1. On the **Filters for** *Log_Group_Name* page, next to the filter name, choose **Create Alarm**.

2. On the **Create Alarm** page, provide the following values.

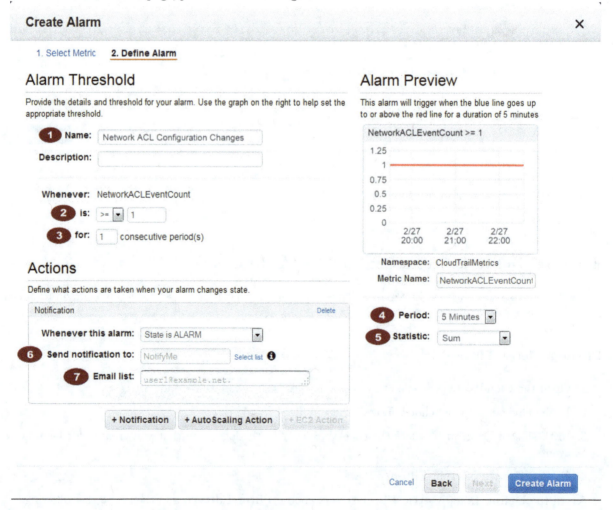

[See the AWS documentation website for more details]

1. Choose **Create Alarm**.

Example: Network Gateway Changes

Follow this procedure to create an Amazon CloudWatch alarm that is triggered when an API call is made to create, update, or delete a customer or Internet gateway.

Create a Metric Filter

1. Open the CloudWatch console at https://console.aws.amazon.com/cloudwatch/.

2. In the navigation pane, choose **Logs**.

3. In the list of log groups, select the check box next to the log group that you created for CloudTrail log events.

4. Choose **Create Metric Filter**.

5. On the **Define Logs Metric Filter** screen, choose **Filter Pattern** and then type the following:

```
1 { ($.eventName = CreateCustomerGateway) || ($.eventName = DeleteCustomerGateway) || ($.
      eventName = AttachInternetGateway) || ($.eventName = CreateInternetGateway) || ($.
      eventName = DeleteInternetGateway) || ($.eventName = DetachInternetGateway) }
```

6. Choose **Assign Metric**.

7. For **Filter Name**, type **GatewayChanges**.

8. For **Metric Namespace**, type **CloudTrailMetrics**.

9. For **Metric Name**, type **GatewayEventCount**.

10. Choose **Show advanced metric settings**.

11. For **Metric Value**, type **1**.

12. Choose **Create Filter**.

Example: Create an Alarm

After you create the metric filter, follow this procedure to create an alarm.

1. On the **Filters for *Log_Group_Name*** page, next to the filter name, choose **Create Alarm**.

2. On the **Create Alarm** page, provide the following values.

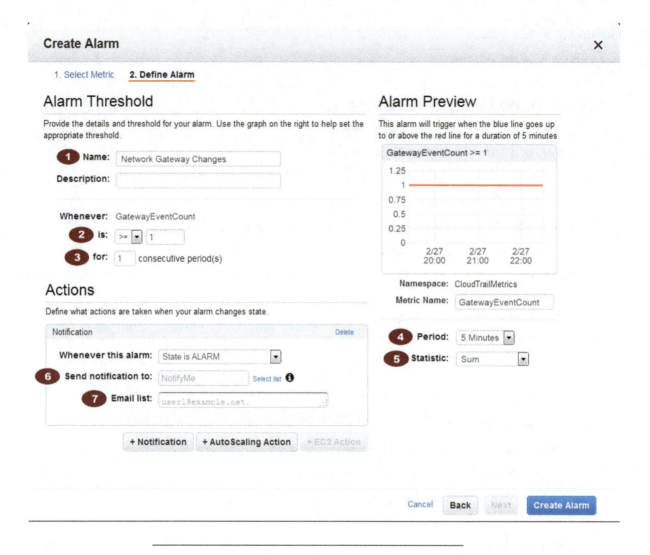

[See the AWS documentation website for more details]

1. Choose **Create Alarm**.

Example: Amazon Virtual Private Cloud (VPC) Changes

Follow this procedure to create an Amazon CloudWatch alarm that is triggered when an API call is made to create, update, or delete an Amazon VPC, an Amazon VPC peering connection, or an Amazon VPC connection to classic Amazon EC2 instances.

Create a Metric Filter

1. Open the CloudWatch console at https://console.aws.amazon.com/cloudwatch/.

2. In the navigation pane, choose **Logs**.

3. In the list of log groups, select the check box next to the log group that you created for CloudTrail log events.

4. Choose **Create Metric Filter**.

5. On the **Define Logs Metric Filter** screen, choose **Filter Pattern** and then type the following:

```
1 { ($.eventName = CreateVpc) || ($.eventName = DeleteVpc) || ($.eventName =
    ModifyVpcAttribute) || ($.eventName = AcceptVpcPeeringConnection) || ($.eventName =
    CreateVpcPeeringConnection) || ($.eventName = DeleteVpcPeeringConnection) || ($.
    eventName = RejectVpcPeeringConnection) || ($.eventName = AttachClassicLinkVpc) || ($.
    eventName = DetachClassicLinkVpc) || ($.eventName = DisableVpcClassicLink) || ($.
    eventName = EnableVpcClassicLink) }
```

6. Choose **Assign Metric**.

7. For **Filter Name**, type **VpcChanges**.

8. For **Metric Namespace**, type **CloudTrailMetrics**.

9. For **Metric Name**, type **VpcEventCount**.

10. Choose **Show advanced metric settings**.

11. For **Metric Value**, type **1**.

12. Choose **Create Filter**.

Create an Alarm

After you create the metric filter, follow this procedure to create an alarm.

1. On the **Filters for *Log_Group_Name*** page, next to the filter name, choose **Create Alarm**.

2. On the **Create Alarm** page, provide the following values.

```
Create Alarm                                                    ✕

  1. Select Metric    2. Define Alarm

Alarm Threshold                                    Alarm Preview

Provide the details and threshold for your alarm. Use the graph on the right to help set the    This alarm will trigger when the blue line goes up
appropriate threshold.                                              to or above the red line for a duration of 5 minutes

    ①  Name:   VPC Changes                         VpcEventCount >= 1

        Description:                                  1.25
                                                         1  ━━━━━━━━━━━━━━━━━━
                                                      0.75
        Whenever:  VpcEventCount                       0.5
                                                      0.25
    ②    is:   >=  ▾   1                                0
                                                          2/27    2/27    2/27
    ③    for:  1   consecutive period(s)                20:00   21:00   22:00

Actions                                             Namespace:  CloudTrailMetrics
                                                    Metric Name:  VpcEventCount
Define what actions are taken when your alarm changes state.

  Notification                              Delete
                                                    ④  Period:   5 Minutes ▾
     Whenever this alarm:  State is ALARM  ▾
                                                    ⑤  Statistic:  Sum       ▾
 ⑥  Send notification to:  NotifyMe    Select list ⓘ

   ⑦   Email list:  user1@example.net.

        + Notification   + AutoScaling Action  + EC2 Action

                          Cancel   Back   Next   Create Alarm
```

[See the AWS documentation website for more details]

1. Choose **Create Alarm**.

Example: Amazon EC2 Instance Changes

Follow this procedure to create an Amazon CloudWatch alarm that is triggered when an API call is made to create, terminate, start, stop, or reboot an Amazon EC2 instance.

Create a Metric Filter

1. Open the CloudWatch console at https://console.aws.amazon.com/cloudwatch/.

2. In the navigation pane, choose **Logs**.

3. In the list of log groups, select the check box next to the log group that you created for CloudTrail log events.

4. Choose **Create Metric Filter**.

5. On the **Define Logs Metric Filter** screen, choose **Filter Pattern** and then type the following:

```
1 { ($.eventName = RunInstances) || ($.eventName = RebootInstances) || ($.eventName =
     StartInstances) || ($.eventName = StopInstances) || ($.eventName = TerminateInstances)
     }
```

6. Choose **Assign Metric**.

7. For **Filter Name**, type **EC2InstanceChanges**.

8. For **Metric Namespace**, type **CloudTrailMetrics**.

9. For **Metric Name**, type **EC2InstanceEventCount**.

10. Choose **Show advanced metric settings**.

11. For **Metric Value**, type **1**.

12. Choose **Create Filter**.

Create an Alarm

After you create the metric filter, follow this procedure to create an alarm.

1. On the **Filters for** *Log_Group_Name* page, next to the filter name, choose **Create Alarm**.

2. On the **Create Alarm** page, provide the following values.

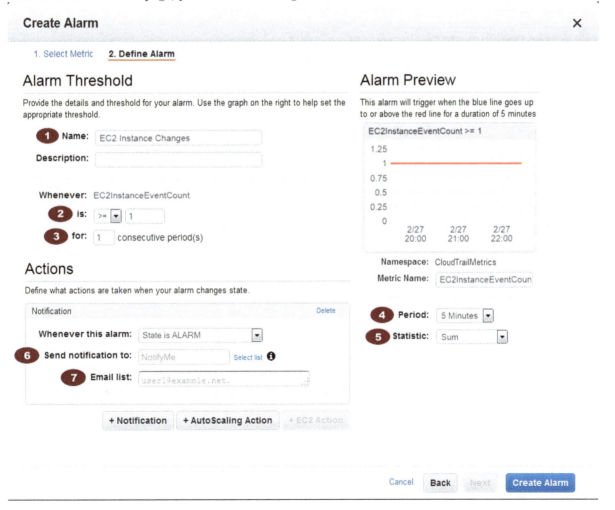

[See the AWS documentation website for more details]

1. Choose **Create Alarm**.

Example: EC2 Large Instance Changes

Follow this procedure to create an Amazon CloudWatch alarm that is triggered when an API call is made to create a 4x or 8x-large Amazon EC2 instance.

Create a Metric Filter

1. Open the CloudWatch console at https://console.aws.amazon.com/cloudwatch/.

2. In the navigation pane, choose **Logs**.

3. In the list of log groups, select the check box next to the log group that you created for CloudTrail log events.

4. Choose **Create Metric Filter**.

5. On the **Define Logs Metric Filter** screen, choose **Filter Pattern** and then type the following:

```
1 { ($.eventName = RunInstances) && (($.requestParameters.instanceType = *.8xlarge) || ($.
    requestParameters.instanceType = *.4xlarge)) }
```

6. Choose **Assign Metric**.

7. For **Filter Name**, type **EC2LargeInstanceChanges**.

8. For **Metric Namespace**, type **CloudTrailMetrics**.

9. For **Metric Name**, type **EC2LargeInstanceEventCount**.

10. Choose **Show advanced metric settings**.

11. For **Metric Value**, type **1**.

12. Choose **Create Filter**.

Create an Alarm

After you create the metric filter, follow this procedure to create an alarm.

1. On the **Filters for *Log_Group_Name*** page, next to the filter name, choose **Create Alarm**.

2. On the **Create Alarm** page, provide the following values.

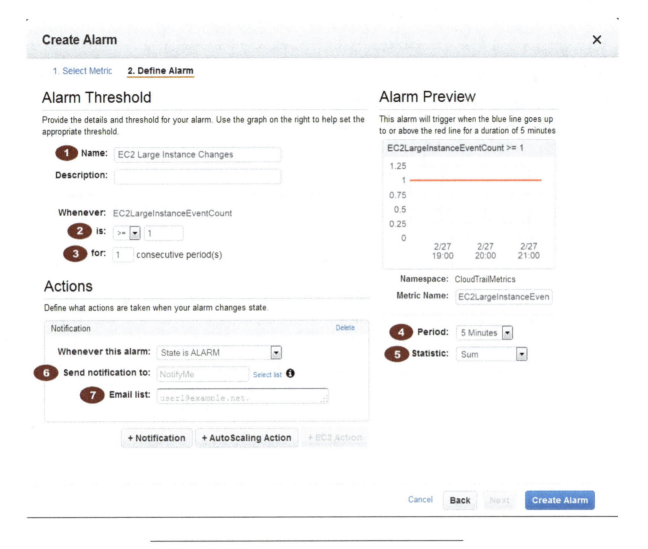

[See the AWS documentation website for more details]

1. Choose **Create Alarm**.

Example: CloudTrail Changes

Follow this procedure to create an Amazon CloudWatch alarm that is triggered when an API call is made to create, update, or delete a CloudTrail trail, or to start or stop logging a trail.

Create a Metric Filter

1. Open the CloudWatch console at https://console.aws.amazon.com/cloudwatch/.

2. In the navigation pane, choose **Logs**.

3. In the list of log groups, select the check box next to the log group that you created for CloudTrail log events.

4. Choose **Create Metric Filter**.

5. On the **Define Logs Metric Filter** screen, choose **Filter Pattern** and then type the following:

127

```
1 { ($.eventName = CreateTrail) || ($.eventName = UpdateTrail) || ($.eventName = DeleteTrail)
    || ($.eventName = StartLogging) || ($.eventName = StopLogging) }
```

6. Choose **Assign Metric**.

7. For **Filter Name**, type **CloudTrailChanges**.

8. For **Metric Namespace**, type **CloudTrailMetrics**.

9. For **Metric Name**, type **CloudTrailEventCount**.

10. Choose **Show advanced metric settings**.

11. For **Metric Value**, type **1**.

12. Choose **Create Filter**.

Create an Alarm

After you create the metric filter, follow this procedure to create an alarm.

1. On the **Filters for *Log_Group_Name*** page, next to the filter name, choose **Create Alarm**.

2. On the **Create Alarm** page, provide the following values.

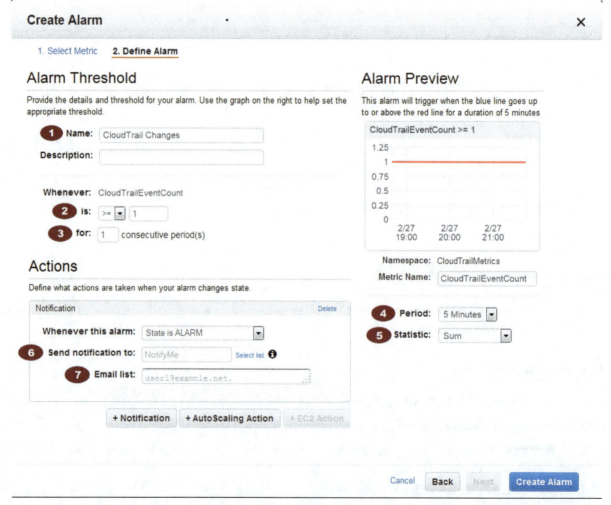

[See the AWS documentation website for more details]

1. Choose **Create Alarm**.

Example: Console Sign-In Failures

Follow this procedure to create an Amazon CloudWatch alarm that is triggered when there are three or more sign-in failures during a five minute period.

Create a Metric Filter

1. Open the CloudWatch console at https://console.aws.amazon.com/cloudwatch/.
2. In the navigation pane, choose **Logs**.
3. In the list of log groups, select the check box next to the log group that you created for CloudTrail log events.
4. Choose **Create Metric Filter**.
5. On the **Define Logs Metric Filter** screen, choose **Filter Pattern** and then type the following:

```
1  { ($.eventName = ConsoleLogin) && ($.errorMessage = "Failed authentication") }
```

6. Choose **Assign Metric**.
7. For **Filter Name**, type **ConsoleSignInFailures**.
8. For **Metric Namespace**, type **CloudTrailMetrics**.
9. For **Metric Name**, type **ConsoleSigninFailureCount**.
10. Choose **Show advanced metric settings**.
11. For **Metric Value**, type **1**.
12. Choose **Create Filter**.

Create an Alarm

After you create the metric filter, follow this procedure to create an alarm.

1. On the **Filters for *Log_Group_Name*** page, next to the filter name, choose **Create Alarm**.
2. On the **Create Alarm** page, provide the following values.

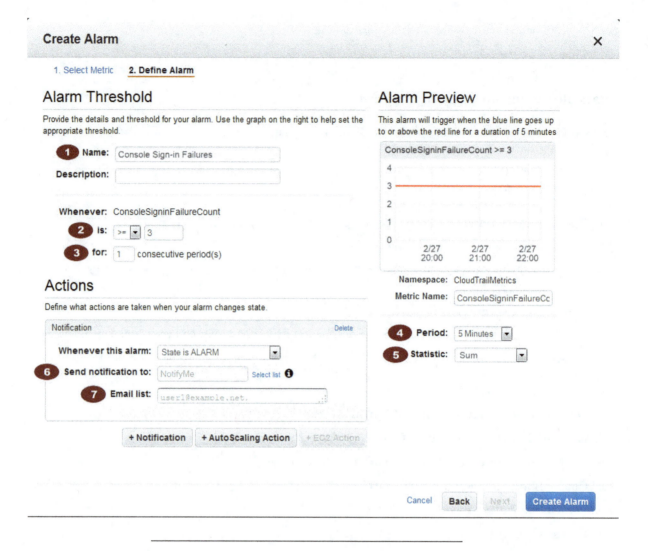

[See the AWS documentation website for more details]

1. Choose **Create Alarm**.

Example: Authorization Failures

Follow this procedure to create an Amazon CloudWatch alarm that is triggered when an unauthorized API call is made.

Create a Metric Filter

1. Open the CloudWatch console at https://console.aws.amazon.com/cloudwatch/.

2. In the navigation pane, choose **Logs**.

3. In the list of log groups, select the check box next to the log group that you created for CloudTrail log events.

4. Choose **Create Metric Filter**.

5. On the **Define Logs Metric Filter** screen, choose **Filter Pattern** and then type the following:

```
1 { ($.errorCode = "*UnauthorizedOperation") || ($.errorCode = "AccessDenied*") }
```

6. Choose **Assign Metric**.

7. For **Filter Name**, type **AuthorizationFailures**.

8. For **Metric Namespace**, type **CloudTrailMetrics**.

9. For **Metric Name**, type **AuthorizationFailureCount**.

10. Choose **Show advanced metric settings**.

11. For **Metric Value**, type **1**.

12. Choose **Create Filter**.

Create an Alarm

After you create the metric filter, follow this procedure to create an alarm.

1. On the **Filters for *Log_Group_Name*** page, next to the filter name, choose **Create Alarm**.

2. On the **Create Alarm** page, provide the following values.
   ![[CloudWatch Logs Create Alarm Wizard]](http://docs.aws.amazon.com/awscloudtrail/latest/userguide/images/cw_alarm_wizard_ authorizationfailures.png)

[See the AWS documentation website for more details]

1. Choose **Create Alarm**.

Example: IAM Policy Changes

Follow this procedure to create an Amazon CloudWatch alarm that is triggered when an API call is made to change an IAM policy.

Create a Metric Filter

1. Open the CloudWatch console at https://console.aws.amazon.com/cloudwatch/.

2. In the navigation pane, choose **Logs**.

3. In the list of log groups, select the check box next to the log group that you created for CloudTrail log events.

4. Choose **Create Metric Filter**.

5. On the **Define Logs Metric Filter** screen, choose **Filter Pattern** and then type the following:

```
1 {($.eventName=DeleteGroupPolicy)||($.eventName=DeleteRolePolicy)||($.eventName=
    DeleteUserPolicy)||($.eventName=PutGroupPolicy)||($.eventName=PutRolePolicy)||($.
    eventName=PutUserPolicy)||($.eventName=CreatePolicy)||($.eventName=DeletePolicy)||($.
    eventName=CreatePolicyVersion)||($.eventName=DeletePolicyVersion)||($.eventName=
    AttachRolePolicy)||($.eventName=DetachRolePolicy)||($.eventName=AttachUserPolicy)||($.
    eventName=DetachUserPolicy)||($.eventName=AttachGroupPolicy)||($.eventName=
    DetachGroupPolicy)}
```

6. Choose **Assign Metric**.

7. For **Filter Name**, type **IAMPolicyChanges**.

8. For **Metric Namespace**, type **CloudTrailMetrics**.

9. For **Metric Name**, type **IAMPolicyEventCount**.

10. Choose **Show advanced metric settings**.

11. For **Metric Value**, type **1**.

12. Choose **Create Filter**.

Create an Alarm

After you create the metric filter, follow this procedure to create an alarm.

1. On the **Filters for *Log_Group_Name*** page, next to the filter name, choose **Create Alarm**.

2. On the **Create Alarm** page, provide the following values.
   ![[CloudWatch Logs Create Alarm Wizard]](http://docs.aws.amazon.com/awscloudtrail/latest/userguide/images/cw_alarm_wizard_ iampolicychanges.png)

[See the AWS documentation website for more details]

1. Choose **Create Alarm**.

Creating CloudWatch Alarms for CloudTrail Events: Additional Examples

AWS Identity and Access Management (IAM) best practices recommend that you do not use your root account credentials to access AWS. Instead, you should create individual IAM users so that you can give each user a unique set of security credentials. The IAM Best Practices also recommend that you enable multi-factor authentication (MFA) for IAM users who are allowed access to sensitive resources or APIs.

You can monitor whether activity in your AWS account adheres to these best practices by creating the CloudWatch alarms that notify you when root account credentials have been used to access AWS, or when API activity or console sign-ins without MFA have occurred. These alarms are described in this document.

Configuring an alarm involves two main steps:

- Create a metric filter
- Create an alarm based on the filter
- Example: Monitor for Root Usage
- Example: Monitor for API Activity Without Multi-factor Authentication (MFA)
- Example: Monitor for Console Sign In Without Multi-factor Authentication (MFA)

Example: Monitor for Root Usage

This scenario walks you through how to use the AWS Management Console to create an Amazon CloudWatch alarm that is triggered when root (account) credentials are used.

Create a Metric Filter

1. Open the CloudWatch console at https://console.aws.amazon.com/cloudwatch/.

2. In the navigation pane, choose **Logs**.

3. In the list of log groups, select the check box next to the log group that you created for CloudTrail log events.

4. Choose **Create Metric Filter**.

5. On the **Define Logs Metric Filter** screen, choose **Filter Pattern** and then type the following:

```
1 { $.userIdentity.type = "Root" && $.userIdentity.invokedBy NOT EXISTS && $.eventType != "
    AwsServiceEvent" }
```

Note
For more information about syntax for metric filters and patterns for CloudTrail log events, see the JSON-related sections of Filter and Pattern Syntax in the Amazon CloudWatch User Guide.

1. Choose **Assign Metric**, and then on the **Create Metric Filter and Assign a Metric** screen, in the **Filter Name** box, enter **RootAccountUsage**

2. Under **Metric Details**, in the **Metric Namespace** box, enter **CloudTrailMetrics**.

3. In the **Metric Name** field, enter **RootAccountUsageCount**.

4. Choose **Metric Value**, and then type **1**. **Note**
   If **Metric Value** does not appear, choose **Show advanced metric settings** first.

5. When you are finished, choose **Create Filter**.

Create an Alarm

These steps are a continuation of the previous steps for creating a metric filter.

1. On the **Filters for *Log__Group__Name*** page, next to the filter name, choose **Create Alarm**.

2. On the **Create Alarm** page, provide the following values.

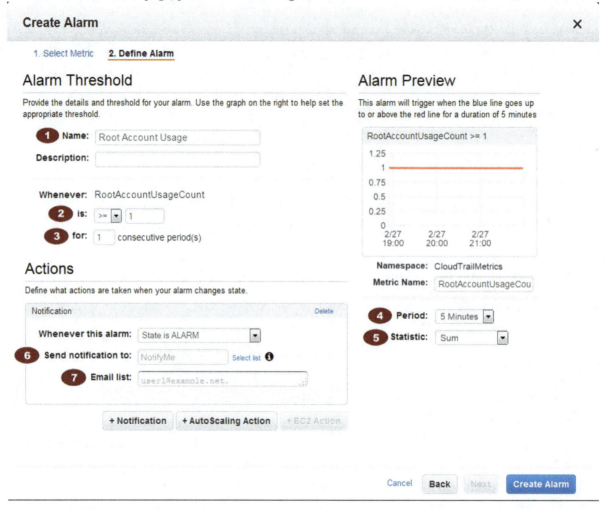

[See the AWS documentation website for more details]

1. When you are finished, choose **Create Alarm**.

Example: Monitor for API Activity Without Multi-factor Authentication (MFA)

This scenario walks you through how to use the AWS Management Console to create an Amazon CloudWatch alarm that is triggered when API calls are made without the use of multi-factor authentication (MFA).

Create a Metric Filter

1. Open the CloudWatch console at https://console.aws.amazon.com/cloudwatch/.

2. In the navigation pane, choose **Logs**.

3. In the list of log groups, select the check box next to the log group that you created for CloudTrail log events.

4. Choose **Create Metric Filter**.

5. On the **Define Logs Metric Filter** screen, choose **Filter Pattern** and then type the following:

```
1 { $.userIdentity.sessionContext.attributes.mfaAuthenticated != "true" }
```

Note

For more information about syntax for metric filters and patterns for CloudTrail log events, see the JSON-related sections of Filter and Pattern Syntax in the Amazon CloudWatch User Guide.

1. Choose **Assign Metric**, and then on the **Create Metric Filter and Assign a Metric** screen, in the **Filter Name** box, enter **ApiActivityWithoutMFA**.

2. Under **Metric Details**, in the **Metric Namespace** box, enter **CloudTrailMetrics**.

3. In the **Metric Name** box, enter **ApiActivityWithoutMFACount**.

4. Choose **Metric Value**, and then type **1**. **Note**
   If **Metric Value** does not appear, choose **Show advanced metric settings** first.

5. When you are finished, choose **Create Filter**.

Create an Alarm

These steps are a continuation of the previous steps for creating a metric filter.

1. On the **Filters for _Log_Group_Name_** page, next to the filter name, choose **Create Alarm**.

2. On the **Create Alarm** page, provide the following values.

135

Create Alarm ✕

1. Select Metric   **2. Define Alarm**

Alarm Threshold

Provide the details and threshold for your alarm. Use the graph on the right to help set the appropriate threshold.

① **Name:** Api Activity Without MFA

Description:

Whenever: ApiActivityWithoutMFACount

② **is:** >= ▾ 1

③ **for:** 1   consecutive period(s)

Actions

Define what actions are taken when your alarm changes state.

Notification   Delete

Whenever this alarm: State is ALARM ▾

⑥ **Send notification to:** NotifyMe   Select list ⓘ

⑦ **Email list:** user1@example.net.

[+ Notification]   [+ AutoScaling Action]   [+ EC2 Action]

Alarm Preview

This alarm will trigger when the blue line goes up to or above the red line for a duration of 5 minutes

ApiActivityWithoutMFACount >= 1

```
1.25
   1  ──────────────────────────
0.75
 0.5
0.25
   0
      2/27    2/27    2/27
     19:00   20:00   21:00
```

Namespace: CloudTrailMetrics

Metric Name: ApiActivityWithoutMFAC

④ **Period:** 5 Minutes ▾

⑤ **Statistic:** Sum ▾

Cancel   [Back]   [Next]   [**Create Alarm**]

[See the AWS documentation website for more details]

1. When you are finished, choose **Create Alarm**.

Example: Monitor for Console Sign In Without Multi-factor Authentication (MFA)

This scenario walks you through how to use the AWS Management Console to create an Amazon CloudWatch alarm that is triggered when a console sign in is made without multi-factor authentication.

Create a Metric Filter

1. Open the CloudWatch console at https://console.aws.amazon.com/cloudwatch/.

2. In the navigation pane, choose **Logs**.

3. In the list of log groups, select the check box next to the log group that you created for CloudTrail log events.

4. Choose **Create Metric Filter**.

5. On the **Define Logs Metric Filter** screen, choose **Filter Pattern** and then type the following:

```
1 { $.eventName = "ConsoleLogin" && $.additionalEventData.MFAUsed = "No" }
```

Note

For more information about syntax for metric filters and patterns for CloudTrail log events, see the JSON-related sections of Filter and Pattern Syntax in the Amazon CloudWatch User Guide.

1. Choose **Assign Metric**, and then on the **Create Metric Filter and Assign a Metric** screen, in the **Filter Name** box, enter **ConsoleSignInWithoutMfa**

2. Under **Metric Details**, in the **Metric Namespace** box, enter **CloudTrailMetrics**.

3. In the **Metric Name** field, enter **ConsoleSignInWithoutMfaCount**.

4. Choose **Metric Value**, and then type **1**. **Note**
   If **Metric Value** does not appear, choose **Show advanced metric settings** first.

5. When you are finished, choose **Create Filter**.

Example: Create an Alarm

These steps are a continuation of the previous steps for creating a metric filter.

1. On the **Filters for *Log_Group_Name*** page, next to the filter name, choose **Create Alarm**.

2. On the **Create Alarm** page, provide the following values.

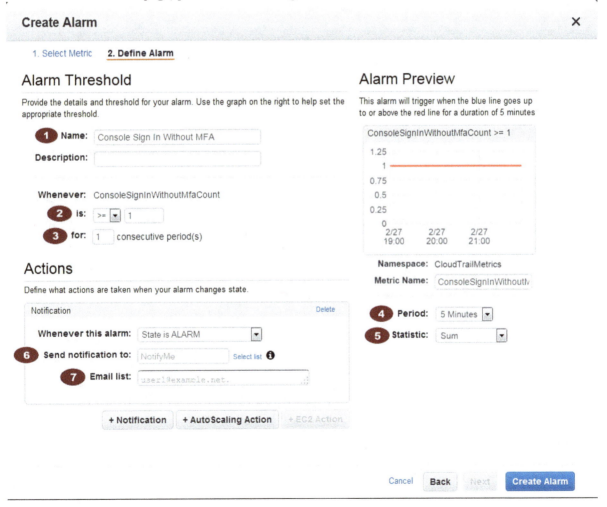

[See the AWS documentation website for more details]

1. When you are finished, choose **Create Alarm**.

Configuring Notifications for CloudWatch Logs Alarms

You can configure CloudWatch Logs to send a notification whenever an alarm is triggered for CloudTrail. Doing so enables you to respond quickly to critical operational events captured in CloudTrail events and detected by CloudWatch Logs. CloudWatch uses Amazon Simple Notification Service (SNS) to send email. For more information, see Set Up Amazon SNS in the CloudWatch Developer Guide.

Stopping CloudTrail from Sending Events to CloudWatch Logs

You can stop sending events to CloudWatch Logs by deleting the delivery endpoint.

AWS Management Console

To remove the CloudWatch Logs delivery endpoint using the AWS Management Console

1. Sign in to the AWS Management Console.
2. Navigate to the CloudTrail console.
3. In the navigation pane, click **Configuration**.
4. In the **CloudWatch Logs (optional)** section, click the **Delete** (trash can) icon.
5. Click **Continue** to confirm.

AWS Command Line Interface (CLI)

You can remove the CloudWatch Logs log group as a delivery endpoint using the `update-trail` command. The following command clears the log group and role from the trail configuration.

```
1 aws cloudtrail update-trail --name trailname --cloud-watch-logs-log-group-arn="" --cloud-watch-
      logs-role-arn=""
```

CloudWatch Log Group and Log Stream Naming for CloudTrail

Amazon CloudWatch will display the log group that you created for CloudTrail events alongside any other log groups you have in a region. We recommend that you use a log group name that helps you easily distinguish the log group from others. For example, **CloudTrail/logs**. Log group names can be between 1 and 512 characters long. Allowed characters include a-z, A-Z, 0-9, '_' (underscore), '-' (hyphen), '/' (forward slash), and '.' (period).

When CloudTrail creates the log stream for the log group, it names the log stream according to the following format: *account_ID_CloudTrail_source_region*.

Note
If the volume of CloudTrail logs is large, multiple log streams may be created to deliver log data to your log group.

Role Policy Document for CloudTrail to Use CloudWatch Logs for Monitoring

This section describes the trust policy required for the CloudTrail role to send log events to CloudWatch Logs. You can attach a policy document to a role when you configure CloudTrail to send events, as described in Sending Events to CloudWatch Logs. You can also create a role using IAM. For more information, see Creating a Role for an AWS Service (AWS Management Console) or Creating a Role (CLI and API).

The following example policy document contains the permissions required to create a CloudWatch log stream in the log group that you specify and to deliver CloudTrail events to that log stream in the US East (Ohio) region. (This is the default policy for the default IAM role `CloudTrail_CloudWatchLogs_Role`.)

```
 1 {
 2   "Version": "2012-10-17",
 3   "Statement": [
 4     {
 5
 6       "Sid": "AWSCloudTrailCreateLogStream2014110",
 7       "Effect": "Allow",
 8       "Action": [
 9         "logs:CreateLogStream"
10       ],
11       "Resource": [
12         "arn:aws:logs:us-east-2:accountID:log-group:log_group_name:log-stream:
             CloudTrail_log_stream_name_prefix*"
13       ]
14
15     },
16     {
17       "Sid": "AWSCloudTrailPutLogEvents20141101",
18       "Effect": "Allow",
19       "Action": [
20         "logs:PutLogEvents"
21       ],
22       "Resource": [
23         "arn:aws:logs:us-east-2:accountID:log-group:log_group_name:log-stream:
             CloudTrail_log_stream_name_prefix*"
24       ]
25     }
26   ]
27 }
```

Receiving CloudTrail Log Files from Multiple Accounts

You can have CloudTrail deliver log files from multiple AWS accounts into a single Amazon S3 bucket. For example, you have four AWS accounts with account IDs 111111111111, 222222222222, 333333333333, and 444444444444, and you want to configure CloudTrail to deliver log files from all four of these accounts to a bucket belonging to account 111111111111. To accomplish this, complete the following steps in order:

1. Turn on CloudTrail in the account where the destination bucket will belong (111111111111 in this example). Do not turn on CloudTrail in any other accounts yet.

   For instructions, see Creating a Trail.

2. Update the bucket policy on your destination bucket to grant cross-account permissions to CloudTrail.

   For instructions, see Setting Bucket Policy for Multiple Accounts.

3. Turn on CloudTrail in the other accounts you want (222222222222, 333333333333, and 444444444444 in this example). Configure CloudTrail in these accounts to use the same bucket belonging to the account that you specified in step 1 (111111111111 in this example).

   For instructions, see Turning on CloudTrail in Additional Accounts.

- Setting Bucket Policy for Multiple Accounts
- Turning on CloudTrail in Additional Accounts

Setting Bucket Policy for Multiple Accounts

For a bucket to receive log files from multiple accounts, its bucket policy must grant CloudTrail permission to write log files from all the accounts you specify. This means that you must modify the bucket policy on your destination bucket to grant CloudTrail permission to write log files from each specified account.

To modify bucket permissions so that files can be received from multiple accounts

1. Sign in to the AWS Management Console using the account that owns the bucket (111111111111 in this example) and open the Amazon S3 console.

2. Choose the bucket where CloudTrail delivers your log files and then choose **Properties**.

3. Choose **Permissions**.

4. Choose **Edit Bucket Policy**.

5. Modify the existing policy to add a line for each additional account whose log files you want delivered to this bucket. See the following example policy and note the underlined `Resource` line specifying a second account ID. **Note**
An AWS account ID is a twelve-digit number, and leading zeros must not be omitted.

```
1  {
2    "Version": "2012-10-17",
3    "Statement": [
4      {
5        "Sid": "AWSCloudTrailAclCheck20131101",
6        "Effect": "Allow",
7        "Principal": {
8          "Service": "cloudtrail.amazonaws.com"
9        },
10       "Action": "s3:GetBucketAcl",
11       "Resource": "arn:aws:s3:::myBucketName"
12     },
13     {
14       "Sid": "AWSCloudTrailWrite20131101",
15       "Effect": "Allow",
16       "Principal": {
17         "Service": "cloudtrail.amazonaws.com"
18       },
19       "Action": "s3:PutObject",
20       "Resource": [
21         "arn:aws:s3:::myBucketName/[optional] myLogFilePrefix/AWSLogs/111111111111/*",
22         "arn:aws:s3:::myBucketName/[optional] myLogFilePrefix/AWSLogs/222222222222/*"
23       ],
24       "Condition": {
25         "StringEquals": {
26           "s3:x-amz-acl": "bucket-owner-full-control"
27         }
28       }
29     }
30   ]
31 }
```

Turning on CloudTrail in Additional Accounts

You can use the console or the command line interface to turn on CloudTrail in additional AWS accounts.

Using the Console to Turn on CloudTrail in Additional AWS Accounts

You can use the CloudTrail console to turn on CloudTrail in additional accounts.

1. Sign into the AWS management console using account 222222222222 credentials and open the AWS CloudTrail console. In the navigation bar, select the region where you want to turn on CloudTrail.

2. Choose **Get Started Now**.

3. On the following page, type a name for your trail in the **Trail name** box.

4. For **Create a new S3 bucket?**, choose **No**. Use the text box to enter the name of the bucket you created previously for storing log files when you signed in using account 111111111111 credentials. CloudTrail displays a warning asking you if you are sure that you want to specify an S3 bucket in another account. Verify the name of the bucket you entered.

5. Choose **Advanced**.

6. In the **Log file prefix** field, enter the same prefix you entered for storing log files when you turned on CloudTrail using account 111111111111 credentials. If you choose to use a prefix that is different from the one you entered when you turned on CloudTrail in the first account, you must edit the bucket policy on your destination bucket to allow CloudTrail to write log files to your bucket using this new prefix.

7. (Optional) Choose **Yes** or **No** for **SNS notification for every log file delivery?**. If you chose **Yes**, type a name for your Amazon SNS topic in the **SNS topic (new) field**. **Note**
Amazon SNS is a regional service, so if you choose to create a topic, that topic will exist in the same region in which you turn on CloudTrail. If you have a trail that applies to all regions, you can pick an Amazon SNS topic in any region as long as you have the correct policy applied to the topic. For more information, see Amazon SNS Topic Policy for CloudTrail.

8. Choose **Turn On**.

In about 15 minutes, CloudTrail starts publishing log files that show the AWS calls made in your accounts in this region since you completed the preceding steps.

Using the CLI to Turn on CloudTrail in Additional AWS Accounts

You can use the AWS command line tools to turn on CloudTrail in additional accounts and aggregate their log files to one Amazon S3 bucket. For more information about these tools, see the AWS Command Line Interface User Guide.

Turn on CloudTrail in your additional accounts by using the `create-subscription` command. Use the following options to specify additional settings:

- `--name` specifies the name of the trail.

- `--s3-use-bucket` specifies the existing Amazon S3 bucket, created when you turned on CloudTrail in your first account (111111111111 in this example).

- `--s3-prefix` specifies a prefix for the log file delivery path (optional).

- `--sns-new-topic` specifies the name of the Amazon SNS topic to which you can subscribe for notification of log file delivery to your bucket (optional).

In contrast to trails that you create using the console, you must give every trail you create with the AWS CLI a name. You can create one trail for each region in which an account is running AWS resources.

The following example command shows how to create a trail for your additional accounts by using the AWS CLI. To have log files for these account delivered to the bucket you created in your first account (111111111111 in this example), specify the bucket name in the `--s3-new-bucket` option. Amazon S3 bucket names are globally unique.

```
1 aws cloudtrail create-subscription --name AWSCloudTrailExample --s3-use-bucket
    MyBucketBelongingToAccount111111111111 --s3-prefix AWSCloudTrailPrefixExample --sns-new-
    topic AWSCloudTrailLogDeliveryTopicExample
```

When you run the command, you will see output similar to the following:

```
1 CloudTrail configuration:
2 {
3   "trailList": [
4     {
5       "S3KeyPrefix": "AWSCloudTrailPrefixExample",
6       "IncludeGlobalServiceEvents": true,
7       "Name": "AWSCloudTrailExample",
8       "SnsTopicName": "AWSCloudTrailLogDeliveryTopicExample",
9       "S3BucketName": "MyBucketBelongingToAccount111111111111"
10    }
11  ]
12 }
```

For more information about using CloudTrail from the AWS command line tools, see the CloudTrail command line reference.

Sharing CloudTrail Log Files Between AWS Accounts

This section explains how to share CloudTrail log files between multiple AWS accounts. We will assume that the log files have all been received in a single Amazon S3 bucket, which is the default setting for a trail created in the CloudTrail console. In the first scenario, you will learn how to grant read-only access to the accounts that generated the log files that have been placed into your Amazon S3 bucket. In the second scenario, you will learn how to grant access to all of the log files to a third-party account that can analyze the files for you.

To share log files between multiple AWS accounts, you must perform the following general steps. These steps are explained in detail later in this section.

- Create an IAM role for each account that you want to share log files with.

- For each of these IAM roles, create an access policy that grants read-only access to the account you want to share the log files with.

- Have an IAM user in each account programmatically assume the appropriate role and retrieve the log files.

This section walks you through the preceding steps in the context of two different sharing scenarios: granting access to the log files to each account that generated those files, and sharing log files with a third party. Most of the steps you take for the two scenarios are the same; the important difference is in what kind of permissions the IAM role grants to each account. That is, you can grant permission for an account to read only its own log files, or you can grant an account permission to read all log files. For details about permissions management for IAM roles, see Roles (Delegation and Federation) in *IAM User Guide*.

Scenario 1: Granting Access to the Account that Generated the Log Files

In this scenario, we'll assume that your enterprise is made up of two business units and that it maintains three AWS accounts. The first account, Account A, is the top-level account. For example, it might be managed by your enterprise's IT department and therefore be responsible for collecting log files from all other departments and business units into a single bucket. The other two accounts, B and C, correspond to your enterprise's business units.

This scenario assumes that you have already configured the log files from all three accounts to be delivered to a single Amazon S3 bucket, and that account A has full control over that bucket, as shown in the following illustration.

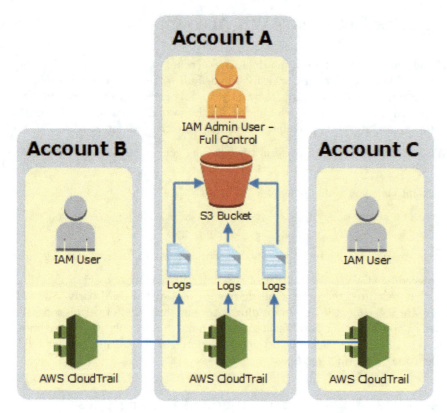

Although the Amazon S3 bucket contains log files that were generated by Accounts A, B and C, accounts B and C do not initially have access to the log files that accounts B and C generated. You will give each business unit read-only access to the log files that it generated, as shown in the following illustration.

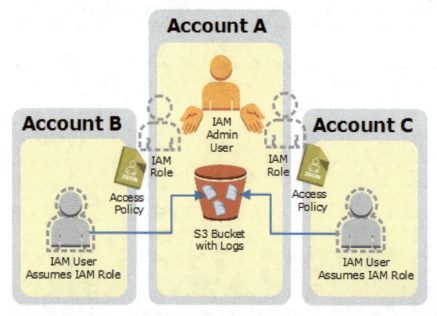

To grant read-only access to the log files generated by accounts B and C, you must do the following in the account Account A. Remember that Account A has full control of the Amazon S3 bucket.

- Create an IAM role for account B and another IAM role for account C. How: Creating a Role

- For the IAM role created for account B, create an access policy that grants read-only access to the log files generated by account B. For the IAM role created for account C, create an access policy that grants read-only access to the log files generated by account C. How: Creating an Access Policy to Grant Access to Accounts You Own

- Have an IAM user in account B programmatically assume the role created for account B. Have an IAM user in account C programmatically assume the role created for account C. Each IAM user must be given permission to assume the role by the respective account owner. How: Creating permissions policies for IAM users.

- Finally, the account owner who grants the permission must be an administrator, and must know the ARN of the role in account A that is being assumed. How: Calling AssumeRole.

The IAM users in accounts B and C can then programmatically retrieve their own log files, but not the log files of any other account.

Scenario 2: Granting Access to All Logs

In this scenario, we'll assume that your enterprise is structured as it was in the previous scenario, that is, it is made up of two business units and it maintains three AWS accounts. The first account, Account A, is the top-level account. For example, it might be managed by your enterprise's IT department and therefore be responsible for placing all other log files into a single bucket. The other two accounts, B and C, correspond to each of your enterprise's business units.

Like the previous scenario, this scenario assumes that you have already placed the log files from all three accounts into a single Amazon S3 bucket, and that account A has full control over that bucket.

Finally, we'll also assume that your enterprise wants to share all the log files from all accounts (A, B, and C) with a third party. We'll say that the third party has an AWS account called Account Z, as shown in the following illustration.

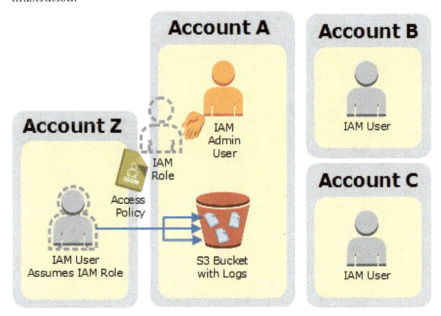

To share all of the log files from your enterprise with Account Z, you must do the following in the Account A, the account that has full control over the Amazon S3 bucket.

- Create an IAM role for Account Z. How: Creating a Role

- For the IAM role created for Account Z, create an access policy that grants read-only access to the log files generated by accounts A, B, and C. How: Creating an Access Policy to Grant Access to a Third Party

- Have an IAM user in Account Z programmatically assume the role and then retrieve the appropriate log files. The IAM user must be given permission to assume the role by the owner of Account Z. How: Creating permissions policies for IAM users. Further, the account owner who grants the permission must

149

be an administrator and know the ARN of the role in Account A that is being assumed. How: Calling AssumeRole.

Creating a Role

When you aggregate log files from multiple accounts into a single Amazon S3 bucket, only the account that has full control of the bucket, Account A in our example, has full read access to all of the log files in the bucket. Accounts B, C, and Z in our example do not have any rights until granted. Therefore, to share your AWS CloudTrail log files from one account to another (that is, to complete either Scenario 1 or Scenario 2 described previously in this section), you must *enable cross-account access*. You can do this by creating IAM roles and their associated access policies.

Roles

Create an IAM *role* for each account to which you want to give access. In our example, you will have three roles, one each for accounts B, C, and Z. Each IAM role defines an access or permissions policy that enables the accounts to access the resources (log files) owned by account A. The permissions are attached to each role and are associated with each account (B, C, or Z) only when the role is assumed. For details about permissions management for IAM roles, see IAM Roles in the *IAM User Guide*. For more information about how to assume a role, see Assuming a Role.

Policies

There are two policies for each IAM role you create. The *trust policy* specifies a * trusted entity* or *principal*. In our example, accounts B, C, and Z are trusted entities, and an IAM user with the proper permissions in those accounts can assume the role.

The *trust policy* is automatically created when you use the console to create the role. If you use the SDK to create the role, you must supply the trust policy as a parameter to the `CreateRole` API. If you use the CLI to create the role, you must specify the trust policy in the `create-role` CLI command.

The *role access (or permissions) policy* that you must create as the owner of Account A defines what actions and resources the principal or trusted entity is allowed access to (in this case, the CloudTrail log files). For Scenario 1 that grants log file access to the account that generated the log files, as discussed in Creating an Access Policy to Grant Access to Accounts You Own. For Scenario 2 that grants read access to all log files to a third party, as discussed in Creating an Access Policy to Grant Access to a Third Party .

For further details about creating and working with IAM policies, see Access Management in the *IAM User Guide*.

Creating a Role

To Create a Role by Using the Console

1. Sign into the AWS Management Console as an administrator of Account A.

2. Navigate to the IAM console.

3. In the navigation pane, choose **Roles**.

4. Choose **Create New Role**.

5. Type a name for the new role, and then choose **Next Step**.

6. Choose **Role for Cross-Account Access**.

7. For Scenario 1, do the following to provide access between accounts you own:

    1. Choose **Provide access between AWS accounts you own.**

2. Enter the twelve-digit account ID of the account (B, C, or Z) to be granted access.

3. Check the **Require MFA** box if you want the user to provide multi-factor authentication before assuming the role.

For Scenario 2, do the following to provide access to a third-party account. In our example, you would perform these steps for Account Z, the third-party log analyzer:

1. Choose **Allows IAM users from a 3rd party AWS account to access this account.**

2. Enter the twelve-digit account ID of the account (Account Z) to be granted access.

3. Enter an external ID that provides additional control over who can assume the role. For more information, see How to Use an External ID When Granting Access to Your AWS Resources to a Third Party in the *IAM User Guide*.

8. Choose **Next Step** to attach a policy that sets the permissions for this role.

9. Under **Attach Policy**, choose the **AmazonS3ReadOnlyAccess** policy. **Note**
By default, the **AmazonS3ReadOnlyAccess** policy grants retrieval and list rights to all Amazon S3 buckets within your account.

   - To grant an account access to only that account's log files (Scenario 1), see Creating an Access Policy to Grant Access to Accounts You Own.

   - To grant an account access to all of the log files in the Amazon S3 bucket (Scenario 2), see Creating an Access Policy to Grant Access to a Third Party .

10. Choose **Next Step**

11. Review the role information. **Note**
You can edit the role name at this point if you wish, but if you do so, you will be taken back to the **Step 2: Select Role Type** page where you must reenter the information for the role.

12. Choose **Create Role**. When the role creation process completes, the role you created appears in the role list.

Creating an Access Policy to Grant Access to Accounts You Own

In Scenario 1, as an administrative user in Account A, you have full control over the Amazon S3 bucket to which CloudTrail writes log files for accounts B and C. You want to share each business unit's log files back to business unit that created them. But, you don't want a unit to be able to read any other unit's log files.

For example, to share Account B's log files with Account B but not with Account C, you must create a new IAM role in Account A that specifies that Account B is a trusted account. This role trust policy specifies that Account B is trusted to assume the role created by Account A, and should look like the following example. The trust policy is automatically created if you create the role by using the console. If you use the SDK to create the role, you must supply the trust policy as a parameter to the `CreateRole` API. If you use the CLI to create the role, you must specify the trust policy in the `create-role` CLI command.

```
1  {
2    "Version": "2012-10-17",
3    "Statement": [
4      {
5        "Sid": "",
6        "Effect": "Allow",
7        "Principal": {
8          "AWS": "arn:aws:iam::account-B-id:root"
9        },
10       "Action": "sts:AssumeRole"
11     }
12   ]
13 }
```

You must also create an access policy to specify that Account B can read from only the location to which B wrote its log files. The access policy will look something like the following. Note that the **Resource** ARN includes the twelve-digit account ID for Account B, and the prefix you specified, if any, when you turned on CloudTrail for Account B during the aggregation process. For more information about specifying a prefix, see Turning on CloudTrail in Additional Accounts.

Important

You must ensure that the prefix in the access policy is exactly the same as the prefix that you specified when you turned on CloudTrail for Account B. If it is not, then you must edit the IAM role access policy in Account A to incorporate the actual prefix for Account B. If the prefix in the role access policy is not exactly the same as the prefix you specified when you turned on CloudTrail in Account B, then Account B will not be able to access its log files.

```
1  {
2    "Version": "2012-10-17",
3    "Statement": [
4      {
5        "Effect": "Allow",
6        "Action": [
7          "s3:Get*",
8          "s3:List*"
9        ],
10       "Resource": "arn:aws:s3:::bucket-name/prefix/AWSLogs/account-B-id/*"
11     },
12     {
13       "Effect": "Allow",
14       "Action": [
15         "s3:Get*",
16         "s3:List*"
```

```
17      ],
18      "Resource": "arn:aws:s3:::bucket-name"
19    }
20  ]
21 }
```

The role you create for Account C will be nearly identical to the one you created for Account B. The access policy for each role must include the appropriate account ID and prefix so that each account can read from only the location to which CloudTrail wrote that account's log files.

After you have created roles for each account and specified the appropriate trust and access policies, and after an IAM user in each account has been granted access by the administrator of that account, an IAM user in accounts B or C can programmatically assume the role.

After you have created roles for each account and specified the appropriate trust and access policies, an IAM user in one of the newly trusted accounts (B or C) must programmatically assume the role in order to read log files from the Amazon S3 bucket.

For more information, see Assuming a Role.

Creating an Access Policy to Grant Access to a Third Party

Account A must create a separate IAM role for Account Z, the third-party analyzer in Scenario 2. When you create the role, AWS automatically creates the trust relationship, which specifies that Account Z will be trusted to assume the role. The access policy for the role specifies what actions Account Z can take. For more information about creating roles and role policies, see Creating a Role.

For example, the trust relationship created by AWS specifies that Account Z is trusted to assume the role created by Account A. The following is an example trust policy:

```
1  {
2      "Version": "2012-10-17",
3      "Statement": [{
4          "Sid": "",
5          "Effect": "Allow",
6          "Principal": {"AWS": "arn:aws:iam::account-Z-id:root"},
7          "Action": "sts:AssumeRole"
8      }]
9  }
```

If you specified an external ID when you created the role for Account Z, your access policy contains an added `Condition` element that tests the unique ID assigned by Account Z. The test is performed when the role is assumed. The following example access policy has a `Condition` element.

For more information, see How to Use an External ID When Granting Access to Your AWS Resources to a Third Party in the *IAM User Guide*.

```
1   {
2       "Version": "2012-10-17",
3       "Statement": [{
4           "Sid": "",
5           "Effect": "Allow",
6           "Principal": {"AWS": "arn:aws:iam::account-Z-id:root"},
7           "Action": "sts:AssumeRole",
8           "Condition": {"StringEquals": {"sts:ExternalId": "external-ID-issued-by-account-Z"}}
9       }]
10  }
```

You must also create an access policy for the Account A role to specify that Account Z can read all logs from the Amazon S3 bucket. The access policy should look something like the following example. The wild card (*) at the end of the `Resource` value indicates that Account Z can access any log file in the S3 bucket to which it has been granted access.

```
1   {
2       "Version": "2012-10-17",
3       "Statement": [
4           {
5               "Effect": "Allow",
6               "Action": [
7                   "s3:Get*",
8                   "s3:List*"
9               ],
10              "Resource": "arn:aws:s3:::bucket-name/*"
11          },
12          {
13              "Effect": "Allow",
14              "Action": [
```

```
15          "s3:Get*",
16          "s3:List*"
17        ],
18        "Resource": "arn:aws:s3:::bucket-name"
19      }
20    ]
21 }
```

After you have created a role for Account Z and specified the appropriate trust relationship and access policy, an IAM user in Account Z must programmatically assume the role to be able to read log files from the bucket. For more information, see Assuming a Role.

Assuming a Role

You must designate a separate IAM user to assume each role you've created in each account, and ensure that each IAM user has appropriate permissions.

IAM Users and Roles

After you have created the necessary roles and policies in Account A for scenarios 1 and 2, you must designate an IAM user in each of the accounts B, C, and Z. Each IAM user will programmatically assume the appropriate role to access the log files. That is, the user in account B will assume the role created for account B, the user in account C will assume the role created for account C, and the user in account Z will assume the role created for account Z. When a user assumes a role, AWS returns temporary security credentials that can be used to make requests to list, retrieve, copy, or delete the log files depending on the permissions granted by the access policy associated with the role.

For more information about working with IAM users, see Working with IAM Users and Groups .

The primary difference between scenarios 1 and 2 is in the access policy that you create for each IAM role in each scenario.

- In scenario 1, the access policies for accounts B and C limit each account to reading only its own log files. For more information, see Creating an Access Policy to Grant Access to Accounts You Own.

- In scenario 2, the access policy for Account Z allows it to read all the log files that are aggregated in the Amazon S3 bucket. For more information, see Creating an Access Policy to Grant Access to a Third Party .

Creating permissions policies for IAM users

To perform the actions permitted by the roles, the IAM user must have permission to call the AWS STS `AssumeRole` API. You must edit the *user-based policy* for each IAM user to grant them the appropriate permissions. That is, you set a **Resource** element in the policy that is attached to the IAM user. The following example shows a policy for an IAM user in Account B that allows the user to assume a role named "Test" created earlier by Account A.

To attach the required policy to the IAM role

1. Sign in to the AWS Management Console and open the IAM console.

2. Choose the user whose permissions you want to modify.

3. Choose the **Permissions** tab.

4. Choose **Custom Policy**.

5. Choose **Use the policy editor to customize your own set of permissions**.

6. Type a name for the policy.

7. Copy the following policy into the space provided for the policy document.

```
1 {
2   "Version": "2012-10-17",
3   "Statement": [
4     {
5       "Effect": "Allow",
6       "Action": ["sts:AssumeRole"],
7       "Resource": "arn:aws:iam::account-A-id:role/Test"
8     }
9   ]
```

```
10 }
```

Important

Only IAM users can assume a role. If you attempt to use AWS root account credentials to assume a role, access will be denied.

Calling AssumeRole

A user in accounts B, C, or Z can assume a role by creating an application that calls the AWS STS http: //docs.aws.amazon.com/STS/latest/APIReference/API_AssumeRole.html API and passes the role session name, the Amazon Resource Number (ARN) of the role to assume, and an optional external ID. The role session name is defined by Account A when it creates the role to assume. The external ID, if any, is defined by Account Z and passed to Account A for inclusion during role creation. For more information, see How to Use an External ID When Granting Access to Your AWS Resources to a Third Party in the *IAM User Guide*. You can retrieve the ARN from the Account A by opening the IAM console.

To find the ARN Value in Account A with the IAM console

1. Choose **Roles**

2. Choose the role you want to examine.

3. Look for the **Role ARN** in the **Summary** section.

The AssumeRole API returns temporary credentials that a user in accounts B, C, or Z can use to access resources in Account A. In this example, the resources you want to access are the Amazon S3 bucket and the log files that the bucket contains. The temporary credentials have the permissions that you defined in the role access policy.

The following Python example (using the AWS SDK for Python (Boto)) shows how to call `AssumeRole` and how to use the temporary security credentials returned to list all Amazon S3 buckets controlled by Account A.

```python
1  import boto
2  from boto.sts import STSConnection
3  from boto.s3.connection import S3Connection
4
5  # The calls to AWS STS AssumeRole must be signed using the access key ID and secret
6  # access key of an IAM user or using existing temporary credentials. (You cannot call
7  # AssumeRole using the access key for an account.) The credentials can be in
8  # environment variables or in a configuration file and will be discovered automatically
9  # by the STSConnection() function. For more information, see the Python SDK
10 # documentation: http://boto.readthedocs.org/en/latest/boto_config_tut.html
11
12 sts_connection = STSConnection()
13 assumedRoleObject = sts_connection.assume_role(
14     role_arn="arn:aws:iam::account-of-role-to-assume:role/name-of-role",
15     role_session_name="AssumeRoleSession1"
16 )
17
18 # Use the temporary credentials returned by AssumeRole to call Amazon S3
19 # and list the bucket in the account that owns the role (the trusting account)
20 s3_connection = S3Connection(
21     aws_access_key_id=assumedRoleObject.credentials.access_key,
22     aws_secret_access_key=assumedRoleObject.credentials.secret_key,
23     security_token=assumedRoleObject.credentials.session_token
24 )
25 bucket = s3_connection.get_bucket(bucketname)
26 print bucket.name
```

Stop Sharing CloudTrail Log Files Between AWS Accounts

To stop sharing log files to another AWS account, simply delete the role that you created for that account in Creating a Role.

1. Sign in to the AWS Management Console as an IAM user with administrative-level permissions for Account A.

2. Navigate to the IAM console.

3. In the navigation pane, click **Roles**.

4. Select the role you want to delete.

5. Right-click and select **Delete Role** from the context menu.

Encrypting CloudTrail Log Files with AWS KMS–Managed Keys (SSE-KMS)

By default, the log files delivered by CloudTrail to your bucket are encrypted by Amazon server-side encryption with Amazon S3-managed encryption keys (SSE-S3). To provide a security layer that is directly manageable, you can instead use server-side encryption with AWS KMS–managed keys (SSE-KMS) for your CloudTrail log files.

Note
Enabling server-side encryption encrypts the log files but not the digest files with SSE-KMS. Digest files are encrypted with Amazon S3-managed encryption keys (SSE-S3).

To use SSE-KMS with CloudTrail, you create and manage a KMS key, also known as a customer master key (CMK). You attach a policy to the key that determines which users can use the key for encrypting and decrypting CloudTrail log files. The decryption is seamless through S3. When authorized users of the key read CloudTrail log files, S3 manages the decryption, and the authorized users are able to read log files in unencrypted form.

This approach has the following advantages:

- You can create and manage the CMK encryption keys yourself.

- You can use a single CMK to encrypt and decrypt log files for multiple accounts across all regions.

- You have control over who can use your key for encrypting and decrypting CloudTrail log files. You can assign permissions for the key to the users in your organization according to your requirements.

- You have enhanced security. With this feature, in order to read log files, you now need to meet two conditions:

- You must have S3 read permission on the bucket.

- You must be granted decrypt permission by the CMK policy.

- Because S3 automatically decrypts the log files for requests from users authorized to use the CMK, SSE-KMS encryption for CloudTrail log files is backward-compatible with applications that read CloudTrail log data.

Note
The key that you choose must be in the same region as the S3 bucket that receives your log files. To verify the region for an S3 bucket, inspect its properties in the S3 console.

Enabling Log File Encryption

Note
If you create a CMK in the CloudTrail console, CloudTrail adds the required CMK policy sections for you. Follow these procedures if you created a key in the IAM console or AWS CLI and you need to manually add the required policy sections.

To enable SSE-KMS encryption for CloudTrail log files, perform the following high-level steps:

1. Create a CMK.

- For information about creating a CMK with the AWS Management Console, see Creating Keys in the *AWS Key Management Service Developer Guide.*

- For information about creating a CMK with the AWS CLI, see create-key. **Note**
  The CMK that you choose must be in the same region as the S3 bucket that receives your log files. To verify the region for an S3 bucket, inspect the bucket's properties in the S3 console.

1. Add policy sections to the key that enable CloudTrail to encrypt and users to decrypt log files.

- For information about what to include in the policy, see AWS KMS Key Policy for CloudTrail.
  Warning
  Be sure to include decrypt permissions in the policy for all users who need to read log files. If you do not perform this step before adding the key to your trail configuration, users without decrypt permissions cannot read encrypted files.

- For information about editing a policy with the IAM console, see Editing a Key Policy in the *AWS Key Management Service Developer Guide*.

- For information about attaching a policy to a CMK with the AWS CLI, see put-key-policy.

2. Update your trail to use the CMK whose policy you modified for CloudTrail.

   - To update your trail configuration by using the CloudTrail console, see Updating a Trail to Use Your CMK.

   - To update your trail configuration by using the AWS CLI, see Enabling and disabling CloudTrail log file encryption with the AWS CLI.

The next section describes the policy sections that your CMK policy requires for use with CloudTrail.

Granting Permissions to Create a CMK

You can grant users permission to create a customer master key (CMK) with the AWSKeyManagementService-PowerUser policy.

To grant permission to create a CMK

1. Open the IAM console at https://console.aws.amazon.com/iam.

2. Choose the group or user that you want to give permission.

3. Choose **Permissions**, and then choose **Attach Policy**.

4. Search for **AWSKeyManagementServicePowerUser**, choose the policy, and then choose **Attach policy**.

   The user now has permission to create a CMK. If you want to create custom policies for your users, see Creating Customer Managed Policies in the *IAM User Guide*.

AWS KMS Key Policy for CloudTrail

You can create a customer master key (CMK) in three ways:

- The CloudTrail console
- The IAM console
- The AWS CLI

If you create a CMK in the CloudTrail console, CloudTrail adds the required CMK policy sections for you. You do not need to complete the following steps.

If you create a CMK in the IAM console or the AWS CLI, you need to add policy sections to the key so that you can use it with CloudTrail. The policy must allow CloudTrail to use the key to encrypt your log files, and allow the users you specify to read log files in unencrypted form.

See the following resources:

- To create a CMK with the AWS CLI, see create-key.
- To edit a CMK policy for CloudTrail, see Editing a Key Policy in the *AWS Key Management Service Developer Guide*.
- For technical details on how CloudTrail uses AWS KMS, see How AWS CloudTrail Uses AWS KMS in the *AWS Key Management Service Developer Guide*.

Required CMK policy sections for use with CloudTrail

If you created a CMK in the CloudTrail console, CloudTrail adds the required CMK policy for you. You do not need to manually add the policy statements. See Default Key Policy Created in CloudTrail Console.

If you created a CMK with the IAM console or the AWS CLI, then you must, at minimum, add three statements to your CMK policy for it to work with CloudTrail.

1. Enable CloudTrail log encrypt permissions. See Granting encrypt permissions.

2. Enable CloudTrail log decrypt permissions. See Granting decrypt permissions.

3. Enable CloudTrail to describe CMK properties. See Enable CloudTrail to describe CMK properties.

Note
When you add the new sections to your CMK policy, do not change any existing sections in the policy.

Warning
If encryption is enabled on a trail and the CMK is disabled or the CMK policy is not correctly configured for CloudTrail, CloudTrail will not deliver logs until the CMK issue is corrected.

Granting encrypt permissions

Example Allow CloudTrail to encrypt logs on behalf of specific accounts

CloudTrail needs explicit permission to use the CMK to encrypt logs on behalf of specific accounts. To specify an account, add the following required statement to your CMK policy, modifying *aws-account-id* as necessary. You can add additional account IDs to the `EncryptionContext` section to enable those accounts to use CloudTrail to use your CMK to encrypt log files.

```
1  {
2    "Sid": "Allow CloudTrail to encrypt logs",
3    "Effect": "Allow",
4    "Principal": {
5      "Service": "cloudtrail.amazonaws.com"
6    },
7    "Action": "kms:GenerateDataKey*",
8    "Resource": "*",
9    "Condition": {
10     "StringLike": {
11       "kms:EncryptionContext:aws:cloudtrail:arn": [
12         "arn:aws:cloudtrail:*:aws-account-id:trail/*"
13       ]
14     }
15   }
16 }
```

Example

The following example policy statement illustrates how another account can use your CMK to encrypt CloudTrail logs.

Scenario

- Your CMK is in account 111111111111.

- Both you and account 222222222222 will encrypt logs.

In the policy, you add one or more accounts that will encrypt with your key to the CloudTrail **Encryption-Context**. This restricts CloudTrail to using your key to encrypt logs only for those accounts that you specify. Giving the root of account 222222222222 permission to encrypt logs delegates the administrator of that account to allocate encrypt permissions as required to other users in account 222222222222 by changing their IAM user policies.

CMK policy statement:

```
1  {
2    "Sid": "Enable CloudTrail Encrypt Permissions",
3    "Effect": "Allow",
4    "Principal": {
5      "Service": "cloudtrail.amazonaws.com"
6    },
7    "Action": "kms:GenerateDataKey*",
8    "Resource": "*",
9    "Condition": {
10     "StringLike": {
11       "kms:EncryptionContext:aws:cloudtrail:arn": [
12         "arn:aws:cloudtrail:*:111111111111:trail/*",
13         "arn:aws:cloudtrail:*:222222222222:trail/*"
14       ]
15     }
```

```
16     }
17 }
```

For steps on editing a CMK policy for use with CloudTrail, see Editing a Key Policy in the AWS Key Management Service Developer Guide.

Granting decrypt permissions

Before you add your CMK to your CloudTrail configuration, it is important to give decrypt permissions to all users who require them. Users who have encrypt permissions but no decrypt permissions will not be able to read encrypted logs.

Enable CloudTrail log decrypt permissions

Users of your key must be given explicit permissions to read the log files that CloudTrail has encrypted. To enable users to read encrypted logs, add the following required statement to your CMK policy, modifying the `Principal` section to add a line for every principal (role or user) that you want to be able decrypt by using your CMK.

```
1  {
2    "Sid": "Enable CloudTrail log decrypt permissions",
3    "Effect": "Allow",
4    "Principal": {
5      "AWS": "arn:aws:iam::aws-account-id:user/username"
6    },
7    "Action": "kms:Decrypt",
8    "Resource": "*",
9    "Condition": {
10     "Null": {
11       "kms:EncryptionContext:aws:cloudtrail:arn": "false"
12     }
13   }
14 }
```

Allow users in your account to decrypt with your CMK

Example

This policy statement illustrates how to allow an IAM user or role in your account to use your key to read the encrypted logs in your account's S3 bucket.

Example Scenario

- Your CMK, S3 bucket, and IAM user Bob are in account 111111111111.

- You give IAM user Bob permission to decrypt CloudTrail logs in the S3 bucket.

In the key policy, you enable CloudTrail log decrypt permissions for IAM user Bob.

CMK policy statement:

```
1  {
2    "Sid": "Enable CloudTrail log decrypt permissions",
3    "Effect": "Allow",
4    "Principal": {
5      "AWS": "arn:aws:iam::111111111111:user/Bob"
6    },
7    "Action": "kms:Decrypt",
8    "Resource": "*",
9    "Condition": {
10     "Null": {
11       "kms:EncryptionContext:aws:cloudtrail:arn": "false"
12     }
13   }
14 }
```

Allow users in other accounts to decrypt with your CMK

You can allow users in other accounts to use your CMK to decrypt logs. The changes required to your key policy depend on whether the S3 bucket is in your account or in another account.

Allow users of a bucket in a different account to decrypt logs

Example
This policy statement illustrates how to allow an IAM user or role in another account to use your key to read encrypted logs from an S3 bucket in the other account.

Scenario

- Your CMK is in account 111111111111.

- The IAM user Alice and S3 bucket are in account 222222222222.

In this case, you give CloudTrail permission to decrypt logs under account 222222222222, and you give Alice's IAM user policy permission to use your key KeyA, which is in account 111111111111.

CMK policy statement:

```
1  {
2    "Sid": "Enable encrypted CloudTrail log read access",
3    "Effect": "Allow",
4    "Principal": {
5      "AWS": [
6        "arn:aws:iam::222222222222:root"
7      ]
8    },
9    "Action": "kms:Decrypt",
10   "Resource": "*",
11   "Condition": {
12     "Null": {
13       "kms:EncryptionContext:aws:cloudtrail:arn": "false"
14     }
15   }
16 }
```

Alice's IAM user policy statement:

```
1  {
2    "Version": "2012-10-17",
3    "Statement": [
4      {
5        "Effect": "Allow",
6        "Action": "kms:Decrypt",
7        "Resource": "arn:aws:kms:us-east-1:111111111111:key/keyA"
8      }
9    ]
10 }
```

Allow users in a different account to decrypt logs from your bucket

Example
This policy illustrates how another account can use your key to read encrypted logs from your S3 bucket.

Example Scenario

- Your CMK and S3 bucket are in account 111111111111.

- The user who will read logs from your bucket is in account 222222222222.

To enable this scenario, you enable decrypt permissions for the IAM role **CloudTrailReadRole** in your account, and then give the other account permission to assume that role.

CMK policy statement:

```
1  {
2    "Sid": "Enable encrypted CloudTrail log read access",
3    "Effect": "Allow",
4    "Principal": {
5      "AWS": [
6        "arn:aws:iam::11111111111:role/CloudTrailReadRole"
7      ]
8    },
9    "Action": "kms:Decrypt",
10   "Resource": "*",
11   "Condition": {
12     "Null": {
13       "kms:EncryptionContext:aws:cloudtrail:arn": "false"
14     }
15   }
16 }
```

CloudTrailReadRole trust entity policy statement:

```
1  {
2    "Version": "2012-10-17",
3    "Statement": [
4      {
5        "Sid": "",
6        "Effect": "Allow",
7        "Principal": {
8          "AWS": "arn:aws:iam::222222222222:root"
9        },
10       "Action": "sts:AssumeRole"
11     }
12   ]
13 }
```

For steps on editing a CMK policy for use with CloudTrail, see Editing a Key Policy in the *AWS Key Management Service Developer Guide*.

Enable CloudTrail to describe CMK properties

CloudTrail requires the ability to describe the properties of the CMK. To enable this functionality, add the following required statement as is to your CMK policy. This statement does not grant CloudTrail any permissions beyond the other permissions that you specify.

```
1 {
2   "Sid": "Allow CloudTrail access",
3   "Effect": "Allow",
4   "Principal": {
5     "Service": "cloudtrail.amazonaws.com"
6   },
7   "Action": "kms:DescribeKey",
8   "Resource": "*"
9 }
```

For steps on editing a CMK policy for use with CloudTrail, see Editing a Key Policy in the *AWS Key Management Service Developer Guide.*

Default Key Policy Created in CloudTrail Console

If you create a customer master key (CMK) in the CloudTrail console, the following policy is automatically created for you. The policy allows these permissions:

- Allows AWS account (root) permissions for the CMK

- Allows CloudTrail to encrypt log files under the CMK and describe the CMK

- Allows all users in the specified accounts to decrypt log files

- Allows all users in the specified account to create a KMS alias for the CMK

```
1  {
2      "Version": "2012-10-17",
3      "Id": "Key policy created by CloudTrail",
4      "Statement": [
5          {
6              "Sid": "Enable IAM User Permissions",
7              "Effect": "Allow",
8              "Principal": {"AWS": [
9                  "arn:aws:iam::aws-account-id:root",
10                 "arn:aws:iam::aws-account-id:user/username"
11             ]},
12             "Action": "kms:*",
13             "Resource": "*"
14         },
15         {
16             "Sid": "Allow CloudTrail to encrypt logs",
17             "Effect": "Allow",
18             "Principal": {"Service": ["cloudtrail.amazonaws.com"]},
19             "Action": "kms:GenerateDataKey*",
20             "Resource": "*",
21             "Condition": {"StringLike": {"kms:EncryptionContext:aws:cloudtrail:arn": "arn:aws:
                   cloudtrail:*:aws-account-id:trail/*"}}
22         },
23         {
24             "Sid": "Allow CloudTrail to describe key",
25             "Effect": "Allow",
26             "Principal": {"Service": ["cloudtrail.amazonaws.com"]},
27             "Action": "kms:DescribeKey",
28             "Resource": "*"
29         },
30         {
31             "Sid": "Allow principals in the account to decrypt log files",
32             "Effect": "Allow",
33             "Principal": {"AWS": "*"},
34             "Action": [
35                 "kms:Decrypt",
36                 "kms:ReEncryptFrom"
37             ],
38             "Resource": "*",
39             "Condition": {
40                 "StringEquals": {"kms:CallerAccount": "aws-account-id"},
41                 "StringLike": {"kms:EncryptionContext:aws:cloudtrail:arn": "arn:aws:cloudtrail
                       :*:aws-account-id:trail/*"}
```

```
42                    }
43              },
44              {
45                    "Sid": "Allow alias creation during setup",
46                    "Effect": "Allow",
47                    "Principal": {"AWS": "*"},
48                    "Action": "kms:CreateAlias",
49                    "Resource": "*",
50                    "Condition": {"StringEquals": {
51                        "kms:ViaService": "ec2.region.amazonaws.com",
52                        "kms:CallerAccount": "aws-account-id"
53                    }}
54              },
55              {
56                    "Sid": "Enable cross account log decryption",
57                    "Effect": "Allow",
58                    "Principal": {"AWS": "*"},
59                    "Action": [
60                        "kms:Decrypt",
61                        "kms:ReEncryptFrom"
62                    ],
63                    "Resource": "*",
64                    "Condition": {
65                        "StringEquals": {"kms:CallerAccount": "aws-account-id"},
66                        "StringLike": {"kms:EncryptionContext:aws:cloudtrail:arn": "arn:aws:cloudtrail
                            :*:aws-account-id:trail/*"}
67                    }
68              }
69        ]
70 }
```

Note
The policy's final statement allows cross accounts to decrypt log files with the CMK.

Updating a Trail to Use Your CMK

To update a trail to use the customer master key (CMK) that you modified for CloudTrail, complete the following steps in the CloudTrail console.

Note
Updating a trail with the following procedure encrypts the log files but not the digest files with SSE-KMS. Digest files are encrypted with Amazon S3-managed encryption keys (SSE-S3).

To update a trail using the AWS CLI, see Enabling and disabling CloudTrail log file encryption with the AWS CLI.

To update a trail to use your CMK

1. Sign in to the AWS Management Console and open the CloudTrail console at https://console.aws.amazon. com/cloudtrail/.

2. Choose **Trails** and then choose a trail.

3. For **Storage location**, choose the pencil icon.

4. Choose **Advanced**.

5. For **Encrypt log files**, choose **Yes** to have CloudTrail encrypt your log files with the CMK.

6. For **Create a new KMS key**, choose **No**.

7. For **KMS key**, choose the CMK alias whose policy you modified for use with CloudTrail. **Note**
   Choose a CMK that is in the same region as the S3 bucket that receives your log files. To verify the region for an S3 bucket, inspect its properties in the S3 console.

   You can type the alias name, ARN, or the globally unique key ID. If the CMK belongs to another account, verify that the key policy has permissions that enable you to use it. The value can be one of the following formats:

   - **Alias Name**: `alias/MyAliasName`

   - **Alias ARN**: `arn:aws:kms:region:123456789012:alias/MyAliasName`

   - **Key ARN**: `arn:aws:kms:region:123456789012:key/12345678-1234-1234-1234-123456789012`

   - **Globally unique key ID**: `12345678-1234-1234-1234-123456789012`

8. Choose **Save**. **Note**
   If the CMK that you chose is disabled or is pending deletion, you cannot save the trail with that CMK. You can enable the CMK or choose another one. For more information, see How Key State Affects Use of a Customer Master Key.

Enabling and disabling CloudTrail log file encryption with the AWS CLI

This topic describes how to enable and disable SSE-KMS log file encryption for CloudTrail by using the AWS CLI. For background information, see Encrypting CloudTrail Log Files with AWS KMS–Managed Keys (SSE-KMS).

Enabling CloudTrail log file encryption by using the AWS CLI

1. Create a key with the AWS CLI. The key that you create must be in the same region as the S3 bucket that receives your CloudTrail log files. For this step, you use the KMS create-key command.

2. Get the existing key policy so that you can modify it for use with CloudTrail. You can retrieve the key policy with the KMS get-key-policy command.

3. Add the necessary sections to the key policy so that CloudTrail can encrypt and users can decrypt your log files. Make sure that all users who will read the log files are granted decrypt permissions. Do not modify any existing sections of the policy. For information on the policy sections to include, see AWS KMS Key Policy for CloudTrail.

4. Attach the modified .json policy file to the key by using the KMS put-key-policy command.

5. Run the CloudTrail `create-trail` or `update-trail` command with the `--kms-key-id` parameter. This command will enable log encryption.

```
1 aws cloudtrail update-trail --name Default --kms-key-id alias/MyKmsKey
```

The `--kms-key-id` parameter specifies the key whose policy you modified for CloudTrail. It can be any one of the following four formats:

- **Alias Name**. Example: `alias/MyAliasName`

- **Alias ARN**. Example: `arn:aws:kms:us-east-2:123456789012:alias/MyAliasName`

- **Key ARN**. Example: `arn:aws:kms:us-east-2:123456789012:key/12345678-1234-1234-1234-123456789012`

- **Globally unique key ID**. Example: `12345678-1234-1234-1234-123456789012`

The response will look like the following:

```
1 {
2     "IncludeGlobalServiceEvents": true,
3     "Name": "Default",
4     "TrailARN": "arn:aws:cloudtrail:us-east-2:123456789012:trail/Default",
5     "LogFileValidationEnabled": false,
6     "KmsKeyId": "arn:aws:kms:us-east-2:123456789012:key
            /12345678-1234-1234-1234-123456789012",
7     "S3BucketName": "my-bucket-name"
8 }
```

The presence of the `KmsKeyId` element indicates that log file encryption has been enabled. The encrypted log files should appear in your bucket in about 10 minutes.

Disabling CloudTrail log file encryption by using the AWS CLI

To stop encrypting logs, call `update-trail` and pass an empty string to the `kms-key-id` parameter:

```
1 aws cloudtrail update-trail --name Default --kms-key-id ""
```

The response will look like the following:

```
1  {
2      "IncludeGlobalServiceEvents": true,
3      "Name": "Default",
4      "TrailARN": "arn:aws:cloudtrail:us-east-2:123456789012:trail/Default",
5      "LogFileValidationEnabled": false,
6      "S3BucketName": "my-bucket-name"
7  }
```

The absence of the `KmsKeyId` element indicates that log file encryption is no longer enabled.

Validating CloudTrail Log File Integrity

To determine whether a log file was modified, deleted, or unchanged after CloudTrail delivered it, you can use CloudTrail log file integrity validation. This feature is built using industry standard algorithms: SHA-256 for hashing and SHA-256 with RSA for digital signing. This makes it computationally infeasible to modify, delete or forge CloudTrail log files without detection. You can use the AWS CLI to validate the files in the location where CloudTrail delivered them.

Why Use It?

Validated log files are invaluable in security and forensic investigations. For example, a validated log file enables you to assert positively that the log file itself has not changed, or that particular user credentials performed specific API activity. The CloudTrail log file integrity validation process also lets you know if a log file has been deleted or changed, or assert positively that no log files were delivered to your account during a given period of time.

How It Works

When you enable log file integrity validation, CloudTrail creates a hash for every log file that it delivers. Every hour, CloudTrail also creates and delivers a file that references the log files for the last hour and contains a hash of each. This file is called a digest file. CloudTrail signs each digest file using the private key of a public and private key pair. After delivery, you can use the public key to validate the digest file. CloudTrail uses different key pairs for each AWS region.

The digest files are delivered to the same Amazon S3 bucket associated with your trail as your CloudTrail log files. If your log files are delivered from all regions or from multiple accounts into a single Amazon S3 bucket, CloudTrail will deliver the digest files from those regions and accounts into the same bucket.

The digest files are put into a folder separate from the log files. This separation of digest files and log files enables you to enforce granular security policies and permits existing log processing solutions to continue to operate without modification. Each digest file also contains the digital signature of the previous digest file if one exists. The signature for the current digest file is in the metadata properties of the digest file Amazon S3 object. For more information about digest file contents, see CloudTrail Digest File Structure.

Storing log and digest files

You can store the CloudTrail log files and digest files in Amazon S3 or Amazon Glacier securely, durably and inexpensively for an indefinite period of time. To enhance the security of the digest files stored in Amazon S3, you can use Amazon S3 MFA Delete.

Enabling Validation and Validating Files

To enable log file integrity validation, you can use the AWS Management Console, the AWS CLI, or CloudTrail API. For more information, see Enabling Log File Integrity Validation for CloudTrail.

To validate the integrity of CloudTrail log files, you can use the AWS CLI or create your own solution. The AWS CLI will validate files in the location where CloudTrail delivered them. If you want to validate logs that you have moved to a different location, either in Amazon S3 or elsewhere, you can create your own validation tools.

For information on validating logs by using the AWS CLI, see Validating CloudTrail Log File Integrity with the AWS CLI. For information on developing custom implementations of CloudTrail log file validation, see Custom Implementations of CloudTrail Log File Integrity Validation .

Enabling Log File Integrity Validation for CloudTrail

You can enable log file integrity validation by using the AWS Management Console, AWS Command Line Interface (AWS CLI), or CloudTrail API. CloudTrail starts delivering digest files in about an hour.

AWS Management Console

To enable log file integrity validation with the CloudTrail console, choose **Yes** for the **Enable log file validation** option when you create or update a trail. By default, this feature is enabled for new trails. For more information, see Creating a Trail with the Console.

AWS CLI

To enable log file integrity validation with the AWS CLI, use the `--enable-log-file-validation` option with the create-trail or update-trail commands. To disable log file integrity validation, use the `--no-enable-log-file-validation` option.

Example

The following `update-trail` command enables log file validation and starts delivering digest files to the Amazon S3 bucket for the specified trail.

```
1 aws cloudtrail update-trail --name your-trail-name --enable-log-file-validation
```

CloudTrail API

To enable log file integrity validation with the CloudTrail API, set the `EnableLogFileValidation` request parameter to `true` when calling `CreateTrail` or `UpdateTrail`.

For more information, see CreateTrail and UpdateTrail in the AWS CloudTrail API Reference.

Validating CloudTrail Log File Integrity with the AWS CLI

To validate logs with the AWS Command Line Interface, use the CloudTrail `validate-logs` command. The command uses the digest files delivered to your Amazon S3 bucket to perform the validation. For information about digest files, see CloudTrail Digest File Structure.

The AWS CLI allows you to detect the following types of changes:

- Modification or deletion of CloudTrail log files
- Modification or deletion of CloudTrail digest files
- Modification or deletion of both of the above

Note
The AWS CLI validates only log files that are referenced by digest files. For more information, see Checking Whether a Particular File was Delivered by CloudTrail .

Prerequisites

To validate log file integrity with the AWS CLI, the following conditions must be met:

- You must have online connectivity to AWS.
- You must have read access to the Amazon S3 bucket that contains the digest and log files.
- The digest and log files must not have been moved from the original Amazon S3 location where CloudTrail delivered them.

Note
Log files that have been downloaded to local disk cannot be validated with the AWS CLI. For guidance on creating your own tools for validation, see Custom Implementations of CloudTrail Log File Integrity Validation .

validate-logs

Syntax

The following is the syntax for `validate-logs`. Optional parameters are shown in brackets.

```
aws cloudtrail validate-logs --trail-arn <trailARN> --start-time <start-time> [--end-time <
end-time>] [--s3-bucket <bucket-name>] [--s3-prefix <prefix>] [--verbose]
```

Options

The following are the command-line options for `validate-logs`. The `--trail-arn` and `--start-time` options are required.

`--start-time`
Specifies that log files delivered on or after the specified UTC timestamp value will be validated. Example: `2015-01-08T05:21:42Z`.

`--end-time`
Optionally specifies that log files delivered on or before the specified UTC timestamp value will be validated. The default value is the current UTC time (`Date.now()`). Example: `2015-01-08T12:31:41Z`.
For the time range specified, the `validate-logs` command checks only the log files that are referenced in their corresponding digest files. No other log files in the Amazon S3 bucket are checked. For more information, see Checking Whether a Particular File was Delivered by CloudTrail .

`--bucket-name`
Optionally specifies the Amazon S3 bucket where the digest files are stored. If a bucket name is not specified, the AWS CLI will retrieve it by calling `DescribeTrails()`.

`--prefix`
Optionally specifies the Amazon S3 prefix where the digest files are stored. If not specified, the AWS CLI will retrieve it by calling `DescribeTrails()`.
You should use this option only if your current prefix is different from the prefix that was in use during the time range that you specify.

`--trailARN`
Specifies the Amazon Resource Name (ARN) of the trail to be validated. The format of a trail ARN follows.

```
1 arn:aws:cloudtrail:us-east-2:111111111111:trail/MyTrailName
```

To obtain the trail ARN for a trail, you can use the `describe-trails` command before running `validate-logs`. You may want to specify the bucket name and prefix in addition to the trail ARN if log files have been delivered to more than one bucket in the time range that you specified, and you want to restrict the validation to the log files in only one of the buckets.

`--verbose`
Optionally outputs validation information for every log or digest file in the specified time range. The output indicates whether the file remains unchanged or has been modified or deleted. In non-verbose mode (the default), information is returned only for those cases in which there was a validation failure.

Example

The following example validates log files from the specified start time to the present, using the Amazon S3 bucket configured for the current trail and specifying verbose output.

```
1 aws cloudtrail validate-logs --start-time 2015-08-27T00:00:00Z --end-time 2015-08-28T00:00:00Z
    --trail-arn arn:aws:cloudtrail:us-east-2:111111111111:trail/my-trail-name --verbose
```


How `validate-logs` Works

The `validate-logs` command starts by validating the most recent digest file in the specified time range. First, it verifies that the digest file has been downloaded from the location to which it claims to belong. In other words, if the CLI downloads digest file `df1` from the S3 location `p1`, validate-logs will verify that `p1 == df1.digestS3Bucket + '/' + df1.digestS3Object`.

If the signature of the digest file is valid, it checks the hash value of each of the logs referenced in the digest file. The command then goes back in time, validating the previous digest files and their referenced log files in succession. It continues until the specified value for `start-time` is reached, or until the digest chain ends. If a digest file is missing or not valid, the time range that cannot be validated is indicated in the output.

Validation Results

Validation results begin with a summary header in the following format:

```
1 Validating log files for trail trail_ARN  between time_stamp and time_stamp
```

Each line of the main output contains the validation results for a single digest or log file in the following format:

```
1 <Digest file | Log file> <S3 path> <Validation Message>
```

The following table describes the possible validation messages for log and digest files.

File Type	Validation Message	Description
Digest file	valid	The digest file signature is valid. The log files it references can be checked. This message is included only in verbose mode.
Digest file	INVALID: has been moved from its original location	The S3 bucket or S3 object from which the digest file was retrieved do not match the S3 bucket or S3 object locations that are recorded in the digest file itself.
Digest file	INVALID: invalid format	The format of the digest file is invalid. The log files corresponding to the time range that the digest file represents cannot be validated.
Digest file	INVALID: not found	The digest file was not found. The log files corresponding to the time range that the digest file represents cannot be validated.
Digest file	INVALID: public key not found for fingerprint fingerprint	The public key corresponding to the fingerprint recorded in the digest file was not found. The digest file cannot be validated.
Digest file	INVALID: signature verification failed	The digest file signature is not valid. Because the digest file is not valid, the log files it references cannot be validated, and no assertions can be made about the API activity in them.
Digest file	INVALID: Unable to load PKCS #1 key with fingerprint fingerprint	Because the DER encoded public key in PKCS #1 format having the specified fingerprint could not be loaded, the digest file cannot be validated.
Log file	valid	The log file has been validated and has not been modified since the time of delivery. This message is included only in verbose mode.
Log file	INVALID: hash value doesn't match	The hash for the log file does not match. The log file has been modified after delivery by CloudTrail.
Log file	INVALID: invalid format	The format of the log file is invalid. The log file cannot be validated.

File Type	Validation Message	Description
Log file	INVALID: not found	The log file was not found and cannot be validated.

The output includes summary information about the results returned.

Example Outputs

Verbose

The following example `validate-logs` command uses the `--verbose` flag and produces the sample output that follows. `[...]` indicates the sample output has been abbreviated.

```
1 aws cloudtrail validate-logs --trail-arn arn:aws:cloudtrail:us-east-2:111111111111:trail/example
    -trail-name --start-time 2015-08-31T22:00:00Z --end-time 2015-09-01T19:17:29Z --verbose
```

```
1 Validating log files for trail arn:aws:cloudtrail:us-east-2:111111111111:trail/example-trail-
    name between 2015-08-31T22:00:00Z and 2015-09-01T19:17:29Z
2
3 Digest file    s3://example-bucket/AWSLogs/111111111111/CloudTrail-Digest/us-east
    -2/2015/09/01/111111111111_CloudTrail-Digest_us-east-2_example-trail-name_us-east-2
    _20150901T201728Z.json.gz    valid
4 Log file       s3://example-bucket/AWSLogs/111111111111/CloudTrail/us-east
    -2/2015/09/01/111111111111_CloudTrail_us-east-2_20150901T1925Z_WZZw1RymnjCRjxXc.json.gz
    valid
5 Log file       s3://example-bucket/AWSLogs/111111111111/CloudTrail/us-east
    -2/2015/09/01/111111111111_CloudTrail_us-east-2_20150901T1915Z_POuvV87nu6pfAV2W.json.gz
    valid
6 Log file       s3://example-bucket/AWSLogs/111111111111/CloudTrail/us-east
    -2/2015/09/01/111111111111_CloudTrail_us-east-2_20150901T1930Z_l2QgXhAKVm1QXiIA.json.gz
    valid
7 Log file       s3://example-bucket/AWSLogs/111111111111/CloudTrail/us-east
    -2/2015/09/01/111111111111_CloudTrail_us-east-2_20150901T1920Z_eQJteBBrfpBCqOqw.json.gz
    valid
8 Log file       s3://example-bucket/AWSLogs/111111111111/CloudTrail/us-east
    -2/2015/09/01/111111111111_CloudTrail_us-east-2_20150901T1950Z_9g5A6qlR2B5KaRdq.json.gz
    valid
9 Log file       s3://example-bucket/AWSLogs/111111111111/CloudTrail/us-east
    -2/2015/09/01/111111111111_CloudTrail_us-east-2_20150901T1920Z_i4DNCC12BuXd6Ru7.json.gz
    valid
10 Log file      s3://example-bucket/AWSLogs/111111111111/CloudTrail/us-east
    -2/2015/09/01/111111111111_CloudTrail_us-east-2_20150901T1915Z_Sg5caf2RH6Jdx0EJ.json.gz
    valid
11 Digest file   s3://example-bucket/AWSLogs/111111111111/CloudTrail-Digest/us-east
    -2/2015/09/01/111111111111_CloudTrail-Digest_us-east-2_example-trail-name_us-east-2
    _20150901T191728Z.json.gz    valid
12 Log file      s3://example-bucket/AWSLogs/111111111111/CloudTrail/us-east
    -2/2015/09/01/111111111111_CloudTrail_us-east-2_20150901T1910Z_YYSFiuFQk4nrtnEW.json.gz
    valid
13 [...]
14 Log file      s3://example-bucket/AWSLogs/144218288521/CloudTrail/us-east
    -2/2015/09/01/144218288521_CloudTrail_us-east-2_20150901T1055Z_0Sfy6m9f6iBzmoPF.json.gz
    valid
```

```
15 Log file        s3://example-bucket/AWSLogs/144218288521/CloudTrail/us-east
        -2/2015/09/01/144218288521_CloudTrail_us-east-2_20150901T1040Z_lLa3QzVLp0ed7igR.json.gz
        valid
16
17 Digest file     s3://example-bucket/AWSLogs/144218288521/CloudTrail-Digest/us-east
        -2/2015/09/01/144218288521_CloudTrail-Digest_us-east-2_example-trail-name_us-east-2
        _20150901T101728Z.json.gz   INVALID: signature verification failed
18
19 Digest file     s3://example-bucket/AWSLogs/144218288521/CloudTrail-Digest/us-east
        -2/2015/09/01/144218288521_CloudTrail-Digest_us-east-2_example-trail-name_us-east-2
        _20150901T091728Z.json.gz   valid
20 Log file        s3://example-bucket/AWSLogs/144218288521/CloudTrail/us-east
        -2/2015/09/01/144218288521_CloudTrail_us-east-2_20150901T0830Z_eaFv03dwHo4NCqqc.json.gz
        valid
21 Digest file     s3://example-bucket/AWSLogs/144218288521/CloudTrail-Digest/us-east
        -2/2015/09/01/144218288521_CloudTrail-Digest_us-east-2_example-trail-name_us-east-2
        _20150901T081728Z.json.gz   valid
22 Digest file     s3://example-bucket/AWSLogs/144218288521/CloudTrail-Digest/us-east
        -2/2015/09/01/144218288521_CloudTrail-Digest_us-east-2_example-trail-name_us-east-2
        _20150901T071728Z.json.gz   valid
23 [...]
24 Log file        s3://example-bucket/AWSLogs/111111111111/CloudTrail/us-east
        -2/2015/08/31/111111111111_CloudTrail_us-east-2_20150831T2245Z_mbJkEO5kNcDnVhGh.json.gz
        valid
25 Log file        s3://example-bucket/AWSLogs/111111111111/CloudTrail/us-east
        -2/2015/08/31/111111111111_CloudTrail_us-east-2_20150831T2225Z_IQ6kXy8sKU03RSPr.json.gz
        valid
26 Log file        s3://example-bucket/AWSLogs/111111111111/CloudTrail/us-east
        -2/2015/08/31/111111111111_CloudTrail_us-east-2_20150831T2230Z_eRPVRTxHQ5498ROA.json.gz
        valid
27 Log file        s3://example-bucket/AWSLogs/111111111111/CloudTrail/us-east
        -2/2015/08/31/111111111111_CloudTrail_us-east-2_20150831T2255Z_IlWawYZGvTWB5vYN.json.gz
        valid
28 Digest file     s3://example-bucket/AWSLogs/111111111111/CloudTrail-Digest/us-east
        -2/2015/08/31/111111111111_CloudTrail-Digest_us-east-2_example-trail-name_us-east-2
        _20150831T221728Z.json.gz   valid
29
30 Results requested for 2015-08-31T22:00:00Z to 2015-09-01T19:17:29Z
31 Results found for 2015-08-31T22:17:28Z to 2015-09-01T20:17:28Z:
32
33 22/23 digest files valid, 1/23 digest files INVALID
34 63/63 log files valid
```

Non-verbose

The following example validate-logs command does not use the --verbose flag. In the sample output that follows, one error was found. Only the header, error, and summary information are returned.

```
1 aws cloudtrail validate-logs --trail-arn arn:aws:cloudtrail:us-east-2:111111111111:trail/example
        -trail-name --start-time 2015-08-31T22:00:00Z --end-time 2015-09-01T19:17:29Z
```

```
1 Validating log files for trail arn:aws:cloudtrail:us-east-2:111111111111:trail/example-trail-
        name between 2015-08-31T22:00:00Z and 2015-09-01T19:17:29Z
2
```

```
3  Digest file s3://example-bucket/AWSLogs/144218288521/CloudTrail-Digest/us-east
       -2/2015/09/01/144218288521_CloudTrail-Digest_us-east-2_example-trail-name_us-east-2
       _20150901T101728Z.json.gz  INVALID: signature verification failed
4
5  Results requested for 2015-08-31T22:00:00Z to 2015-09-01T19:17:29Z
6  Results found for 2015-08-31T22:17:28Z to 2015-09-01T20:17:28Z:
7
8  22/23 digest files valid, 1/23 digest files INVALID
9  63/63 log files valid
```

Checking Whether a Particular File was Delivered by CloudTrail

To check if a particular file in your bucket was delivered by CloudTrail, run `validate-logs` in verbose mode for the time period that includes the file. If the file appears in the output of `validate-logs`, then the file was delivered by CloudTrail.

CloudTrail Digest File Structure

Each digest file contains the names of the log files that were delivered to your Amazon S3 bucket during the last hour, the hash values for those log files, and the digital signature of the previous digest file. The signature for the current digest file is stored in the metadata properties of the digest file object. The digital signatures and hashes are used for validating the integrity of the log files and of the digest file itself.

Digest File Location

Digest files are delivered to an Amazon S3 bucket location that follows this syntax.

```
1 s3://s3-bucket-name/AWSLogs/aws-account-id/CloudTrail-Digest/
2   region/digest-end-year/digest-end-month/digest-end-date/
3   aws-account-id_CloudTrail-Digest_region_trail-name_region_digest_end_timestamp.json.gz
```

Sample Digest File Contents

The following example digest file contains information for a CloudTrail log.

```
1  {
2    "awsAccountId": "111122223333",
3    "digestStartTime": "2015-08-17T14:01:31Z",
4    "digestEndTime": "2015-08-17T15:01:31Z",
5    "digestS3Bucket": "S3-bucket-name",
6    "digestS3Object": "AWSLogs/111122223333/CloudTrail-Digest/us-east-2/2015/08/17/111122223333
         _CloudTrail-Digest_us-east-2_your-trail-name_us-east-2_20150817T150131Z.json.gz",
7    "digestPublicKeyFingerprint": "31e8b5433410dfb61a9dc45cc65b22ff",
8    "digestSignatureAlgorithm": "SHA256withRSA",
9    "newestEventTime": "2015-08-17T14:52:27Z",
10   "oldestEventTime": "2015-08-17T14:42:27Z",
11   "previousDigestS3Bucket": "S3-bucket-name",
12   "previousDigestS3Object": "AWSLogs/111122223333/CloudTrail-Digest/us-east
         -2/2015/08/17/111122223333_CloudTrail-Digest_us-east-2_your-trail-name_us-east-2
         _20150817T140131Z.json.gz",
13   "previousDigestHashValue": "97fb791cf91ffc440d274f8190dbdd9aa09c34432aba82739df18b6d3c13df2d",
14   "previousDigestHashAlgorithm": "SHA-256",
15   "previousDigestSignature": "50887
         ccffad4c002b97caa37cc9dc626e3c680207d41d27fa5835458e066e0d3652fc4dfc30937e4d5f4cc7f796e7a258fb5
         ",
16   "logFiles": [
17     {
18       "s3Bucket": "S3-bucket-name",
19       "s3Object": "AWSLogs/111122223333/CloudTrail/us-east-2/2015/08/17/111122223333
           _CloudTrail_us-east-2_20150817T1445Z_9nYN7gp2eWAJHIfT.json.gz",
20       "hashValue": "9bb6196fc6b84d6f075a56548feca262bd99ba3c2de41b618e5b6e22c1fc71f6",
21       "hashAlgorithm": "SHA-256",
22       "newestEventTime": "2015-08-17T14:52:27Z",
23       "oldestEventTime": "2015-08-17T14:42:27Z"
24     }
25   ]
26 }
```

Digest File Field Descriptions

The following are descriptions for each field in the digest file:

`awsAccountId`
The AWS account ID for which the digest file has been delivered.

`digestStartTime`
The starting UTC time range that the digest file covers, taking as a reference the time in which log files have been delivered by CloudTrail. This means that if the time range is [Ta, Tb], the digest will contain all the log files delivered to the customer between Ta and Tb.

`digestEndTime`
The ending UTC time range that the digest file covers, taking as a reference the time in which log files have been delivered by CloudTrail. This means that if the time range is [Ta, Tb], the digest will contain all the log files delivered to the customer between Ta and Tb.

`digestS3Bucket`
The name of the Amazon S3 bucket to which the current digest file has been delivered.

`digestS3Object`
The Amazon S3 object key (that is, the Amazon S3 bucket location) of the current digest file. The first two regions in the string show the region from which the digest file was delivered. The last region (after `your-trail-name`) is the home region of the trail. The home region is the region in which the trail was created. In the case of a multi-region trail, this can be different from the region from which the digest file was delivered.

`newestEventTime`
The UTC time of the most recent event among all of the events in the log files in the digest.

`oldestEventTime`
The UTC time of the oldest event among all of the events in the log files in the digest.
If the digest file is delivered late, the value of `oldestEventTime` will be earlier than the value of `digestStartTime`.

`previousDigestS3Bucket`
The Amazon S3 bucket to which the previous digest file was delivered.

`previousDigestS3Object`
The Amazon S3 object key (that is, the Amazon S3 bucket location) of the previous digest file.

`previousDigestHashValue`
The hexadecimal encoded hash value of the uncompressed contents of the previous digest file.

`previousDigestHashAlgorithm`
The name of the hash algorithm that was used to hash the previous digest file.

`publicKeyFingerprint`
The hexadecimal encoded fingerprint of the public key that matches the private key used to sign this digest file. You can retrieve the public keys for the time range corresponding to the digest file by using the AWS CLI or the CloudTrail API. Of the public keys returned, the one whose fingerprint matches this value can be used for validating the digest file. For information about retrieving public keys for digest files, see the AWS CLI http://docs.aws.amazon.com/cli/latest/reference/cloudtrail/list-public-keys.html command or the CloudTrail http://docs.aws.amazon.com/awscloudtrail/latest/APIReference/API_ListPublicKeys.html API.
CloudTrail uses different private/public key pairs per region. Each digest file is signed with a private key unique to its region. Therefore, when you validate a digest file from a particular region, you must look in the same region for its corresponding public key.

`digestSignatureAlgorithm`
The algorithm used to sign the digest file.

`logFiles.s3Bucket`
The name of the Amazon S3 bucket for the log file.

`logFiles.s3Object`
The Amazon S3 object key of the current log file.

`logFiles.newestEventTime`
The UTC time of the most recent event in the log file. This time also corresponds to the time stamp of the log file itself.

`logFiles.oldestEventTime`
The UTC time of the oldest event in the log file.

`logFiles.hashValue`
The hexadecimal encoded hash value of the uncompressed log file content.

`logFiles.hashAlgorithm`
The hash algorithm used to hash the log file.

Starting Digest File

When log file integrity validation is started, a starting digest file will be generated. A starting digest file will also be generated when log file integrity validation is restarted (by either disabling and then reenabling log file integrity validation, or by stopping logging and then restarting logging with validation enabled). In a starting digest file, the following fields relating to the previous digest file will be null:

- previousDigestS3Bucket

- previousDigestS3Object

- previousDigestHashValue

- previousDigestHashAlgorithm

- previousDigestSignature

'Empty' Digest Files

CloudTrail will deliver a digest file even when there has been no API activity in your account during the one hour period that the digest file represents. This can be useful when you need to assert that no log files were delivered during the hour reported by the digest file.

The following example shows the contents of a digest file that recorded an hour when no API activity occurred. Note that the `logFiles:[ ]` field at the end of the digest file contents is empty.

```
1 {
2    "awsAccountId": "111122223333",
3    "digestStartTime": "2015-08-20T17:01:31Z",
4    "digestEndTime": "2015-08-20T18:01:31Z",
5    "digestS3Bucket": "example-bucket-name",
6    "digestS3Object": "AWSLogs/111122223333/CloudTrail-Digest/us-east-2/2015/08/20/111122223333
          _CloudTrail-Digest_us-east-2_example-trail-name_us-east-2_20150820T180131Z.json.gz",
7    "digestPublicKeyFingerprint": "31e8b5433410dfb61a9dc45cc65b22ff",
8    "digestSignatureAlgorithm": "SHA256withRSA",
9    "newestEventTime": null,
10   "oldestEventTime": null,
11   "previousDigestS3Bucket": "example-bucket-name",
12   "previousDigestS3Object": "AWSLogs/111122223333/CloudTrail-Digest/us-east
          -2/2015/08/20/111122223333_CloudTrail-Digest_us-east-2_example-trail-name_us-east-2
          _20150820T170131Z.json.gz",
13   "previousDigestHashValue": "ed96c4bac9eaa8fe9716ca0e515da51938be651b1db31d781956416a9d05cdfa",
```

```
14    "previousDigestHashAlgorithm": "SHA-256",
15    "previousDigestSignature": "82705525
          fb0fe7f919f9434e5b7138cb41793c776c7414f3520c0242902daa8cc8286b29263d2627f2f259471c745b1654af76e
          ",
16    "logFiles": []
17 }
```

Signature of the Digest File

The signature information for a digest file is located in two object metadata properties of the Amazon S3 digest file object. Each digest file has the following metadata entries:

- x-amz-meta-signature

  The hexadecimal encoded value of the digest file signature. The following is an example signature:

```
1 3
      be472336fa2989ef34de1b3c1bf851f59eb030eaff3e2fb6600a082a23f4c6a82966565b994f9de4a5989d053d9d

2 28
      f1cc237f372264a51b611c01da429565def703539f4e71009051769469231bc22232fa260df02740047af5322298

3 05
      d3ffcb5d2dd5dc28f8bb5b7993938e8a5f912a82b448a367eccb2ec0f198ba71e23eb0b97278cf65f3c8d1e652c6
```

- x-amz-meta-signature-algorithm

  The following shows an example value of the algorithm used to generate the digest signature:

  SHA256withRSA

Digest File Chaining

The fact that each digest file contains a reference to its previous digest file enables a "chaining" that permits validation tools like the AWS CLI to detect if a digest file has been deleted. It also allows the digest files in a specified time range to be successively inspected, starting with the most recent first.

Note

When you disable log file integrity validation, the chain of digest files is broken after one hour. CloudTrail will not create digest files for log files that were delivered during a period in which log file integrity validation was disabled. For example, if you enable log file integrity validation at noon on January 1, disable it at noon on January 2, and re-enable it at noon on January 10, digest files will not be created for the log files delivered from noon on January 2 to noon on January 10. The same applies whenever you stop CloudTrail logging or delete a trail.

If logging is stopped or the trail is deleted, CloudTrail will deliver a final digest file. This digest file can contain information for any remaining log files that cover events up to and including the StopLogging event.

Custom Implementations of CloudTrail Log File Integrity Validation

Because CloudTrail uses industry standard, openly available cryptographic algorithms and hash functions, you can create your own tools to validate the integrity of CloudTrail log files. When log file integrity validation is enabled, CloudTrail delivers digest files to your Amazon S3 bucket. You can use these files to implement your own validation solution. For more information about digest files, see CloudTrail Digest File Structure.

This topic describes how digest files are signed, and then details the steps that you will need to take to implement a solution that validates the digest files and the log files that they reference.

Understanding How CloudTrail Digest Files are Signed

CloudTrail digest files are signed with RSA digital signatures. For each digest file, CloudTrail does the following:

1. Creates a string for data signing based on designated digest file fields (described in the next section).

2. Gets a private key unique to the region.

3. Passes the SHA-256 hash of the string and the private key to the RSA signing algorithm, which produces a digital signature.

4. Encodes the byte code of the signature into hexadecimal format.

5. Puts the digital signature into the `x-amz-meta-signature` metadata property of the Amazon S3 digest file object.

Contents of the Data Signing String

The following CloudTrail objects are included in the string for data signing:

- The ending timestamp of the digest file in UTC extended format (for example, `2015-05-08T07:19:37Z`)

- The current digest file S3 path

- The hexadecimal-encoded SHA-256 hash of the current digest file

- The hexadecimal-encoded signature of the previous digest file

The format for calculating this string and an example string are provided later in this document.

Custom Validation Implementation Steps

When implementing a custom validation solution, you will need to validate the digest file first, and then the log files that it references.

Validate the Digest File

To validate a digest file, you need its signature, the public key whose private key was used to signed it, and a data signing string that you compute.

1. Get the digest file.

2. Verify that the digest file has been retrieved from its original location.

3. Get the hexadecimal-encoded signature of the digest file.

4. Get the hexadecimal-encoded fingerprint of the public key whose private key was used to sign the digest file.

5. Retrieve the public keys for the time range corresponding to the digest file.

6. From among the public keys retrieved, choose the public key whose fingerprint matches the fingerprint in the digest file.

7. Using the digest file hash and other digest file fields, recreate the data signing string used to verify the digest file signature.

8. Validate the signature by passing in the SHA-256 hash of the string, the public key, and the signature as parameters to the RSA signature verification algorithm. If the result is true, the digest file is valid.

Validate the Log Files

If the digest file is valid, validate each of the log files that the digest file references.

1. To validate the integrity of a log file, compute its SHA-256 hash value on its uncompressed content and compare the results with the hash for the log file recorded in hexadecimal in the digest. If the hashes match, the log file is valid.

2. By using the information about the previous digest file that is included in the current digest file, validate the previous digest files and their corresponding log files in succession.

The following sections describe these steps in detail.

A. Get the Digest File

The first steps are to get the most recent digest file, verify that you have retrieved it from its original location, verify its digital signature, and get the fingerprint of the public key.

1. Using http://docs.aws.amazon.com/AmazonS3/latest/API/RESTObjectGET.html or the AmazonS3Client class (for example), get the most recent digest file from your Amazon S3 bucket for the time range that you want to validate.

2. Check that the S3 bucket and S3 object used to retrieve the file match the S3 bucket S3 object locations that are recorded in the digest file itself.

3. Next, get the digital signature of the digest file from the `x-amz-meta-signature` metadata property of the digest file object in Amazon S3.

4. In the digest file, get the fingerprint of the public key whose private key was used to sign the digest file from the `digestPublicKeyFingerprint` field.

B. Retrieve the Public Key for Validating the Digest File

To get the public key to validate the digest file, you can use either the AWS CLI or the CloudTrail API. In both cases, you specify a time range (that is, a start time and end time) for the digest files that you want to validate. One or more public keys may be returned for the time range that you specify. The returned keys may have validity time ranges that overlap.

Note
Because CloudTrail uses different private/public key pairs per region, each digest file is signed with a private key unique to its region. Therefore, when you validate a digest file from a particular region, you must retrieve its public key from the same region.

Use the AWS CLI to Retrieve Public Keys

To retrieve public keys for digest files by using the AWS CLI, use the `cloudtrail list-public-keys` command. The command has the following format:

```
aws cloudtrail list-public-keys [--start-time <start-time>] [--end-time <end-time>]
```

The start-time and end-time parameters are UTC timestamps and are optional. If not specified, the current time is used, and the currently active public key or keys are returned.

Sample Response

The response will be a list of JSON objects representing the key (or keys) returned:

```
 1 {
 2     "publicKeyList": [
 3         {
 4             "ValidityStartTime": "1436317441.0",
 5             "ValidityEndTime": "1438909441.0",
 6             "Value": "MIIBCgKCAQEAn11L2YZ9h7onug2ILi1MWyHiMRsTQjfWE+pHVRLk1QjfWhirG+lpOa8NrwQ/
                r7Ah5bNL6HepznOU9XTDSfmmnP97mqyc7z/upfZdS/AHhYcGaz7n6Wc/RRBU6VmiPCrAUojuSk6/
                GjvA8iOPFsYDuBtviXarvuLPlrT9kAd4Lb+rFfR5peEgBEkhlzc5HuWO7SOy+
                KunqxX6jQBnXGMtxmPBPPOFylgWGNdFtks/4
                YSKcgqwHOYDcawP9GGGDAeCIqPWIXDLG1jOjRRzWfCmDOiJUkz8vTsn4hq/5
                ZxRFE7UBAUiVcGbdnDdvVfhF9C3dQiDq3k7adQIziLTOcShgQIDAQAB",
 7             "Fingerprint": "8eba5db5bea9b640d1c96a77256fe7f2"
 8         },
 9         {
10             "ValidityStartTime": "1434589460.0",
11             "ValidityEndTime": "1437181460.0",
12             "Value": "MIIBCgKCAQEApfYL2FiZhpN74LNWVUzhR+
                VheYhwhYm8wOn5Gf6i95ylW5kBAWKVEmnAQG7BvS5g9SMqFDQx52fW7NWV44IvfJ2xGXT+wT+DgR6ZQ
                +6yxskQNqV5YcXj4Aa5Zz4jJfsYjDuO2MDTZNIzNvBNzaBJ+r2WIWAJ/
                Xq54kyF63B6WE38vKuDE7nSd1FqQuEoNBFLPInvgggYe2Ym1Refe2z71wNcJ2kY+
                q0h1BSHrSM8RWuJIw7MXwF9iQncg9jYzUlNJomozQzAG5wSRfbplcCYNY40xvGd/aAmOOm+Y+
                XFMrKwtLCwseHPvj843qVno6x4BJN9bpWnoPo9sdsbGoiK3QIDAQAB",
13             "Fingerprint": "8933b39ddc64d26d8e14ffbf6566fee4"
14         },
15         {
16             "ValidityStartTime": "1434589370.0",
17             "ValidityEndTime": "1437181370.0",
18             "Value": "
                MIIBIjANBgkqhkiG9w0BAQEFAAOCAQ8AMIIBCgKCAQEAqlzPJbvZJ42UdcmLfPUqXYNfOs6I8lCfao/
                tOs8CmzPOEdtLWugB9xoIUz78qVHdKIqxbaG4jWHfJBiOSSFBMOlt8cdVo4TnRa7oG9io5pysS6DJhBBAeXsi
                +wrUNh8RSLxL4k6G1+BhLX2OtJkZ/
                erT97tDGBujAelqseGg3vPZbTx9SMfOLN65PdLFudLP7GatOZ9p5jw/
                rjpclKfo9Bfc3heeBxWGKwBBOKnFAaN9V57pOaosCvPKmHd9bg7jsQkI9Xp22IzGLsTFJZYVA3KiTAElDMu8O
                +1utKVEiLkR2disdCmPTKOVQIDAQAB",
19             "Fingerprint": "31e8b5433410dfb61a9dc45cc65b22ff"
20         }
21     ]
22 }
```

Use the CloudTrail API to Retrieve Public Keys

To retrieve public keys for digest files by using the CloudTrail API, pass in start time and end time values to the `ListPublicKeys` API. The `ListPublicKeys` API returns the public keys whose private keys were used to sign digest files within the specified time range. For each public key, the API also returns the corresponding fingerprint.

ListPublicKeys

This section describes the request parameters and response elements for the `ListPublicKeys` API.

Note

The encoding for the binary fields for `ListPublicKeys` is subject to change.

Request Parameters

Name	Description
StartTime	Optionally specifies, in UTC, the start of the time range to look up public keys for Cloud-Trail digest files. If StartTime is not specified, the current time is used, and the current public key is returned. Type: DateTime
EndTime	Optionally specifies, in UTC, the end of the time range to look up public keys for Cloud-Trail digest files. If EndTime is not specified, the current time is used. Type: DateTime

Response Elements

`PublicKeyList`, an array of `PublicKey` objects that contains:

Name	Description
Value	The DER encoded public key value in PKCS #1 format. Type: Blob
ValidityStartTime	The starting time of validity of the public key. Type: DateTime
ValidityEndTime	The ending time of validity of the public key. Type: DateTime
Fingerprint	The fingerprint of the public key. The fingerprint can be used to identify the public key that you must use to validate the digest file. Type: String

C. Choose the Public Key to Use for Validation

From among the public keys retrieved by `list-public-keys` or `ListPublicKeys`, choose the public key returned whose fingerprint matches the fingerprint recorded in the `digestPublicKeyFingerprint` field of the digest file. This is the public key that you will use to validate the digest file.

D. Recreate the Data Signing String

Now that you have the signature of the digest file and associated public key, you need to calculate the data signing string. After you have calculated the data signing string, you will have the inputs needed to verify the signature.

The data signing string has the following format:

```
1 Data_To_Sign_String =
2    Digest_End_Timestamp_in_UTC_Extended_format + '\n' +
3    Current_Digest_File_S3_Path + '\n' +
4    Hex(Sha256(current-digest-file-content)) + '\n' +
5    Previous_digest_signature_in_hex
```

An example `Data_To_Sign_String` follows.

```
1 2015-08-12T04:01:31Z
2 S3-bucket-name/AWSLogs/111122223333/CloudTrail-Digest/us-east-2/2015/08/12/111122223333_us-east
     -2_CloudTrail-Digest_us-east-2_20150812T040131Z.json.gz
3 4ff08d7c6ecd6eb313257e839645d20363ee3784a2328a7d76b99b53cc9bcacd
4 6
     e8540b83c3ac86a0312d971a225361d28ed0af20d70c211a2d405e32abf529a8145c2966e3bb47362383a52441545ed09
5 d4c7c09dd152b84e79099ce7a9ec35d2b264eb92eb6e090f1e5ec5d40ec8a0729c02ff57f9e30d5343a8591638f8b794972ce
6 98
     b0aee2c1c8af74ec620261529265e83a9834ebef6054979d3e9a6767dfa6fdb4ae153436c567d6ae208f988047ccfc8e5
```

After you recreate this string, you can validate the digest file.

E. Validate the Digest File

Pass the SHA-256 hash of the recreated data signing string, digital signature, and public key to the RSA signature verification algorithm. If the output is true, the signature of the digest file is verified and the digest file is valid.

F. Validate the Log Files

After you have validated the digest file, you can validate the log files it references. The digest file contains the SHA-256 hashes of the log files. If one of the log files was modified after CloudTrail delivered it, the SHA-256 hashes will change, and the signature of digest file will not match.

The following shows how validate the log files:

1. Do an `S3 Get` of the log file using the S3 location information in the digest file's `logFiles.s3Bucket` and `logFiles.s3Object` fields.

2. If the `S3 Get` operation is successful, iterate through the log files listed in the digest file's logFiles array using the following steps:

   1. Retrieve the original hash of the file from the `logFiles.hashValue` field of the corresponding log in the digest file.

   2. Hash the uncompressed contents of the log file with the hashing algorithm specified in `logFiles.hashAlgorithm`.

   3. Compare the hash value that you generated with the one for the log in the digest file. If the hashes match, the log file is valid.

G. Validate Additional Digest and Log Files

In each digest file, the following fields provide the location and signature of the previous digest file:

- `previousDigestS3Bucket`

- `previousDigestS3Object`

- `previousDigestSignature`

Use this information to visit previous digest files sequentially, validating the signature of each and the log files that they reference by using the steps in the previous sections. The only difference is that for previous digest files, you do not need to retrieve the digital signature from the digest file object's Amazon S3 metadata properties. The signature for the previous digest file is provided for you in the `previousDigestSignature` field.

You can go back until the starting digest file is reached, or until the chain of digest files is broken, whichever comes first.

Validating Digest and Log Files Offline

When validating digest and log files offline, you can generally follow the procedures described in the previous sections. However, you must take into account the following areas:

Handling the Most Recent Digest File

The digital signature of the most recent (that is, "current") digest file is in the Amazon S3 metadata properties of the digest file object. In an offline scenario, the digital signature for the current digest file will not be available.

Two possible ways of handling this are:

- Since the digital signature for the previous digest file is in the current digest file, start validating from the next-to-last digest file. With this method, the most recent digest file cannot be validated.

- As a preliminary step, obtain the signature for the current digest file from the digest file object's metadata properties (for example, by calling the Amazon S3 getObjectMetadata API) and then store it securely offline. This would allow the current digest file to be validated in addition to the previous files in the chain.

Path Resolution

Fields in the downloaded digest files like `s3Object` and `previousDigestS3Object` will still be pointing to Amazon S3 online locations for log files and digest files. An offline solution must find a way to reroute these to the current path of the downloaded log and digest files.

Public Keys

In order to validate offline, all of the public keys that you need for validating log files in a given time range must first be obtained online (by calling `ListPublicKeys`, for example) and then stored securely offline. This step must be repeated whenever you want to validate additional files outside the initial time range that you specified.

Sample Validation Snippet

The following sample snippet provides skeleton code for validating CloudTrail digest and log files. The skeleton code is online/offline agnostic; that is, it is up to you to decide whether to implement it with or without online connectivity to AWS. The suggested implementation uses the Java Cryptography Extension (JCE) and Bouncy Castle as a security provider.

The sample snippet shows:

- How to create the data signing string used to validate the digest file signature.

- How to verify the digest file signature.

- How to verify the log file hashes.

- A code structure for validating a chain of digest files.

```
1  import java.util.Arrays;
2  import java.security.MessageDigest;
3  import java.security.KeyFactory;
4  import java.security.PublicKey;
5  import java.security.Security;
6  import java.security.Signature;
7  import java.security.spec.X509EncodedKeySpec;
8  import org.json.JSONObject;
9  import org.bouncycastle.jce.provider.BouncyCastleProvider;
10 import org.apache.commons.codec.binary.Hex;
11
12 public class DigestFileValidator {
13
14     public void validateDigestFile(String digestS3Bucket, String digestS3Object, String
          digestSignature) {
15
16         // Using the Bouncy Castle provider as a JCE security provider - http://www.bouncycastle
              .org/
17         Security.addProvider(new BouncyCastleProvider());
18
19         // Load the digest file from S3 (using Amazon S3 Client) or from your local copy
20         JSONObject digestFile = loadDigestFileInMemory(digestS3Bucket, digestS3Object);
21
22         // Check that the digest file has been retrieved from its original location
23         if (!digestFile.getString("digestS3Bucket").equals(digestS3Bucket) ||
24                 !digestFile.getString("digestS3Object").equals(digestS3Object)) {
25             System.err.println("Digest file has been moved from its original location.");
26         } else {
27             // Compute digest file hash
28             MessageDigest messageDigest = MessageDigest.getInstance("SHA-256");
29             messageDigest.update(convertToByteArray(digestFile));
30             byte[] digestFileHash = messageDigest.digest();
31             messageDigest.reset();
32
33             // Compute the data to sign
34             String dataToSign = String.format("%s%n%s/%s%n%s%n%s",
35                                 digestFile.getString("digestEndTime"),
36                                 digestFile.getString("digestS3Bucket"), digestFile.getString("
                                    digestS3Object"), // Constructing the S3 path of the digest
                                    file as part of the data to sign
37                                 Hex.encodeHexString(digestFileHash),
38                                 digestFile.getString("previousDigestSignature"));
39
40             byte[] signatureContent = Hex.decodeHex(digestSignature);
41
42             /*
43                 NOTE:
44                 To find the right public key to verify the signature, call CloudTrail
                      ListPublicKey API to get a list
45                 of public keys, then match by the publicKeyFingerprint in the digest file. Also,
```

```
                      the public key bytes
46          returned from ListPublicKey API are DER encoded in PKCS#1 format:
47
48          PublicKeyInfo ::= SEQUENCE {
49              algorithm       AlgorithmIdentifier,
50              PublicKey       BIT STRING
51          }
52
53          AlgorithmIdentifier ::= SEQUENCE {
54              algorithm       OBJECT IDENTIFIER,
55              parameters      ANY DEFINED BY algorithm OPTIONAL
56          }
57      */
58      pkcs1PublicKeyBytes = getPublicKey(digestFile.getString("digestPublicKeyFingerprint
            ")));
59
60      // Transform the PKCS#1 formatted public key to x.509 format.
61      RSAPublicKey rsaPublicKey = RSAPublicKey.getInstance(pkcs1PublicKeyBytes);
62      AlgorithmIdentifier rsaEncryption = new AlgorithmIdentifier(PKCSObjectIdentifiers.
            rsaEncryption, null);
63      SubjectPublicKeyInfo publicKeyInfo = new SubjectPublicKeyInfo(rsaEncryption,
            rsaPublicKey);
64
65      // Create the PublicKey object needed for the signature validation
66      PublicKey publicKey = KeyFactory.getInstance("RSA", "BC").generatePublic(new
            X509EncodedKeySpec(publicKeyInfo.getEncoded()));
67
68      // Verify signature
69      Signature signature = Signature.getInstance("SHA256withRSA", "BC");
70      signature.initVerify(publicKey);
71      signature.update(dataToSign.getBytes("UTF-8"));
72
73      if (signature.verify(signatureContent)) {
74          System.out.println("Digest file signature is valid, validating log …files");
75          for (int i = 0; i < digestFile.getJSONArray("logFiles").length(); i++) {
76
77              JSONObject logFileMetadata = digestFile.getJSONArray("logFiles").
                    getJSONObject(i);
78
79              // Compute log file hash
80              byte[] logFileContent = loadUncompressedLogFileInMemory(
81                                      logFileMetadata.getString("s3Bucket"),
82                                      logFileMetadata.getString("s3Object")
83                                  );
84              messageDigest.update(logFileContent);
85               byte[] logFileHash = messageDigest.digest();
86              messageDigest.reset();
87
88              // Retrieve expected hash for the log file being processed
89              byte[] expectedHash = Hex.decodeHex(logFileMetadata.getString("hashValue"));
90
91              boolean signaturesMatch = Arrays.equals(expectedHash, logFileHash);
92              if (!signaturesMatch) {
93                  System.err.println(String.format("Log file: %s/%s hash doesn't match.\
```

```
                                    tExpected: %s Actual: %s",
94                          logFileMetadata.getString("s3Bucket"), logFileMetadata.getString
                                ("s3Object"),
95                          Hex.encodeHexString(expectedHash), Hex.encodeHexString(
                                logFileHash)));
96                  } else {
97                      System.out.println(String.format("Log file: %s/%s hash match",
98                          logFileMetadata.getString("s3Bucket"), logFileMetadata.getString
                                ("s3Object")));
99                  }
100             }

101
102         } else {
103             System.err.println("Digest signature failed validation.");
104         }

105
106         System.out.println("Digest file validation completed.");

107
108         if (chainValidationIsEnabled()) {
109             // This enables the digests' chain validation
110             validateDigestFile(
111                     digestFile.getString("previousDigestS3Bucket"),
112                     digestFile.getString("previousDigestS3Object"),
113                     digestFile.getString("previousDigestSignature"));
114         }
115     }
116   }
117 }
```

Using the CloudTrail Processing Library

The CloudTrail Processing Library is a Java library that provides an easy way to process AWS CloudTrail logs. You provide configuration details about your CloudTrail SQS queue and write code to process events. The CloudTrail Processing Library does the rest. It polls your Amazon SQS queue, reads and parses queue messages, downloads CloudTrail log files, parses events in the log files, and passes the events to your code as Java objects.

The CloudTrail Processing Library is highly scalable and fault-tolerant. It handles parallel processing of log files so that you can process as many logs as needed. It handles network failures related to network timeouts and inaccessible resources.

The following topic shows you how to use the CloudTrail Processing Library to process CloudTrail logs in your Java projects.

The library is provided as an Apache-licensed open-source project, available on GitHub:

- https://github.com/aws/aws-cloudtrail-processing-library

The library source includes sample code that you can use as a base for your own projects.

- Minimum Requirements
- Processing CloudTrail Logs
- Advanced Topics
- Additional Resources

Minimum Requirements

To use the CloudTrail Processing Library, you must have the following:

- AWS SDK for Java 1.11.135
- Java 1.7

Processing CloudTrail Logs

To process CloudTrail logs in your Java application:

1. Adding the CloudTrail Processing Library to Your Project

2. Configuring the CloudTrail Processing Library

3. Implementing the Events Processor

4. Instantiating and Running the Processing Executor

Adding the CloudTrail Processing Library to Your Project

To use the CloudTrail Processing Library, add it to your Java project's classpath.

Adding the Library to an Apache Ant Project
To add the library to an Apache Ant project

1. Download or clone the CloudTrail Processing Library source code from GitHub:

   - https://github.com/aws/aws-cloudtrail-processing-library

2. Build the .jar file from source as described in the README:

```
1 mvn clean install -Dgpg.skip=true
```

3. Copy the resulting .jar file into your project and add it to your project's `build.xml` file. For example:

```
1 <classpath>
2   <pathelement path="${classpath}"/>
3   <pathelement location="lib/aws-cloudtrail-processing-library-1.1.2.jar"/>
4 </classpath>
```

Adding the Library to an Apache Maven Project

The CloudTrail Processing Library is available for Apache Maven. You can add it to your project by writing a single dependency in your project's `pom.xml` file.

To add the CloudTrail Processing Library to a Maven project

- Open your Maven project's `pom.xml` file and add the following dependency:

```
1 <dependency>
2     <groupId>com.amazonaws</groupId>
3     <artifactId>aws-cloudtrail-processing-library</artifactId>
4     <version>1.1.2</version>
5 </dependency>
```

Adding the Library to an Eclipse Project

To add the CloudTrail Processing Library to an Eclipse project

1. Download or clone the CloudTrail Processing Library source code from GitHub:

   - https://github.com/aws/aws-cloudtrail-processing-library

2. Build the .jar file from source as described in the README:

```
1 mvn clean install -Dgpg.skip=true
```

3. Copy the built aws-cloudtrail-processing-library-1.1.2.jar to a directory in your project (typically `lib`).

4. Right-click your project's name in the Eclipse **Project Explorer**, choose **Build Path**, and then choose **Configure**

5. In the **Java Build Path** window, choose the **Libraries** tab.

6. Choose **Add JARs...** and navigate to the path where you copied aws-cloudtrail-processing-library-1.1.2.jar.

7. Choose **OK** to complete adding the `.jar` to your project.

Adding the Library to an IntelliJ Project

To add the CloudTrail Processing Library to an IntelliJ project

1. Download or clone the CloudTrail Processing Library source code from GitHub:

   - https://github.com/aws/aws-cloudtrail-processing-library

2. Build the .jar file from source as described in the README:

```
1 mvn clean install -Dgpg.skip=true
```

3. From **File**, choose **Project Structure**.

4. Choose **Modules** and then choose **Dependencies**.

5. Choose **+ JARS or Directories** and then go to the path where you built the `aws-cloudtrail-processing-library-1.1.2.jar`.

6. Choose **Apply** and then choose **OK** to complete adding the `.jar` to your project.

Configuring the CloudTrail Processing Library

You can configure the CloudTrail Processing Library by creating a classpath properties file that is loaded at runtime, or by creating a `ClientConfiguration` object and setting options manually.

Providing a Properties File

You can write a classpath properties file that provides configuration options to your application. The following example file shows the options you can set:

```
1  # AWS access key. (Required)
2  accessKey = your_access_key
3
4  # AWS secret key. (Required)
5  secretKey = your_secret_key
6
7  # The SQS URL used to pull CloudTrail notification from. (Required)
8  sqsUrl = your_sqs_queue_url
9
10 # The SQS end point specific to a region.
11 sqsRegion = us-east-1
12
13 # A period of time during which Amazon SQS prevents other consuming components
14 # from receiving and processing that message.
15 visibilityTimeout = 60
16
17 # The S3 region to use.
18 s3Region = us-east-1
19
20 # Number of threads used to download S3 files in parallel. Callbacks can be
21 # invoked from any thread.
22 threadCount = 1
23
24 # The time allowed, in seconds, for threads to shut down after
25 # AWSCloudTrailEventProcessingExecutor.stop() is called. If they are still
26 # running beyond this time, they will be forcibly terminated.
27 threadTerminationDelaySeconds = 60
28
29 # The maximum number of AWSCloudTrailClientEvents sent to a single invocation
30 # of processEvents().
31 maxEventsPerEmit = 10
32
33 # Whether to include raw event information in CloudTrailDeliveryInfo.
34 enableRawEventInfo = false
35
36 # Whether to delete SQS message when the CloudTrail Processing Library is unable to process the
         notification.
37 deleteMessageUponFailure = false
```

The following parameters are required:

- **sqsUrl** – Provides the URL from which to pull your CloudTrail notifications. If you don't specify this value, the `AWSCloudTrailProcessingExecutor` throws an `IllegalStateException`.

- **accessKey** – A unique identifier for your account, such as AKIAIOSFODNN7EXAMPLE.

- **secretKey** – A unique identifier for your account, such as wJalrXUtnFEMI/K7MDENG/bPxRfiCYEX-AMPLEKEY.

The `accessKey` and `secretKey` parameters provide your AWS credentials to the library so the library can access AWS on your behalf.

Defaults for the other parameters are set by the library. For more information, see the AWS CloudTrail Processing Library Reference.

Creating a ClientConfiguration

Instead of setting options in the classpath properties, you can provide options to the `AWSCloudTrailProcessingExecutor` by initializing and setting options on a `ClientConfiguration` object, as shown in the following example:

```
1 ClientConfiguration basicConfig = new ClientConfiguration(
2     "http://sqs.us-east-1.amazonaws.com/123456789012/queue2",
3     new DefaultAWSCredentialsProviderChain());
4
5 basicConfig.setEnableRawEventInfo(true);
6 basicConfig.setThreadCount(4);
7 basicConfig.setnEventsPerEmit(20);
```

Implementing the Events Processor

To process CloudTrail logs, you must implement an `EventsProcessor` that receives the CloudTrail log data. The following is an example implementation:

```
1 public class SampleEventsProcessor implements EventsProcessor {
2
3     public void process(List<CloudTrailEvent> events) {
4         int i = 0;
5         for (CloudTrailEvent event : events) {
6             System.out.println(String.format("Process event %d : %s", i++, event.getEventData())
                    );
7         }
8     }
9 }
```

When implementing an `EventsProcessor`, you implement the `process()` callback that the `AWSCloudTrailProcessingExecutor` uses to send you CloudTrail events. Events are provided in a list of `CloudTrailClientEvent` objects.

The `CloudTrailClientEvent` object provides a `CloudTrailEvent` and `CloudTrailEventMetadata` that you can use to read the CloudTrail event and delivery information.

This simple example prints the event information for each event passed to `SampleEventsProcessor`. In your own implementation, you can process logs as you see fit. The `AWSCloudTrailProcessingExecutor` continues to send events to your `EventsProcessor` as long as it has events to send and is still running.

Instantiating and Running the Processing Executor

After you write an `EventsProcessor` and set configuration values for the CloudTrail Processing Library (either in a properties file or by using the `ClientConfiguration` class), you can use these elements to initialize and use an `AWSCloudTrailProcessingExecutor`.

To use `AWSCloudTrailProcessingExecutor` to process CloudTrail events

1. Instantiate an `AWSCloudTrailProcessingExecutor.Builder` object. Builder's constructor takes an `EventsProcessor` object and a classpath properties file name.

2. Call the Builder's `build()` factory method to configure and obtain an `AWSCloudTrailProcessingExecutor` object.

3. Use the `AWSCloudTrailProcessingExecutor`'s `start()` and `stop()` methods to begin and end CloudTrail event processing.

```
1  public class SampleApp {
2    public static void main(String[] args) throws InterruptedException {
3      AWSCloudTrailProcessingExecutor executor = new
4        AWSCloudTrailProcessingExecutor.Builder(new SampleEventsProcessor(),
5          "/myproject/cloudtrailprocessing.properties").build();
6
7      executor.start();
8      Thread.sleep(24 * 60 * 60 * 1000); // let it run for a while (optional)
9      executor.stop(); // optional
10   }
11 }
```

Advanced Topics

- Filtering the Events to Process
- Reporting Progress
- Handling Errors

Filtering the Events to Process

By default, all logs in your Amazon SQS queue's S3 bucket and all events that they contain are sent to your `EventsProcessor`. The CloudTrail Processing Library provides optional interfaces that you can implement to filter the sources used to obtain CloudTrail logs and to filter the events that you are interested in processing.

SourceFilter
You can implement the `SourceFilter` interface to choose whether you want to process logs from a provided source. `SourceFilter` declares a single callback method, `filterSource()`, that receives a `CloudTrailSource` object. To keep events from a source from being processed, return `false` from `filterSource()`.
The CloudTrail Processing Library calls the `filterSource()` method after the library polls for logs on the Amazon SQS queue. This occurs before the library starts event filtering or processing for the logs.
The following is an example implementation:

```
1  public class SampleSourceFilter implements SourceFilter{
2    private static final int MAX_RECEIVED_COUNT = 3;
3
4    private static List<String> accountIDs ;
5    static {
6      accountIDs = new ArrayList<>();
7      accountIDs.add("123456789012");
```

```
 8      accountIDs.add("234567890123");
 9    }
10
11    @Override
12    public boolean filterSource(CloudTrailSource source) throws CallbackException {
13      source = (SQSBasedSource) source;
14      Map<String, String> sourceAttributes = source.getSourceAttributes();
15
16      String accountId = sourceAttributes.get(
17        SourceAttributeKeys.ACCOUNT_ID.getAttributeKey());
18
19      String receivedCount = sourceAttributes.get(
20        SourceAttributeKeys.APPROXIMATE_RECEIVE_COUNT.getAttributeKey());
21
22      int approximateReceivedCount = Integer.parseInt(receivedCount);
23
24      return approximateReceivedCount <= MAX_RECEIVED_COUNT && accountIDs.contains(accountId);
25    }
26 }
```

If you don't provide your own `SourceFilter`, then `DefaultSourceFilter` is used, which allows all sources to be processed (it always returns `true`).

EventFilter

You can implement the `EventFilter` interface to choose whether a CloudTrail event is sent to your `EventsProcessor`. `EventFilter` declares a single callback method, `filterEvent()`, that receives a `CloudTrailEvent` object. To keep the event from being processed, return `false` from `filterEvent()`.

The CloudTrail Processing Library calls the `filterEvent()` method after the library polls for logs on the Amazon SQS queue and after source filtering. This occurs before the library starts event processing for the logs. See the following example implementation:

```
 1 public class SampleEventFilter implements EventFilter{
 2
 3    private static final String EC2_EVENTS = "ec2.amazonaws.com";
 4
 5    @Override
 6    public boolean filterEvent(CloudTrailClientEvent clientEvent) throws CallbackException {
 7      CloudTrailEvent event = clientEvent.getEvent();
 8
 9      String eventSource = event.getEventSource();
10      String eventName = event.getEventName();
11
12      return eventSource.equals(EC2_EVENTS) && eventName.startsWith("Delete");
13    }
14 }
```

If you don't provide your own `EventFilter`, then `DefaultEventFilter` is used, which allows all events to be processed (it always returns `true`).

Reporting Progress

Implement the `ProgressReporter` interface to customize the reporting of CloudTrail Processing Library progress. `ProgressReporter` declares two methods: `reportStart()` and `reportEnd()`, which are called at the beginning and end of the following operations:

- Polling messages from Amazon SQS

- Parsing messages from Amazon SQS

- Processing an Amazon SQS source for CloudTrail logs

- Deleting messages from Amazon SQS

- Downloading a CloudTrail log file

- Processing a CloudTrail log file

Both methods receive a `ProgressStatus` object that contains information about the operation that was performed. The `progressState` member holds a member of the `ProgressState` enumeration that identifies the current operation. This member can contain additional information in the `progressInfo` member. Additionally, any object that you return from `reportStart()` is passed to `reportEnd()`, so you can provide contextual information such as the time when the event began processing.

The following is an example implementation that provides information about how long an operation took to complete:

```
1  public class SampleProgressReporter implements ProgressReporter {
2    private static final Log logger =
3      LogFactory.getLog(DefaultProgressReporter.class);
4
5    @Override
6    public Object reportStart(ProgressStatus status) {
7      return new Date();
8    }
9
10   @Override
11   public void reportEnd(ProgressStatus status, Object startDate) {
12     System.out.println(status.getProgressState().toString() + " is " +
13       status.getProgressInfo().isSuccess() + " , and latency is " +
14       Math.abs(((Date) startDate).getTime()-new Date().getTime()) + "
15       milliseconds.");
16   }
17 }
```

If you don't implement your own `ProgressReporter`, then `DefaultExceptionHandler`, which prints the name of the state being run, is used instead.

Handling Errors

The `ExceptionHandler` interface allows you to provide special handling when an exception occurs during log processing. `ExceptionHandler` declares a single callback method, `handleException()`, which receives a `ProcessingLibraryException` object with context about the exception that occurred.

You can use the passed-in `ProcessingLibraryException`'s `getStatus()` method to find out what operation was executed when the exception occurred and get additional information about the status of the operation. `ProcessingLibraryException` is derived from Java's standard `Exception` class, so you can also retrieve information about the exception by invoking any of the exception methods.

See the following example implementation:

```
1  public class SampleExceptionHandler implements ExceptionHandler{
2    private static final Log logger =
3      LogFactory.getLog(DefaultProgressReporter.class);
4
5    @Override
6    public void handleException(ProcessingLibraryException exception) {
```

```
7     ProgressStatus status = exception.getStatus();
8     ProgressState state = status.getProgressState();
9     ProgressInfo info = status.getProgressInfo();
10
11    System.err.println(String.format(
12      "Exception. Progress State: %s. Progress Information: %s.", state, info));
13  }
14 }
```

If you don't provide your own `ExceptionHandler`, then `DefaultExceptionHandler`, which prints a standard error message, is used instead.

Note

If the `deleteMessageUponFailure` parameter is `true`, the CloudTrail Processing Library does not distinguish general exceptions from processing errors and may delete queue messages.

For example, you use the `SourceFilter` to filter messages by timestamp. However, you don't have the required permissions to access the S3 bucket that receives the CloudTrail log files. Because you don't have the required permissions, an `AmazonServiceException` is thrown. The CloudTrail Processing Library wraps this in a `CallBackException`. The `DefaultExceptionHandler` logs this as an error, but does not identify the root cause, which is that you don't have the required permissions. The CloudTrail Processing Library considers this a processing error and deletes the message, even if the message includes a valid CloudTrail log file. If you want to filter messages with `SourceFilter`, verify that your `ExceptionHandler` can distinguish service exceptions from processing errors.

Additional Resources

For more information about the CloudTrail Processing Library, see the following:

- CloudTrail Processing Library GitHub project, which includes sample code that demonstrates how to implement a CloudTrail Processing Library application.

- CloudTrail Processing Library Java Package Documentation.

CloudTrail Log Event Reference

A CloudTrail log is a record in JSON format. The log contains information about requests for resources in your account, such as who made the request, the services used, the actions performed, and parameters for the action. The event data is enclosed in a `Records` array.

The following example shows a single log record at the beginning of a log file. The entry shows that an IAM user named Alice called the CloudTrail `StartLogging` API from the CloudTrail console to start the logging process.

```
1  {
2      "Records": [{
3          "eventVersion": "1.01",
4          "userIdentity": {
5              "type": "IAMUser",
6              "principalId": "AIDAJDPLRKLG7UEXAMPLE",
7              "arn": "arn:aws:iam::123456789012:user/Alice",
8              "accountId": "123456789012",
9              "accessKeyId": "AKIAIOSFODNN7EXAMPLE",
10             "userName": "Alice",
11             "sessionContext": {
12                 "attributes": {
13                     "mfaAuthenticated": "false",
14                     "creationDate": "2014-03-18T14:29:23Z"
15                 }
16             }
17         },
18         "eventTime": "2014-03-18T14:30:07Z",
19         "eventSource": "cloudtrail.amazonaws.com",
20         "eventName": "StartLogging",
21         "awsRegion": "us-west-2",
22         "sourceIPAddress": "72.21.198.64",
23         "userAgent": "signin.amazonaws.com",
24         "requestParameters": {
25             "name": "Default"
26         },
27         "responseElements": null,
28         "requestID": "cdc73f9d-aea9-11e3-9d5a-835b769c0d9c",
29         "eventID": "3074414d-c626-42aa-984b-68ff152d6ab7"
30     },
31     ... additional entries ...
32     ]
```

The following topics list the data fields that CloudTrail captures for each AWS API call and sign-in event.

- CloudTrail Record Contents
- CloudTrail userIdentity Element
- Non-API Events Captured by CloudTrail

CloudTrail Record Contents

The body of the record contains fields that help you determine the requested action as well as when and where the request was made.

eventTime
The date and time the request was made, in coordinated universal time (UTC).

eventVersion
The version of the log event format. The current version is 1.06.

userIdentity
Information about the user that made a request. For more information, see CloudTrail userIdentity Element.

eventSource
The service that the request was made to. This name is typically a short form of the service name without spaces plus `.amazonaws.com`. For example:

- AWS CloudFormation is `cloudformation.amazonaws.com`.

- Amazon EC2 is `ec2.amazonaws.com`.

- Amazon Simple Workflow Service is `swf.amazonaws.com`. This convention has some exceptions. For example, the `eventSource` for Amazon CloudWatch is `monitoring.amazonaws.com`.

eventName
The requested action, which is one of the actions in the API for that service.

awsRegion
The AWS region that the request was made to, such as `us-east-2`. See CloudTrail Supported Regions.

sourceIPAddress
The IP address that the request was made from. For actions that originate from the service console, the address reported is for the underlying customer resource, not the console web server. For services in AWS, only the DNS name is displayed.

userAgent
The agent through which the request was made, such as the AWS Management Console, an AWS service, the AWS SDKs or the AWS CLI. The following are example values:

- `signin.amazonaws.com` – The request was made by an IAM user with the AWS Management Console.

- `console.amazonaws.com`– The request was made by a root user with the AWS Management Console.

- `lambda.amazonaws.com` – The request was made with AWS Lambda.

- `aws-sdk-java` – The request was made with the AWS SDK for Java.

- `aws-sdk-ruby` – The request was made with the AWS SDK for Ruby.

- `aws-cli/1.3.23 Python/2.7.6 Linux/2.6.18-164.el5` – The request was made with the AWS CLI installed on Linux. For events originated by AWS, this field is usually `aws-internal/#` where `#` is a number used for internal purposes.

errorCode
The AWS service error if the request returns an error.

errorMessage
If the request returns an error, the description of the error. This message includes messages for authorization failures. CloudTrail captures the message logged by the service in its exception handling. For an example, see Error Code and Message Log Example.
Some AWS services provide the `errorCode` and `errorMessage` as top-level fields in the event. Other AWS services provide error information as part of `responseElements`.

requestParameters
The parameters, if any, that were sent with the request. These parameters are documented in the API reference documentation for the appropriate AWS service.

responseElements
The response element for actions that make changes (create, update, or delete actions). If an action does not change state (for example, a request to get or list objects), this element is omitted. These actions are documented in the API reference documentation for the appropriate AWS service.

additionalEventData
Additional data about the event that was not part of the request or response.
Support for this field begins with eventVersion 1.00.

requestID
The value that identifies the request. The service being called generates this value.
Support for this field begins with eventVersion 1.01.

eventID
GUID generated by CloudTrail to uniquely identify each event. You can use this value to identify a single event. For example, you can use the ID as a primary key to retrieve log data from a searchable database.
Support for this field begins with eventVersion 1.01.

eventType
Identifies the type of event that generated the event record. This can be the one of the following values:

- AwsApiCall – An API was called.

- AwsServiceEvent – The service generated an event related to your trail. For example, this can occur when another account made a call with a resource that you own.

- ConsoleSignin – A user in your account (root, IAM, federated, SAML, or SwitchRole) signed in to the AWS Management Console. Support for this field begins with eventVersion 1.02.

apiVersion
Identifies the API version associated with the AwsApiCall eventType value.
Support for this field begins with eventVersion 1.02.

managementEvent
A Boolean value that identifies whether the event is a management event.
Support for this field begins with eventVersion 1.06.

readOnly
Identifies whether this operation is a read-only operation. This can be one of the following values:

- true – The operation is read-only (for example, DescribeTrails).

- false – The operation is write-only (for example, DeleteTrail). Support for this field begins with eventVersion 1.01.

resources
A list of resources accessed in the event. The field can contain the following information:

- Resource ARNs

- Account ID of the resource owner

- Resource type identifier in the format: AWS::aws-service-name::data-type-name For example, when an AssumeRole event is logged, the resources field can appear like the following:

- ARN: arn:aws:iam::123456789012:role/myRole

- Account ID: 123456789012

- Resource type identifier: `AWS::IAM::Role` For example logs with the `resources` field, see AWS STS API Event in CloudTrail Log File in the *IAM User Guide* or Logging AWS KMS API Calls in the *AWS Key Management Service Developer Guide*.

  Support for this field begins with `eventVersion 1.01`.

recipientAccountID

Represents the account ID that received this event. The `recipientAccountID` may be different from the CloudTrail userIdentity Element `accountId`. This can occur in cross-account resource access. For example, if a KMS key, also known as a customer master key (CMK), was used by a separate account to call the Encrypt API, the `accountId` and `recipientAccountID` values will be the same for the event delivered to the account that made the call, but the values will be different for the event that is delivered to the account that owns the CMK. Support for this field begins with `eventVersion 1.02`.

serviceEventDetails

Identifies the service event, including what triggered the event and the result. For more information, see AWS Service Events.

Support for this field begins with `eventVersion 1.05`.

sharedEventID

GUID generated by CloudTrail to uniquely identify CloudTrail events from the same AWS action that is sent to different AWS accounts.

For example, when an account uses a KMS key, also known as a customer master key (CMK), that belongs to another account, the account that used the CMK and the account that owns the CMK receive separate CloudTrail events for the same action. Each CloudTrail event delivered for this AWS action shares the same `sharedEventID`, but also has a unique `eventID` and `recipientAccountID`.

For more information, see sharedEventID Example.

The `sharedEventID` field is present only when CloudTrail events are delivered to multiple accounts. If the caller and owner are the same AWS account, CloudTrail sends only one event, and the `sharedEventID` field is not present. Support for this field begins with `eventVersion 1.03`.

vpcEndpointId

Identifies the VPC endpoint in which requests were made from a VPC to another AWS service, such as Amazon S3.

Support for this field begins with `eventVersion 1.04`.

sharedEventID Example

The following is an example that describes how CloudTrail delivers two events for the same action:

1. Alice has AWS account (111111111111) and creates a customer master key (CMK). She is the owner of this CMK.

2. Bob has AWS account (222222222222). Alice gives Bob permission to use the CMK.

3. Each account has a trail and a separate bucket.

4. Bob uses the CMK to call the `Encrypt` API.

5. CloudTrail sends two separate events.

- One event is sent to Bob. The event shows that he used the CMK.

- One event is sent to Alice. The event shows that Bob used the CMK.

- The events have the same `sharedEventID`, but the `eventID` and `recipientAccountID` are unique.

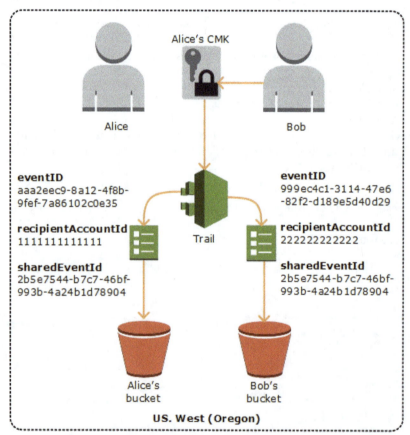

CloudTrail userIdentity Element

AWS Identity and Access Management (IAM) provides different types of identities. The `userIdentity` element contains details about the type of IAM identity that made the request, and which credentials were used. If temporary credentials were used, the element shows how the credentials were obtained.

Examples

userIdentity with IAM user credentials

The following example shows the `userIdentity` element of a simple request made with the credentials of the IAM user named `Alice`.

```
1  "userIdentity": {
2    "type": "IAMUser",
3    "principalId": "AIDAJ45Q7YFFAREXAMPLE",
4    "arn": "arn:aws:iam::123456789012:user/Alice",
5    "accountId": "123456789012",
6    "accessKeyId": "AKIAIOSFODNN7EXAMPLE",
7    "userName": "Alice"
8  }
```

userIdentity with temporary security credentials

The following example shows a `userIdentity` element for a request made with temporary security credentials obtained by assuming an IAM role. The element contains additional details about the role that was assumed to get credentials.

```
1   "userIdentity": {
2     "type": "AssumedRole",
3     "principalId": "AROAIDPPEZS35WEXAMPLE:AssumedRoleSessionName",
4     "arn": "arn:aws:sts::123456789012:assumed-role/RoleToBeAssumed/MySessionName",
5     "accountId": "123456789012",
6     "accessKeyId": "AKIAIOSFODNN7EXAMPLE",
7     "sessionContext": {
8       "attributes": {
9         "mfaAuthenticated": "false",
10        "creationDate": "20131102T010628Z"
11      },
12      "sessionIssuer": {
13        "type": "Role",
14        "principalId": "AROAIDPPEZS35WEXAMPLE",
15        "arn": "arn:aws:iam::123456789012:role/RoleToBeAssumed",
16        "accountId": "123456789012",
17        "userName": "RoleToBeAssumed"
18      }
19    }
20  }
```

Fields

The following fields can appear in a `userIdentity` element.

type
The type of the identity. The following values are possible:

- **Root** – The request was made with your AWS account credentials. If the **userIdentity** type is **Root** and you set an alias for your account, the **userName** field contains your account alias. For more information, see Your AWS Account ID and Its Alias.

- **IAMUser** – The request was made with the credentials of an IAM user.

- **AssumedRole** – The request was made with temporary security credentials that were obtained with a role via a call to the AWS Security Token Service (AWS STS) http://docs.aws.amazon.com/STS/latest/APIReference/API_AssumeRole.html API. This can include roles for Amazon EC2 and cross-account API access.

- **FederatedUser** – The request was made with temporary security credentials that were obtained via a call to the AWS STS http://docs.aws.amazon.com/STS/latest/APIReference/API_GetFederationToken.html API. The **sessionIssuer** element indicates if the API was called with root or IAM user credentials.

  For more information about temporary security credentials, see Temporary Security Credentials in the *IAM User Guide.*

- **AWSAccount** – The request was made by another AWS account.

- **AWSService** – The request was made by an AWS account that belongs to an AWS service. For example, AWS Elastic Beanstalk assumes an IAM role in your account to call other AWS services on your behalf. **AWSAccount** and **AWSService** appear for **type** in your logs when there is cross-account access using an IAM role that you own.

Example: Cross-account access initiated by another AWS account

1. You own an IAM role in your account.

2. Another AWS account switches to that role to assume the role for your account.

3. Because you own the IAM role, you receive a log that shows the other account assumed the role. The **type** is **AWSAccount**. For an example log entry, see AWS STS API Event in CloudTrail Log File.

Example: Cross-account access initiated by an AWS service

1. You own an IAM role in your account.

2. An AWS account owned by an AWS service assumes that role.

3. Because you own the IAM role, you receive a log that shows the AWS service assumed the role. The **type** is **AWSService**.

userName
The friendly name of the identity that made the call. The value that appears in **userName** is based on the value in **type**. The following table shows the relationship between **type** and **userName**:

_____

[See the AWS documentation website for more details] The **userName** field contains the string **HIDDEN_DUE_TO_SECURITY_REASONS** when the recorded event is a console sign-in failure caused by incorrect user name input. CloudTrail does not record the contents in this case because the text could contain sensitive information, as in the following examples:

- A user accidentally types a password in the user name field.

- A user clicks the link for one AWS account's sign-in page, but then types the account number for a different one.

- A user accidentally types the account name of a personal email account, a bank sign-in identifier, or some other private ID.

principalId
A unique identifier for the entity that made the call. For requests made with temporary security credentials,

this value includes the session name that is passed to the `AssumeRole`, `AssumeRoleWithWebIdentity`, or `GetFederationToken` API call.

arn
The Amazon Resource Name (ARN) of the principal that made the call. The last section of the arn contains the user or role that made the call.

accountId
The account that owns the entity that granted permissions for the request. If the request was made with temporary security credentials, this is the account that owns the IAM user or role that was used to obtain credentials.

accessKeyId
The access key ID that was used to sign the request. If the request was made with temporary security credentials, this is the access key ID of the temporary credentials.

sessionContext
If the request was made with temporary security credentials, an element that provides information about the session that was created for those credentials. Sessions are created when any API is called that returns temporary credentials. Sessions are also created when users work in the console and when users make a request with APIs that include multi-factor authentication. Attributes for this element are:

- `creationDate` – The date and time when the temporary security credentials were issued. Represented in ISO 8601 basic notation.

- `mfaAuthenticated` – The value is `true` if the root user or IAM user whose credentials were used for the request also was authenticated with an MFA device; otherwise, `false`.

invokedBy
The name of the AWS service that made the request, such as Amazon EC2 Auto Scaling or AWS Elastic Beanstalk.

sessionIssuer
If the request was made with temporary security credentials, an element that provides information about how the credentials were obtained. For example, if the temporary security credentials were obtained by assuming a role, this element provides information about the assumed role. If the credentials were obtained with root or IAM user credentials to call AWS STS `GetFederationToken`, the element provides information about the root account or IAM user. Attributes for this element are:

- `type` – The source of the temporary security credentials, such as `Root`, `IAMUser`, or `Role`.

- `userName` – The friendly name of the user or role that issued the session. The value that appears depends on the `sessionIssuer` identity `type`. The following table shows the relationship between `sessionIssuer` type and `userName`:

[See the AWS documentation website for more details]

- `principalId` – The internal ID of the entity that was used to get credentials.

- `arn` – The ARN of the source (account, IAM user, or role) that was used to get temporary security credentials.

- `accountId` – The account that owns the entity that was used to get credentials.

webIdFederationData
If the request was made with temporary security credentials obtained by web identity federation, an element that lists information about the identity provider. Attributes for this element are:

- `federatedProvider` – The principal name of the identity provider (for example, `www.amazon.com` for Login with Amazon or `accounts.google.com` for Google).

- **attributes** – The application ID and user ID as reported by the provider (for example, `www.amazon.com:app_id` and `www.amazon.com:user_id` for Login with Amazon). For more information, see Available Keys for Web Identity Federation in the *IAM User Guide*.

Values for AWS STS APIs with SAML and Web Identity Federation

AWS CloudTrail supports logging AWS Security Token Service (AWS STS) API calls made with Security Assertion Markup Language (SAML) and web identity federation. When a call is made to the http://docs.aws.amazon.com/STS/latest/APIReference/API_AssumeRoleWithSAML.html and http://docs.aws.amazon.com/STS/latest/APIReference/API_AssumeRoleWithWebIdentity.html APIs, CloudTrail records the call and delivers the event to your Amazon S3 bucket.

The `userIdentity` element for these APIs contains the following values.

type
The identity type.

- **SAMLUser** – The request was made with SAML assertion.

- **WebIdentityUser** – The request was made by a web identity federation provider.

principalId
A unique identifier for the entity that made the call.

- For **SAMLUser**, this is a combination of the `saml:namequalifier` and `saml:sub` keys.

- For **WebIdentityUser**, this is a combination of the issuer, application ID, and user ID.

userName
The name of the identity that made the call.

- For **SAMLUser**, this is the `saml:sub` key. See Available Keys for SAML-Based Federation.

- For **WebIdentityUser**, this is the user ID. See Available Keys for Web Identity Federation.

identityProvider
The principal name of the external identity provider. This field appears only for **SAMLUser** or **WebIdentityUser** types.

- For **SAMLUser**, this is the `saml:namequalifier` key for the SAML assertion.

- For **WebIdentityUser**, this is the issuer name of the web identity federation provider. This can be a provider that you configured, such as the following:

- `cognito-identity.amazon.com` for Amazon Cognito

- `www.amazon.com` for Login with Amazon

- `accounts.google.com` for Google

- `graph.facebook.com` for Facebook

The following is an example `userIdentity` element for the `AssumeRoleWithWebIdentity` action.

```
1  "userIdentity": {
2      "type": "WebIdentityUser",
3      "principalId": "accounts.google.com:application-id.apps.googleusercontent.com:user-id",
4      "userName": "user-id",
5      "identityProvider": "accounts.google.com"
6  }
```

For example logs of how the `userIdentity` element appears for `SAMLUser` and `WebIdentityUser` types, see Logging IAM Events with AWS CloudTrail.

Non-API Events Captured by CloudTrail

In addition to logging AWS API calls, CloudTrail captures other related events that might have a security or compliance impact on your AWS account or that might help you troubleshoot operational problems.

- AWS Service Events
- AWS Console Sign-in Events

AWS Service Events

CloudTrail supports logging non-API service events to your Amazon S3 bucket. These events are related to AWS services but are not directly triggered by a request to a public AWS API. For these events, the `eventType` field is `AwsServiceEvent`. The following is an example scenario of an AWS service event.

---

1. You want to run a Spot Instance for your application and submit a bid for a specified number and type of EC2 instances.

2. Your bid price exceeds the current Spot price, and the EC2 instances are created for you.

3. When the Spot price exceeds your bid price, your EC2 Spot Instances are terminated and given to other customers.

In the example, CloudTrail logs the service event activity to your Amazon S3 bucket. One event shows that the EC2 Spot Instance was created and another event shows when the EC2 Spot Instance was terminated. For information related to the event, see the `serviceEventDetails` field.

The following example event shows that a bid was accepted for an EC2 Spot Instance. The instance ID appears in the `serviceEventDetails` field.

```
1  {
2        "eventVersion": "1.05",
3        "userIdentity": {
4          "accountId": "123456789012",
5          "invokedBy": "ec2.amazonaws.com"
6        },
7        "eventTime": "2016-08-16T22:30:00Z",
8        "eventSource": "ec2.amazonaws.com",
9        "eventName": "BidFulfilledEvent",
10       "userAgent": "ec2.amazonaws.com",
11       "sourceIPAddress": "ec2.amazonaws.com",
12       "awsRegion": "us-east-2",
13       "eventID": "d27a6096-807b-4bd0-8c20-a33a83375055",
14       "eventType": "AwsServiceEvent",
15       "recipientAccountId": "123456789012",
16       "RequestParameters": null,
17       "ResponseElements": null,
18       "serviceEventDetails": {
19         "instanceIdSet": [
20           "i-04cf7ed6b11ccfac5"
21         ]
22       }
23     }
```

The following example event shows that the EC2 Spot Instance was terminated when the Spot price exceeded your bid price. The instance ID appears in the `serviceEventDetails` field.

```
1  {
2        "eventVersion": "1.05",
3        "userIdentity": {
4          "accountId": "123456789012",
5          "invokedBy": "ec2.amazonaws.com"
6        },
7        "eventTime": "2016-08-16T22:30:00Z",
8        "eventSource": "ec2.amazonaws.com",
```

```
 9      "userAgent": "ec2.amazonaws.com",
10      "sourceIPAddress": "ec2.amazonaws.com",
11      "eventName": "BidEvictedEvent",
12      "awsRegion": "us-east-2",
13      "eventID": "d27a6096-807b-4bd0-8c20-a33a83375054",
14    "eventType": "AwsServiceEvent",
15      "recipientAccountId": "123456789012",
16      "RequestParameters": null,
17      "ResponseElements": null,
18      "serviceEventDetails": {
19        "instanceIdSet": [
20          "i-1eb2ac8e"
21        ]
22      }
23    }
```

AWS Console Sign-in Events

CloudTrail records attempts to sign into the AWS Management Console, the AWS Discussion Forums and the AWS Support Center. All IAM user sign-in attempts (successes and failures), all federated user sign-in events (successes and failures) and all successful AWS root account sign-in attempts generate records in CloudTrail log files. Note, however, that CloudTrail does not record root sign-in failures.

The following record shows that an IAM user named Alice successfully signed into the AWS console without using multi-factor authentication.

```
 1  {
 2    "Records":[
 3      {
 4        "eventVersion":"1.02",
 5        "userIdentity":{
 6          "type":"IAMUser",
 7          "principalId":"AIDAELOPP77CWZEXAMPLE",
 8          "arn":"arn:aws:iam::12345679012:user/alice",
 9          "accountId":"12345679012",
10          "userName":"alice"
11        },
12        "eventTime":"2014-07-08T17:35:32Z",
13        "eventSource":"signin.amazonaws.com",
14        "eventName":"ConsoleLogin",
15        "awsRegion":"us-east-2",
16        "sourceIPAddress":"192.0.2.0",
17        "userAgent":"Mozilla/5.0 (Windows; U; Windows NT 5.0; en-US; rv:1.4b) Gecko/20030516
                   Mozilla Firebird/0.6",
18        "requestParameters":null,
19        "responseElements":{
20          "ConsoleLogin":"Success"
21        },
22        "additionalEventData":{
23          "MobileVersion":"No",
24          "LoginTo":"https://console.aws.amazon.com/sns",
25          "MFAUsed":"No"
26        },
27        "eventID":"3fcfb182-98f8-4744-bd45-10a395ab61cb",
28        "eventType": "AwsConsoleSignin"
29      }
30    ]
31  }
```

The following record shows that an IAM user named Alice logged into the AWS console by using multi-factor authentication.

```
 1  {
 2
 3    "Records":[
 4      {
 5        "eventVersion":"1.02",
 6        "userIdentity":{
 7          "type":"IAMUser",
 8          "principalId":"AIDAEZ7VBM6PDZEXAMPLE",
 9          "arn":"arn:aws:iam::12345679012:user/Alice",
10          "accountId":"12345679012",
```

```
11         "userName":"Alice"
12       },
13       "eventTime":"2014-07-08T17:36:03Z",
14       "eventSource":"signin.amazonaws.com",
15       "eventName":"ConsoleLogin",
16       "awsRegion":"us-east-2",
17       "sourceIPAddress":"192.0.2.0",
18       "userAgent":"Mozilla/5.0 (Windows; U; Windows NT 5.0; en-US; rv:1.4b) Gecko/20030516
             Mozilla Firebird/0.6",
19       "requestParameters":null,
20       "responseElements":{
21         "ConsoleLogin":"Success"
22       },
23       "additionalEventData":{
24         "MobileVersion":"Yes",
25         "LoginTo":"https://console.aws.amazon.com/sns",
26         "MFAUsed":"Yes"
27       },
28       "eventID":"5d2c2f55-3d1e-4336-b940-dbf8e66f588c",
29       "eventType": "AwsConsoleSignin"
30     }
31   ]
32 }
```

The following record shows an unsuccessful AWS console sign-in attempt because of an authentication failure.

```
1 {
2   "Records":[
3     {
4       "eventVersion":"1.02",
5       "userIdentity":{
6         "type":"IAMUser",
7         "principalId":"AIDAELOPP77CWZEXAMPLE",
8         "accountId":"12345679012",
9         "accessKeyId":"",
10        "userName":"alice"
11       },
12       "eventTime":"2014-07-08T17:35:27Z",
13       "eventSource":"signin.amazonaws.com",
14       "eventName":"ConsoleLogin",
15       "awsRegion":"us-east-2",
16       "sourceIPAddress":"192.0.2.0",
17       "userAgent":"Mozilla/5.0 (Windows; U; Windows NT 5.0; en-US; rv:1.4b) Gecko/20030516
             Mozilla Firebird/0.6",
18       "errorMessage":"Failed authentication",
19       "requestParameters":null,
20       "responseElements":{
21         "ConsoleLogin":"Failure"
22       },
23       "additionalEventData":{
24         "MobileVersion":"No",
25         "LoginTo":"https://console.aws.amazon.com/sns",
26         "MFAUsed":"No"
27       },
28       "eventID":"11ea990b-4678-4bcd-8fbe-62509088b7cf",
```

219

```
29          "eventType": "AwsConsoleSignin"
30      }
31    ]
32 }
```

Document History

The following table describes the documentation release history of AWS CloudTrail.

- **API version**: 2013-11-01
- **Latest documentation update**: June 14, 2018

Change	Description	Release Date
Added functionality	This release supports logging all CloudTrail management events in Event history. For more information, see Viewing Events with CloudTrail Event History.	June 14, 2018
Added service support	This release supports AWS Billing and Cost Management. See CloudTrail Supported Services and Integrations.	June 7, 2018
Added service support	This release supports Amazon Elastic Container Service for Kubernetes (Amazon EKS). See CloudTrail Supported Services and Integrations.	June 5, 2018
Updated documentation	This update supports the following patch release for the CloudTrail Processing Library: [See the AWS documentation website for more details] For more information, see Using the CloudTrail Processing Library and the CloudTrail Processing Library on GitHub.	May 16, 2018
Added service support	This release supports AWS Billing and Cost Management. See CloudTrail Supported Services and Integrations.	June 7, 2018
Added service support	This release supports Amazon Elastic Container Service for Kubernetes (Amazon EKS). See CloudTrail Supported Services and Integrations.	June 5, 2018
Updated documentation	This update supports the following patch release for the CloudTrail Processing Library: [See the AWS documentation website for more details] For more information, see Using the CloudTrail Processing Library and the CloudTrail Processing Library on GitHub.	May 16, 2018

Change	Description	Release Date
Added service support	This release supports AWS X-Ray. See CloudTrail Supported Services and Integrations.	April 25, 2018
Added service support	This release supports AWS IoT Analytics. See CloudTrail Supported Services and Integrations.	April 23, 2018
Added service support	This release supports Secrets Manager. See CloudTrail Supported Services and Integrations.	April 10, 2018
Added service support	This release supports Amazon Rekognition. See CloudTrail Supported Services and Integrations.	April 6, 2018
Added service support	This release supports AWS Private Certificate Authority (PCA). See CloudTrail Supported Services and Integrations.	April 4, 2018
Added functionality	This release supports making it easier to search CloudTrail log files with Amazon Athena. You can automatically create tables for querying logs directly from the CloudTrail console, and use those tables to run queries in Athena. For more information, see CloudTrail Supported Services and Integrations and Creating a Table for CloudTrail Logs in the CloudTrail Console.	March 15, 2018
Added service support	This release supports AWS AppSync. See CloudTrail Supported Services and Integrations.	February 13, 2018
Added region support	This release supports an additional region: Asia Pacific (Osaka-Local) (ap-northeast-3). See CloudTrail Supported Regions.	February 12, 2018
Added service support	This release supports AWS Shield. See CloudTrail Supported Services and Integrations.	Februrary 12, 2018
Added service support	This release supports Amazon SageMaker. See CloudTrail Supported Services and Integrations.	January 11, 2018

Change	Description	Release Date
Added service support	This release supports AWS Batch. See CloudTrail Supported Services and Integrations.	January 10, 2018
Added functionality	This release supports extending the amount of account activity that is available in CloudTrail event history to 90 days. You can also customize the display of columns to improve the view of your CloudTrail events. For more information, see Viewing Events with CloudTrail Event History.	December 12, 2017
Added service support	This release supports Amazon WorkMail. See CloudTrail Supported Services and Integrations.	December 12, 2017
Added service support	This release supports Alexa for Business, AWS Elemental MediaConvert, and AWS Elemental MediaStore. See CloudTrail Supported Services and Integrations.	December 1, 2017
Added functionality and documentation	This release supports logging data events for AWS Lambda functions. For more information, see Logging Data and Management Events for Trails.	November 30, 2017
Added functionality and documentation	This release supports logging data events for AWS Lambda functions. For more information, see Logging Data and Management Events for Trails.	November 30, 2017
Added functionality and documentation	This release supports the following updates to the CloudTrail Processing Library: [See the AWS documentation website for more details] For more information, see Using the CloudTrail Processing Library and the CloudTrail Processing Library on GitHub.	November 30, 2017
Added service support	This release supports AWS Glue. See CloudTrail Supported Services and Integrations.	November 7, 2017
New documentation	This release adds a new topic, Limits in AWS CloudTrail.	October 19, 2017

Change	Description	Release Date
Updated documentation	This release updates the documentation of APIs supported in CloudTrail event history for Amazon Athena, AWS CodeBuild, Amazon Elastic Container Registry, and AWS Migration Hub.	October 13, 2017
Added service support	This release supports Amazon Chime. See CloudTrail Supported Services and Integrations.	September 27, 2017
Added functionality and documentation	This release supports configuring data event logging for all Amazon S3 buckets in your AWS account. See Logging Data and Management Events for Trails.	September 20, 2017
Added service support	This release supports Amazon Lex. See CloudTrail Supported Services and Integrations.	August 15, 2017
Added service support	This release supports AWS Migration Hub. See CloudTrail Supported Services and Integrations.	August 14, 2017
Added functionality and documentation	This release supports CloudTrail being enabled by default for all AWS accounts. The past seven days of account activity are available in CloudTrail event history, and the most recent events appear on the console dashboard. The feature formerly known as **API activity history** has been replaced by **Event history**. For more information, see How CloudTrail Works.	August 14, 2017
Added functionality and documentation	This release supports downloading events from the CloudTrail console on the API activity history page. You can download events in JSON or CSV format. For more information, see Downloading Events.	July 27, 2017

Change	Description	Release Date
Added functionality	This release supports logging Amazon S3 object level API operations in two additional regions, EU (London) and Canada (Central). For more information, see Logging Data and Management Events for Trails.	July 19, 2017
Added service support	This release supports looking up APIs for Amazon CloudWatch Events in the CloudTrail API activity history feature.	June 27, 2017
Added functionality and documentation	This release supports additional APIs in the CloudTrail API activity history feature for the following services: [See the AWS documentation website for more details]	June 27, 2017
Added service support	This release supports AWS CodeStar. See CloudTrail Supported Services and Integrations.	June 14, 2017
Added functionality and documentation	This release supports the following updates to the CloudTrail Processing Library: [See the AWS documentation website for more details] For more information, see Using the CloudTrail Processing Library and the CloudTrail Processing Library on GitHub.	June 1, 2017
Added service support	This release supports Amazon Athena. See CloudTrail Supported Services and Integrations.	May 19, 2017
Added functionality	This release supports sending data events to Amazon CloudWatch Logs. For more information about configuring your trail to log data events, see Data Events. For more information about sending events to CloudWatch Logs, see Monitoring CloudTrail Log Files with Amazon CloudWatch Logs.	May 9, 2017
Added service support	This release supports the AWS Marketplace Metering Service. See CloudTrail Supported Services and Integrations.	May 2, 2017

Change	Description	Release Date
Added service support	This release supports Amazon QuickSight. See CloudTrail Supported Services and Integrations.	April 28, 2017
Added functionality and documentation	This release supports an updated console experience for creating new trails. You can now configure a new trail to log management and data events. For more information, see Creating a Trail.	April 11, 2017
Added documentation	If CloudTrail is not delivering logs to your S3 bucket or sending SNS notifications from some regions in your account, you may need to update the policies. To learn more about updating your S3 bucket policy, see Common S3 Policy Configuration Errors. To learn more about updating your SNS topic policy, see Common SNS Policy Configuration Errors.	March 31, 2017
Added service support	This release supports AWS Organizations. See CloudTrail Supported Services and Integrations.	February 27, 2017
Added functionality and documentation	This release supports an updated console experience for configuring trails for logging management and data events. For more information, see Logging Data and Management Events for Trails.	February 10, 2017
Added service support	This release supports Amazon Cloud Directory. See CloudTrail Supported Services and Integrations.	January 26, 2017
Added functionality and documentation	This release supports looking up APIs for AWS CodeCommit, Amazon GameLift, and AWS Managed Services in the CloudTrail API activity history.	January 26, 2017

Change	Description	Release Date
Added functionality	This release supports integration with the AWS Personal Health Dashboard. You can use the Personal Health Dashboard to identify if your trails are unable to deliver logs to an SNS topic or S3 bucket. This can occur when there is an issue with the policy for the S3 bucket or SNS topic. Personal Health Dashboard notifies you about the affected trails and recommends ways to fix the policy.For more information, see the AWS Health User Guide.	January 24, 2017
Added functionality and documentation	This release supports filtering by event source in the CloudTrail console. Event source shows the AWS service to which the request was made. For more information, see Viewing CloudTrail Events in the CloudTrail Console.	January 12, 2017
Added service support	This release supports AWS CodeCommit. See CloudTrail Supported Services and Integrations.	January 11, 2017
Added service support	This release supports Amazon Lightsail. See CloudTrail Supported Services and Integrations.	December 23, 2016
Added service support	This release supports AWS Managed Services. See CloudTrail Supported Services and Integrations.	December 21, 2016
Added region support	This release supports the EU (London) Region. See CloudTrail Supported Regions.	December 13, 2016
Added region support	This release supports the Canada (Central) Region. See CloudTrail Supported Regions.	December 8, 2016
Added service support	This release supports AWS CodeBuild See CloudTrail Supported Services and Integrations. This release supports AWS Health. See CloudTrail Supported Services and Integrations. This release supports AWS Step Functions. See CloudTrail Supported Services and Integrations.	December 1, 2016

Change	Description	Release Date
Added service support	This release supports Amazon Polly. See CloudTrail Supported Services and Integrations.	November 30, 2016
Added service support	This release supports AWS OpsWorks for Chef Automate. See CloudTrail Supported Services and Integrations.	November 23, 2016
Added functionality and documentation	This release supports configuring your trail to log read-only, write-only, or all events. CloudTrail supports logging Amazon S3 object level API operations such as `GetObject`, `PutObject`, and `DeleteObject`. You can configure your trails to log object level API operations. For more information, see Logging Data and Management Events for Trails.	November 21, 2016
Added functionality and documentation	This release supports additional values for the type field in the userIdentity element: AWSAccount and AWSService. For more information, see the Fields for userIdentity.	November 16, 2016
Added service support	This release supports AWS Server Migration Service. See CloudTrail Supported Services and Integrations.	November 14, 2016
Added service support	This release supports Application Auto Scaling. See CloudTrail Supported Services and Integrations.	October 31, 2016
Added region support	This release supports the US East (Ohio) Region. See CloudTrail Supported Regions.	October 17, 2016
Added functionality and documentation	This release supports logging non-API AWS service events. For more information, see AWS Service Events.	September 23, 2016
Added functionality and documentation	This release supports using the CloudTrail console to view resource types that are supported by AWS Config. For more information, see Viewing Resources Referenced with AWS Config.	July 7, 2016

Change	Description	Release Date
Added service support	This release supports AWS Service Catalog. See Cloud-Trail Supported Services and Integrations.	July 6, 2016
Added service support	This release supports Amazon Elastic File System (Amazon EFS). See CloudTrail Supported Services and Integrations.	June 28, 2016
Added region support	This release supports one additional region: ap-south-1 (Asia Pacific (Mumbai)). See CloudTrail Supported Regions.	June 27, 2016
Added service support	This release supports AWS Application Discovery Service. See CloudTrail Supported Services and Integrations.	May 12, 2016
Added service support	This release supports Cloud-Watch Logs in the South America (São Paulo) Region. For more information, see Monitoring CloudTrail Log Files with Amazon Cloud-Watch Logs.	May 6, 2016
Added service support	This release supports AWS WAF. See CloudTrail Supported Services and Integrations.	April 28, 2016
Added service support	This release supports AWS Support. See CloudTrail Supported Services and Integrations.	April 21, 2016
Added service support	This release supports Amazon Inspector. See CloudTrail Supported Services and Integrations.	April 20, 2016
Added service support	This release supports AWS IoT. See CloudTrail Supported Services and Integrations.	April 11, 2016
Added functionality and documentation	This release supports logging AWS Security Token Service (AWS STS) API calls made with Security Assertion Markup Language (SAML) and web identity federation. For more information, see Values for AWS STS APIs with SAML and Web Identity Federation.	March 28, 2016

Change	Description	Release Date
Added service support	This release supports AWS Certificate Manager. See CloudTrail Supported Services and Integrations.	March 25, 2016
Added service support	This release supports Amazon Kinesis Data Firehose. See CloudTrail Supported Services and Integrations.	March 17, 2016
Added service support	This release supports Amazon CloudWatch Logs. See CloudTrail Supported Services and Integrations.	March 10, 2016
Added service support	This release supports Amazon Cognito. See CloudTrail Supported Services and Integrations.	February 18, 2016
Added service support	This release supports AWS Database Migration Service. See CloudTrail Supported Services and Integrations.	February 4, 2016
Added service support	This release supports Amazon GameLift (GameLift). See CloudTrail Supported Services and Integrations.	January 27, 2016
Added service support	This release supports Amazon CloudWatch Events. See CloudTrail Supported Services and Integrations.	January 16, 2016
Added region support	This release supports one additional region: ap-northeast-2 (Asia Pacific (Seoul)). See CloudTrail Supported Regions.	January 6, 2016
Added service support	This release supports Amazon Elastic Container Registry (Amazon ECR). See CloudTrail Supported Services and Integrations.	December 21, 2015
Added functionality and documentation	This release supports turning on CloudTrail across all regions and support for multiple trails per region. For more information, see How Does CloudTrail Behave Regionally and Globally?.	December 17, 2015
Added service support	This release supports Amazon Machine Learning. See CloudTrail Supported Services and Integrations.	December 10, 2015

Change	Description	Release Date
Added functionality and documentation	This release supports log file encryption, log file integrity validation, and tagging. For more information, see Encrypting CloudTrail Log Files with AWS KMS–Managed Keys (SSE-KMS), Validating CloudTrail Log File Integrity, and Updating a Trail.	October 1, 2015
Added service support	This release supports Amazon Elasticsearch Service. See CloudTrail Supported Services and Integrations.	October 1, 2015
Added service support	This release supports Amazon S3 bucket level events. See CloudTrail Supported Services and Integrations.	September 1, 2015
Added service support	This release supports AWS Device Farm. See CloudTrail Supported Services and Integrations.	July 13, 2015
Added service support	This release supports Amazon API Gateway. See CloudTrail Supported Services and Integrations.	July 9, 2015
Added service support	This release supports AWS CodePipeline. See CloudTrail Supported Services and Integrations.	July 9, 2015
Added service support	This release supports Amazon DynamoDB. See CloudTrail Supported Services and Integrations.	May 28, 2015
Added service support	This release supports CloudWatch Logs in the US West (N. California) region. See the CloudTrail release notes. For more information about CloudTrail support for CloudWatch Logs monitoring, see Monitoring CloudTrail Log Files with Amazon CloudWatch Logs.	May 19, 2015
Added service support	This release supports AWS Directory Service. See CloudTrail Supported Services and Integrations.	May 14, 2015
Added service support	This release supports Amazon Simple Email Service (Amazon SES). See CloudTrail Supported Services and Integrations.	May 7, 2015

Change	Description	Release Date
Added service support	This release supports Amazon Elastic Container Service See CloudTrail Supported Services and Integrations.	April 9, 2015
Added service support	This release supports AWS Lambda. See CloudTrail Supported Services and Integrations.	April 9, 2015
Added service support	This release supports Amazon WorkSpaces. See CloudTrail Supported Services and Integrations.	April 9, 2015
	This release supports the lookup of AWS activity captured by CloudTrail (CloudTrail events). You can look up and filter events in your account related to creation, modification, or deletion. To look up these events, you can use the CloudTrail console, the AWS Command Line Interface (AWS CLI), or the AWS SDK. For more information, see Viewing Events with CloudTrail Event History.	March 12, 2015
Added service support and new documentation	This release supports Amazon CloudWatch Logs in the Asia Pacific (Singapore), Asia Pacific (Sydney), Asia Pacific (Tokyo), and EU (Frankfurt) regions. Additional CloudWatch alarm examples have been added to Creating CloudWatch Alarms for CloudTrail Events, and a new page has been added: Using a AWS CloudFormation Template to Create CloudWatch Alarms.	March 5, 2015
Added API support	This release supports Amazon EC2 Systems Manager (SSM). SSM lets you configure, manage and easily deploy custom Windows instance configurations. For more information about SSM, see Managing Windows Instance Configuration. For information about the SSM API calls logged by CloudTrail, see Logging SSM API Calls Using AWS CloudTrail.	February 17, 2015

Change	Description	Release Date
New documentation	A new section that describes CloudTrail support for AWS Security Token Service (AWS STS) regional endpoints has been added to the CloudTrail Concepts page.	February 17, 2015
Added service support	This release supports Amazon Route 53. See CloudTrail Supported Services and Integrations.	February 11, 2015
Added service support	This release supports AWS Config. See CloudTrail Supported Services and Integrations.	February 10, 2015
Added service support	This release supports AWS CloudHSM. See CloudTrail Supported Services and Integrations.	January 8, 2015
Added service support	This release supports AWS CodeDeploy. See CloudTrail Supported Services and Integrations.	December 17, 2014
Added service support	This release supports AWS Storage Gateway. See CloudTrail Supported Services and Integrations.	December 16, 2014
Added region support	This release supports one additional region: us-gov-west-1 (AWS GovCloud (US)). See CloudTrail Supported Regions.	December 16, 2014
Added service support	This release supports Amazon Glacier. See CloudTrail Supported Services and Integrations.	December 11, 2014
Added service support	This release supports AWS Data Pipeline. See CloudTrail Supported Services and Integrations.	December 2, 2014
Added service support	This release supports AWS Key Management Service. See CloudTrail Supported Services and Integrations.	November 12, 2014
New documentation	A new section, Monitoring CloudTrail Log Files with Amazon CloudWatch Logs, has been added to the guide. It describes how to use Amazon CloudWatch Logs to monitor CloudTrail log events.	November 10, 2014

Change	Description	Release Date
New documentation	A new section, Using the CloudTrail Processing Library, has been added to the guide. It provides information about how to write a CloudTrail log processor in Java using the AWS CloudTrail Processing Library.	November 5, 2014
Added service support	This release supports Amazon Elastic Transcoder. See CloudTrail Supported Services and Integrations.	October 27, 2014
Added region support	This release supports one additional region: eu-central-1 (EU (Frankfurt)). See CloudTrail Supported Regions.	October 23, 2014
Added service support	This release supports Amazon CloudSearch. See CloudTrail Supported Services and Integrations.	October 16, 2014
Added service support	This release supports Amazon Simple Notification Service. See CloudTrail Supported Services and Integrations.	October 09, 2014
Added service support	This release supports Amazon ElastiCache. See CloudTrail Supported Services and Integrations.	September 15, 2014
Added service support	This release supports Amazon WorkDocs. See CloudTrail Supported Services and Integrations.	August 27, 2014
Added new content	This release includes a topic that discusses logging sign-in events. See AWS Console Sign-in Events.	July 24, 2014
Added new content	The **eventVersion** element for this release has been upgraded to version 1.02 and three new fields have been added. See CloudTrail Record Contents.	July 18, 2014
Added service support	This release supports Auto Scaling (see CloudTrail Supported Services and Integrations).	July 17, 2014

Change	Description	Release Date
Added region support	This release supports three additional regions: ap-southeast-1 (Asia Pacific (Singapore)), ap-northeast-1 (Asia Pacific (Tokyo)), sa-east-1 (South America (São Paulo)). See CloudTrail Supported Regions.	June 30, 2014
Additional service support	This release supports Amazon Redshift. See CloudTrail Supported Services and Integrations.	June 10, 2014
Added service support	This release supports AWS OpsWorks. See CloudTrail Supported Services and Integrations.	June 5, 2014
Added service support	This release supports Amazon CloudFront. See CloudTrail Supported Services and Integrations.	May 28, 2014
Added region support	This release supports three additional regions: us-west-1 (US West (N. California)), eu-west-1 (EU (Ireland)), ap-southeast-2 (Asia Pacific (Sydney)). See CloudTrail Supported Regions.	May 13, 2014
Added service support	This release supports Amazon Simple Workflow Service. See CloudTrail Supported Services and Integrations.	May 9, 2014
Added new content	This release includes topics that discuss sharing log files between accounts. See Sharing CloudTrail Log Files Between AWS Accounts.	May 2, 2014
Added service support	This release supports Amazon CloudWatch. See CloudTrail Supported Services and Integrations.	April 28, 2014
Added service support	This release supports Amazon Kinesis. See CloudTrail Supported Services and Integrations.	April 22, 2014
Added service support	This release supports AWS Direct Connect. See CloudTrail Supported Services and Integrations.	April 11, 2014
Added service support	This release supports Amazon EMR. See CloudTrail Supported Services and Integrations.	April 4, 2014

Change	Description	Release Date
Added service support	This release supports Elastic Beanstalk. See CloudTrail Supported Services and Integrations.	April 2, 2014
Additional service support	This release supports AWS CloudFormation. See CloudTrail Supported Services and Integrations.	March 7, 2014
New guide	This release introduces AWS CloudTrail.	November 13, 2013

AWS Glossary

For the latest AWS terminology, see the AWS Glossary in the *AWS General Reference*.